D1712881

# Weapons Don't Make War

# Modern War Studies

Theodore A. Wilson
*General Editor*

Raymond A. Callahan
J. Garry Clifford
Jacob W. Kipp
Jay Luvaas
Allan R. Millett
*Series Editors*

# WEAPONS DON'T MAKE WAR

## Policy, Strategy, and Military Technology

COLIN S. GRAY

University Press of Kansas

Published by the University Press of Kansas (Lawrence, Kansas 66049), which was
organized by the Kansas Board of Regents and is operated and funded by Emporia
State University, Fort Hays State University, Kansas State University, Pittsburg State
University, the University of Kansas, and Wichita State University

Library of Congress Cataloging-in-Publication Data

Gray, Colin S.
  Weapons don't make war : policy, strategy, and military technology
by Colin S. Gray.
    p.  cm. — (Modern war studies)
Includes bibliographical references and index.
ISBN 0-7006-0559-2 (hard cover)
    1. United States—Military policy.  2. Military doctrine—United
States—History—20th century.  3. United States—Armed Forces—
Weapons systems—History—20th century.  4. Military art and
science—United States—History—20th century.  5. Military art and
science—History—20th century.  6. Military policy.  7. Strategy.
8. Military equipment.  9. Arms control.  I. Title.  II. Series.
UA23.G786   1992
355′.0335′73—dc20                                                            92-10090

British Library Cataloguing in Publication Data is available.

Printed in the United States of America
10 9 8 7 6 5 4 3 2 1

The paper used in this publication meets the minimum requirements of the American
National Standard for Permanence of Paper for Printed Library Materials
Z39.48-1984.

TO THE MEMORY OF MY FATHER, BILL GRAY

# CONTENTS

| | |
|---|---|
| ABM | Antiballistic missile. |
| ASAT/DSAT | Antisatellite weapons or measures/weapons or measures for the defense of satellites. ASAT does not refer solely to weapons designed to intercept satellites in orbit. Any measures intended to destroy or impair the functioning of satellite systems (in any of their three segments—orbital, up and down links, and ground) fall within the purview of ASAT. |
| ASW | Antisubmarine warfare. |
| ATBM | Antitactical ballistic missile. |
| ATGW | Antitank guided weapon. |
| ATTU | Atlantic to the Urals, geographical scope of applicability of CFE treaty. |
| BMD | Ballistic missile defense. |
| CFE | Conventional Forces in Europe, treaty signed on November 19, 1990 (see ATTU). |
| C$^3$I | Command, control, communications, and intelligence. |
| GPALS | Global Protection against Limited Strikes. The Bush Administration's preferred ballistic missile defense program for the 1990s. GPALS is designed to thwart accidental or other small-scale missile launches, not massive attacks by a superpower. |
| ICBM | Intercontinental ballistic missile. A land-based ballistic missile with a range in excess of 3,400 miles. |

IMU — Inertial Measurement Unit; the guidance system for a ballistic missile.

INF — Intermediate-range nuclear forces; ground launched ballistic and cruise missiles with ranges between 625 and 3,400 miles. An INF treaty, banning all such missiles, was signed by the United States and the USSR on December 8, 1987.

IOC — Initial operating capability; the achievement of combat readiness by the first tactical unit equipped with a new weapon system (e.g., an ICBM squadron).

MX/MPS — MX (missile, experimental) ICBM, eventually named *Peacekeeper,* to be housed in multiple protective shelters. This was an ICBM basing scheme briefly favored by the Carter Administration in 1980. President Reagan abandoned this concept in 1981.

MX Rail Garrison — In 1986 the Reagan Administration announced a scheme to deploy fifty MX ICBMs on board twenty-five trains (two per train), with the trains normally in a garrison mode on bases of the U.S. Strategic Air Command. In a period of high political tension, or on receipt of strategic warning of attack, the MX trains would move out of garrison onto the nation's railroad system. The ICBMs could be launched from presurveyed sites.

"Overkill" — The idea that in a nuclear war targets would be destroyed several times over.

"Red Team" — A formal or an ad hoc group of experts convened or self-appointed to critique a particular idea or defense program.

RISOP — Russian Integrated Operational Plan; the Russian nuclear war plan deduced by the U.S. defense community from capabilities, for the purpose of testing the practicality of the SIOP. The RISOP was *not* a prediction of how the USSR most likely would wage central nuclear war. The RISOP's function, rather, was akin to an exercise machine for U.S. strategic forces and command arrangements.

SDI — Strategic Defense Initiative. The defense research effort launched by the Reagan Administration in 1983,

|  | concentrated under an SDI Organization (or SDIO) in 1984. |
|---|---|
| SIOP | Single Integrated Operational Plan; the U.S. nuclear war plan. |
| SLBM | Submarine-launched ballistic missile. |
| SSBN | Nuclear-powered ballistic missile submarine. |
| SSN | Nuclear-powered (attack) submarine. |
| START | Strategic Arms Reduction Talks; begun in 1982 out of the wreckage of the SALT II treaty, signed on June 18, 1979, but never ratified. START produced a treaty which was signed by Presidents Bush and Gorbachev on July 31, 1991. |

# Introduction

It is a supremely dangerous error to suppose that technology is a solution for the problems of war. A strategy devised by technocrats,
based solely on superiority in weaponry is no strategy at all. Machines do not win wars.

—Barry S. Strauss and Josiah Ober
*The Anatomy of Error*

American strategic culture is very, indeed excessively, machine-
minded,[1] and it is not surprising that the relationship between weapons and strategy remains poorly understood in U.S. public debate.
Noteworthy works on strategy in the English language, let alone works
on strategy and war, strategy and weapons, or strategy and technology,
are as severely limited in number as the literature on all aspects of military technology is burgeoning. If one looks for works that seek system-
atically to explore the connections among policy, strategy, and weapons, the hunt is poorly rewarded indeed. In a major study of World War
II, the military historian John Ellis complains appropriately about

> the enormous number of books and magazines that seem to con-
> centrate almost exclusively on the hardware deployed in the war.
> Illustrations and specifications of tanks, aircraft, warships, sub-
> marines and all manner of electronic devices are presented in lov-
> ing detail, the accretion of which has now laid on a technological
> gloss so thick that the reader inevitably loses sight of the essen-
> tial character of military operations.[2]

Certainly, many American strategic studies betray a weakness similar to that flagged by Ellis, and specifically, weapons tend to be confused with strategy. Instruments and their intended effects are merged by references to "strategic weapons" or to "the deterrent." It is the central purpose of this book to explain the properly subordinate—though still two-way—relationships of weaponry to strategy and to policy. As a subtheme, I emphasize also the necessary synergism of weapons with people in weapon systems, with other weapons in combined arms teams, and—in particular—of weapons operating in several geographical environments for common military and political purposes.

The works of Carl von Clausewitz and Alfred Thayer Mahan are not as widely read as they should be, but the advice they proffer on the correct relationship between policy and war, let alone between policy and weaponry, has long been recognized as true.

> We maintain . . . that war is simply a continuation of political intercourse, with the addition of other means.[3]

> The office of the statesman is to determine, and to indicate to the military authorities, the national interests most vital to be defended, as well as the objects of conquest or destruction most injurious to the enemy, in view of the political exigencies which the military power only subserves.[4]

Clausewitz advised that

> the first, the supreme, the most far reaching act of judgment that the statesman and commander have to make is to establish by that test [of war as an instrument of policy—i.e., what is the policy?] the kind of war on which they are embarking; neither mistaking it for, nor trying to turn it into, something that is alien to its nature. This is the first of all strategic questions and the most comprehensive.[5]

Seven of the chapters in this book present complementary explorations into an important aspect of the broad subject on which Clausewitz and Mahan have just been quoted: the relationships among policy, strategy, and weapons (rather than war). Taken in order, these seven chapters examine the relationships between or among policy and offensive or defensive strategies (Chapter 1); policy, strategy, and allegedly offensive or defensive weapons (Chapter 2); policy, weapons, and the so-called arms races (Chapter 3); policy, strategy, and the weapons acquisition process (Chapter 4); policy, strategy, and defense planning for uncertainty (Chapter 5); policy, strategy, and arms control (Chapter 6); and the historical record of the connections among policy, strategy, and weapons in the nuclear age to date (Chapter 7).

The thread of argument that binds these seven explorations together also reflects my discontent with much mainstream strategic theory, defense analysis, and policy practice; namely, weapons, weapons and military forces "processed" through operational or war plans, military strategies, competitive arms relationships, and arms control processes are all frequently treated as things apart. When Clausewitz wrote that "war should never be thought of as *something autonomous* but always as an *instrument of policy*,"[6] he provided the guiding light that can drive away darkness on the complex subject of this book. For "war" substitute weapons, arms races and arms control processes, and the thrust of the text of this book is revealed.

Clausewitz's observation about the proper dominance of policy and strategy over military means is so familiar as to be a cliché, and unfortunately, the familiarity of clichés often means that both critical intelligence and appreciation of an author's qualifying ideas are neglected. Necessarily, policy has to be supreme in and over war, but war has its own "grammar"[7] and can reshape policy. It is the connections between the logic of policy and the alleged "grammar" of strategies, weapons, arms races, and arms control processes that form the basis of this book.

Polities as more or less distinctive strategic cultures tend to commit characteristic errors; indeed, their errors may be caused by some of their virtues. For example, the leading American student of Byzantine military history has judged as follows:

The conviction that there was utility in using the mind to devise cunning stratagems, ruses, and techniques of war to wage war effectively yet cheaply was a two-edged inheritance from antiquity. It encouraged an admirable proclivity to use one's head in thinking about war, yet it also many times created a dangerous even disastrous overconfidence in the ability of the strategist to offset, through cleverness, quantitatively and perhaps also qualitatively superior material and human resources and power.[8]

The same author goes on to say that "excessive overconfidence and intellectualism in military operations" resulted in "an underestimation of basic underlying forces, such as the role of numbers, in the outcome of war."[9] For a much more recent example, in World War II the Japanese pursued operational dexterity far beyond the point where it would be likely to yield positive returns. The initial Japanese rampage to the south in 1941–1942 was indeed operationally dextrous, but at Midway (June 1942) and Leyte Gulf (November 1944), the Japanese military dexterity deteriorated into mere complexity. Not for nothing are simplicity and maintaining the objective listed as enduring principles of war.

In two world wars, it was the Germans' misfortune to have a cultural inability to function effectively at the strategic level of conflict. That is to say, Germany never succeeded in effecting the necessary mutual adjustments between military prowess and policy ambitions. By and large, German military power was the epitome of military effectiveness—unit for unit—in both world wars,[10] but there was never enough of that power to accomplish the strategic tasks, and the higher strategic direction of that tactical and generally operational German military excellence usually ranged between poor and abysmal.

An undue machine-mindedness is the American cultural equivalent to Byzantine strategic oversubtlety, Japanese operational overcomplexity, and German neglect of strategy. As with the Byzantines, the Japanese, and the Germans, this characteristic American weakness is a paradoxical and pathological consequence of American strengths. It has been the "American way of war" to substitute both weight of material and the power of machines for thought and for military skills (in planning and in execution)[11]—which has meant making a virtue of necessity. The continental and overseas geography of America's wars has required competence, even excellence, in logistic planning and execution. American geography (great distances), some lack of military skills (inexperience), high valuation upon the individual (sensitivity to *American* casualties), and general machine-mindedness have produced a way of war that is above all else technical and logistic in character.[12]

Americans have not thought of war as politics with violence and they have tended to be much better at building the machines of war, and applying them tactically, than they have been at orchestrating tactical effect for operational consequences and operational success for strategic victory. The United States has won its wars through brute force—at least the wars that were winnable by such means. Desert Storm stands in healthy contrast to the direct approach to war typically favored by the United States since the 1860s,[13] but it is sad to observe that even in the military triumph of Desert Storm the United States and the grand coalition it led proved to be stronger in battle than wise in war. It is as if American strategists learned only part of the critical lesson they should have learned from the Vietnam trauma. They learned that the U.S. armed forces must be permitted to select achievable military goals which unquestionably equate with military victory, but they did not fully recognize the need to select military goals compatible with political victory.

In recent years it has been fashionable to demand that the United States as a defense community should "think smarter, not richer" and should develop and apply "competitive strategies." These are excellent ideas. They are not, however, very American ideas. Time and again in this book, reference is made to inappropriately technical approaches to truly strategic or political questions. The primacy of policy as a guide for strategy and of strategy as a guide for military power is incontestable and is unchallenged in American public debate, but in practice, strategies, weapons, arms competitive dynamics (and alleged consequences), weapons acquisition, and arms control processes are all discussed as if technical matters really drive the political and strategic worlds. None of my comments should be interpreted as denigrating technical analysis or the analysis of technical subjects. Defense preparation and war do involve technology, but they also involve politics, economics, psychology, military skill, and a host of other factors. In this book, my central theme is weapons and military technology and their relations with policy and strategy.

If readers approach this volume looking for a single dominant, let alone new, theory, they will be disappointed. The relations among policy, strategy, and weapons are complicated and vary with issue, time, and country. There is, however, one factor that links the seven topics explored here: the conviction that strategies, weapons, arms competition, arms acquisition, military plans, and arms control tend to be approached in the United States too much as technical subjects separate from broader strategic or policy meanings.[14] It is not my purpose to make a case against, and certainly not to serve an indictment upon, defense theorists and practitioners. Instead, the seven chapters should be thought of as seven systematic explorations to "worry" at the complex topics being considered. This is an enquiry, not a trial.

This book is written to help explain the structure of the problem or condition of the complex relations among policy, strategy, and weapons,

not to advocate particular solutions to discrete difficulties. I believe
that there is a great deal of confusion today about offensive and defensive strategies; about weapons with allegedly offensive or defensive
characteristics; about arms races and their consequences; about weapons acquisition; about how military planning should be conducted; and
about the value of arms control. As noted above, this work endeavors to
cut away the confusion by examining the structure of the subjects discussed. I advance no single "wonder thought," no master formula guaranteed to deliver national success.

Even if, as some theorists would argue, the world is in the process of
becoming vastly more "geoeconomical," as opposed to geopolitical[15]
(which seems improbable), the general subject and subordinate topics
addressed here will retain their significance. The identity of adversaries may change and military technologies will evolve, but the relations
among policy, strategy and weapons will remain critical elements of
national security. Americans can benefit from improved understanding
of the subject of this book, whatever the course of future U.S. military
strategy. I have intended this work to be detached and scholarly, but it
is necessary to recognize that strategic studies is an applied social science and that a vital test of excellence in strategic matters is the test of
practicability: can it, does it, work. From time to time, therefore, I
shrug off some detachment and assume an explicit advisory mode.
When that occurs, however, I typically recommend a system of ideas or
an approach to an issue area; I do not advocate this or that operational
idea or weapon program.

The analysis presented here obviously is rooted in a particular time
and place. Although the concrete historical examples that support the
conceptual argument are generally recent or contemporary, I have
made no effort to confine the illustrations to a particular period. This is
a book about the complex sets of relations among policy, strategy, and
weapons technology and, more generally, about the connections between technology and defense. It is not about U.S. nuclear strategy, nuclear war plans, or strategic nuclear force posture. Although those
closely interrelated topics do indeed figure prominently here, their elu-
cidation should be read more as illustrations of argument than as subjects of discussion in their own right.

Five points may be useful in reading the chapters that follow. First,
the policy relevance of this discussion is both desirable and inescapable. Relations among policy, strategy, and weapons can be explored as
matters of defense philosophy, but truth in this area is ultimately prag-

matic. Clausewitz drew a sharp distinction between "real war" and "war on paper."[16] Ideal connections among policy, strategy, and weapons are valuable as standards and as guides, but practical people seek practical assistance from ideas that must be workable in more than the formal, logical sense.

Second, it is easy for defense philosophers, and practical-minded professional defense critics alike to forget that the best is frequently the enemy of the good enough. In order for the purposes of defense effort to be achieved, the right side must win, but it need not win in the most elegant fashion possible. Victory need not be heroic for a Western democracy that seeks to protect a vision of international order. The strategic merit in a military organization is always relative rather than absolute. It is no accident, then, that this text is about policy, strategy, and weapons. Strategies and weapons require assessment in relation to the objectives set for them by high *policy*, which is not to deny that policy can err if it sets goals that are unduly expansive or unduly modest.

Third, unless one endorses some facsimile of Francis Fukuyama's intensely optimistic thesis that "history as such" is ending, or has ended, with "the universalization of Western liberal democracy as the final form of human government,"[17] the subjects of this book are of permanent public and intellectual interest. Technologies and political players will change, but the relationships probed here are not period bound.

Fourth, the international political system has ceased to be bipolar. What is occuring is the redistribution of power and the restructuring of power relationships. What is not occurring is a radical shift in the nature of international politics. The 1990s are registering the end of the postwar world and the ragged, uncertain emergence of a post postwar world, but the evidence for the imminent birth of a thoroughly benign "new world order" is unconvincing.[18] I do not deny the reality and force of change, but I do deny as fantastic the prospect for "the end of history"—at least as history has been described from the time of Thucydides to the present.

Fifth, extreme claims about the implications of the nuclear revolution abound, but they should be treated with reserve. Popular understanding of the effects of nuclear weapons has enabled even stupid or desperate policymakers to appreciate how bad a future war could be. The possibility of prompt mutual catastrophe and the improbability that nuclear strategy will lead to a classic military victory have revolutionized the military terms of the security arrangements among the great powers. However, as Robert Jervis acknowledges, nuclear weapons, though not conducive to the achievement of military victory, are eminently well adapted for the pursuit of political success.[19] It is possible to view any use of nuclear weapons as an irrational act, a view that is central to the thesis of a study by Edward Rhodes.[20] Rhodes recommends that instead of seeking to eliminate irrationality from contingent nuclear employment, the United States should endeavor to build a credible case for behaving irrationally.

I find no merit in Rhodes's argument, traditionally known as the "rationality of irrationality"; I deny the validity of John Mueller's argument that nuclear weapons have been essentially irrelevant to international security;[21] and generally I find the academic literature on nuclear strategy and deterrence to be short on empathy for the real-world dilemmas of policymakers, defense planners, and soldiers. Highly critical appraisals of U.S. policy, strategy, and weapon choices stand in a long line, but their authors offer little more in the way of practical, real-world conclusions than this appraisal of the British navy: "One historian who investigated the British navy in the early eighteenth century was so appalled by what she found that she concluded the empire must have been won by trade, for it could not have been won by the navy."[22]

CHAPTER ONE

# Offensive and Defensive Strategies

Useful distinctions can . . . be drawn between offensive and defensive policy goals, strategies, and capabilities.
—Samuel P. Huntington
"U.S. Defense Strategy"

## POLICY AND STRATEGY

The meaning of a country's weapons is determined more by its policy than by the technical characteristics of its weapons. In evaluating a weapon system, then, we must first distinguish between satisfied and dissatisfied states, or between reformist, perhaps even revolutionary or "rogue" states and status quo powers. Usually it is easier to assess the military value of a country's armed forces than to predict how the country is likely to use them.

Whether a policy is judged offensive or defensive is very much a matter of political perspective. A state with a wholly self-interested view of security can justify to its own satisfaction a bid for world empire. If a strictly national security is deemed the absolute highest good, policymakers can rationalize the imposition of a Carthaginian peace on all actual or potential rivals. Policy goals may be identified as either balance-of-power or hegemonic.[1] The former seeks an international systemic security via the negative condition wherein no state or coalition achieves an "immoderate greatness."[2] The latter seeks unilaterally to achieve an unassailable national security via the achievement of a favorably unbalanced relationship of power.

An offensive strategy is a mode of operation whereby conflict is taken to (or around) the enemy, possibly for the purpose of disarming him forcefully and certainly with the intention of damaging his ability or willingness to continue the struggle. Offensive strategies express determination to set the terms of engagement through exercise of the initiative. A defensive strategy is a mode of operation whereby an enemy is obliged to make at least the first move, to reveal his intentions through action. Competently exercised, a defensive strategy requires the enemy to attack his opponent's strength or abandon hope of achieving a swift decision by arms.

Although the United States is a status quo power whose strategy necessarily must serve defensive policy goals, American political culture is not friendly towards passivity in strategic method. The United States is a problem-solving society, deeply imbued with faith both in progress and in the ability of active people to move progress along. Historically viewed, defensive strategies do not sit well with popular American expectations of their country as an important player in the great game of international security politics.[3]

## THE KEY CONCEPT: STRATEGIC EFFECTIVENESS

Defense debate in the United States is unnecessarily confused and fragmented by the lack of a common currency, a lingua franca in which the outputs of disparate kinds of military and diplomatic activity can be expressed. The concept of strategic effectiveness provides that common language. It is a goal- and adversary-oriented concept that accommodates in a single idea the benefits to be secured via action at sea, on land, in the air, and in or through space, whether such action be offensive or defensive in kind.[4] Strategic effectiveness may be defined as net impact upon the course and outcome of a conflict. For example, the third unrestricted *guerre de course* waged by imperial Germany's U-boats in World War I, in 1917–1918, can be examined in three ways: tactically, operationally at the level of the campaign, or strategically for its net effectiveness upon the course of the war as a whole.

Deterrence and war must be viewed together. It is the goal of U.S. policy to deter war if possible, but to win if need be. Policymakers are interested in success in land combat, or in a missile "exchange," only insofar as such success has favorable meaning for the course and outcome of a war. Strategic effectiveness, unlike tactical effectiveness, cannot be quantified; nonetheless, it is the concept that should be thought of as supervising the mathematics of tactical engagement. The idea behind strategic effectiveness is that tactics (the threat or the actual use of armed forces of any kind) is of interest in strategy and policy making only for its consequences. In and of themselves, the sinking of ships or the destruction of satellites and silo-housed ICBMs is of no particular interest. If, however, these events have important implications for the ability or willingness of the enemy to fight on, then one has entered the world of strategic effectiveness, indeed of strategic consequences.

The fighting power of a military unit, no matter what its size or character, is not necessarily synonymous with its strategic effectiveness. Fighting power is a tactical, not a strategic, concept.[5] For example, the German army typically generated fighting power superior to all adversaries, unit for unit, in both world wars, yet Germany lost those wars. Thus, fighting power must be assayed as a quantitative, as well as a qualitative, concept. (The German army plainly was the best fighting instrument for land warfare, but there was not enough of it for the tasks it was assigned.) Furthermore, environmentally specific fighting power, no matter how impressive in quality and quantity, will usually be restricted in scope geostrategically.

The concept of strategic effectiveness obliges analysts to consider the probable and possible actions and intentions of the enemy. Strategy is a dual-relational idea. Its Janus-like character has at its heart both the dialogue between national means and national ends and the competitive interaction between our performance and the enemy's performance. Strategic questions are means-ends questions. Describing operations as offensive or defensive makes sense only in strategic perspective. What are our objectives? How well endowed are we with the means, the instruments, to achieve them? A temporary deficiency in military means need not necessitate a defensive strategy, because the exercise of the initiative through surprise or surprise effect can function as a great force multiplier. If a defense establishment has slighted questions of the estimated strategic utility and putative strategic effectiveness of tactical behavior, it is likely to be punished severely as a consequence in the event of crisis or war. Professional politicians are, by nature of their expertise, all but certain to treat defense questions astrategically—primarily as opportunity-cost matters of scarce resource allocation. Defense professionals, by contrast, are the would-be guardians of a strategically rational military establishment shaped in its possible duties by policy-anticipating and policy-responsive plans. A defense establishment that speaks the language of strategic utility and strategic effectiveness can, by virtue of that fact alone, help shape debate to ensure a responsible decision. Moreover, unless a plausible strategic utility story is included when a new weapons capability is introduced, the new capability would merit budgetary difficulties.

## STRATEGY, OPERATIONS, AND TACTICS

To understand the relationship between offense and defense in military preparation for deterrence or in the conduct of a particular war, strategy, operations, and tactics must be disaggregated. (For example, an offensive tactical style may serve a bid for offensive success in a theater campaign that is, overall, in support of a defensive strategy.) It is well to remember Clausewitz's point that although defense preparation and war have a policy logic, they also have a military "grammar." The purposes for which armed forces fight, and even some of the terms of engagement, should be determined by politics. However, the details of combat and even the selection of suitable tactical combinations must have *military* integrity in terms of the grammar of war, not the logic of policy. Limited war can no more translate into limited effort in combat than a defensive policy and strategy can dictate a defensive style in operations and tactics.[6] Similarly, the fashionable concept of low-intensity conflict embraces special operations that can involve small numbers of elite soldiers in the most high-risk, desperately personal form of combat.

Clausewitz's distinction between the (policy) logic and the grammar of war finds no better illustration than the problems that faced the disintegrating "Soviet" Union of Sovereign States in 1990. Soviet political leaders solemnly claimed that their country was shifting military doctrinal gears in favor of the defense.[7] Soviet military science, on the other hand, argued that offense is the dominant form of warfare. Since Soviet *military doctrine* was the rough equivalent of U.S. *national security policy*—with political-social and military-technical dimensions—Soviet spokespeople had some room to maneuver in explaining why Western expectations of Soviet postural change rested upon a conceptual, even a linguistic, misapprehension. Nonetheless, even if the advertisement of a defensive defense was intended to mean what optimistic Western observers said it meant, the military instrument still had to function according to rules that made military sense. It is a dilemma for the military professional if his government demands a tactical and operational style of military behavior that mirrors policy motives yet affronts rules of military prudence. Tactically offensive actions undertaken for precautionary reasons of security lend themselves to political interpretation as evidence of offensive policy intentions. Furthermore, a commitment to operational-level counteroffensive prowess would be distinguishable from a thoroughgoing offensive orientation only via the fragile footprints of deployment details.

If a country has any positive objects among its war aims—if it aspires to accomplish anything beyond merely repelling an aggressor— then offensive action is required at some time. The grammar of war in the form, say, of very hot pursuit, might turn a genuinely defensive strategy into an operationally offensive action. In addition, prudence suggests that a repulsed foe should be so punished that he will be unable to resume his aggression for many years to come. It is a cliché, but still true, to affirm that war cannot be won on the defensive. The problem for the statesman and the military leader is to know how to combine offense with defense. Although a defensive mode concedes the initiative to the enemy, it does not mean passivity, even at the tactical level of war. Active and passive defenses are clearly distinguishable, although the former can shade into offensive operations, depending upon their reach and scale.

## OFFENSE AND DEFENSE IN THE FOUR ENVIRONMENTS

The character and extent of a state's physical geography exercise a large influence over the style and objectives of its warfare. The specific strength of one state relative to other states must always be considered important, as must the technologies of war in any particular period. Still, there are enduring features of conflict fairly specific to the distinctive physical geographies of each of the four environments for war.

Offense and defense are terms employed casually in public discussion, though typically with little recognition of how they relate to each other; in ignorance of whether or not they are reliably distinguishable; without sensitivity to the question of whether the nature of competition at the technical-tactical, operational, strategic, and policy levels of conflict should determine the style of combat; and, overall, with little careful thought about the synergisms between offense and defense at each level or between levels (for example, tactical defense in aid of operational offense or operational offense in aid of defensive policy).[8]

It is generally true of land warfare that defense is the stronger form of war. The defender knows the ground to be fought over, is able to prepare it for attack, and obliges the enemy to expose himself physically by movement and to signal his intentions by the direction of his movement. If pressed hard, the defender falls back upon his lines of communication, while the attacker must lengthen his logistic tail as he advances (assuming he cannot live off the country).

By contrast, in war at sea the offense generally is the stronger form of war.[9] Away from fortified coastal bastions or maritime defiles (chokepoints), a tactically overmatched naval force cannot employ terrain as a force multiplier. With only modest qualification—bearing principally upon lake-like (or "closed") seas that can be dominated by land-based military power—a superior navy will be able to secure a working control of *all* of the maritime conflict environment. The continuity and uniformity of the oceans and the inherent maneuvering agility of naval assets provide a substantial premium for an offensive style in tactics. Whether or not superior sea-based power can fulfill offensive, (that is, positive), objectives in operations and strategy must depend upon the course and character of war as a whole. For example, the U.S. Navy might rule most of the world's oceans (subsurface, surface, and in the air), but its strategic function could still be defensive if the United States lacked the means to take the fight from the sea to a preponderantly land-based enemy.

War in the air has more in common with war at sea than with war on land. The air, like the maritime environment, cannot itself be fortified for defense. Similarly, the fact that aircraft are inherently maneuverable yet provide concentrated fixed targets on their (admittedly fortified) bases, renders the continuous "air ocean" a region wherein the offense is the stronger form of war. Tactical and technological circumstances can modify the force, even the applicability, of this general principle (contrast the Battle of Britain in the late summer of 1940 with the air Battle of Germany in spring 1944).

The tactical offense-defense relationship in a war in space is a matter for speculation. Pending the availability of true hybrid, aerospace planes, the space environment would appear, somewhat counterintuitively, to share more combat features with the land and the sea than with the air. The offense may appear to be the stronger form of war in space, given the absence of terrain obstacles, the relative paucity of capital assets (and targets), and the global consequences of military success or failure. But in practice, the space environment near earth is very sharply differentiated by the action, or absence of action, of gravity. Space vehicles of all kinds lack the agility of aircraft and ships. Furthermore, the predictability mandated by the orbital mechanics that express Keppler's three laws of motion, the possible vulnerability of antipodal chokepoints,[10] and the problems of geosynchronous (and far beyond) "parking" alert us to the positional features of space warfare and the fortification of space. Overall, it is by no means self-evident that the offense must be the strongest form of war in space. For the technologies of the 1990s, it is plausible to argue that the offense is the strongest form of war in low earth orbit, but that in high earth and geosynchronous orbits the defense enjoys critical advantages—of distance from credible threats and ability to hide in orbits not easily surveilled.

At present, offense is the strongest form of "strategic" nuclear war, at least in the limited sense that defensive means of all kinds cannot reliably prevent large numbers of offensive weapons either from being launched or from completing their flights. But, in a truly strategic sense—bearing upon means *and ends*—defense is the stronger form of war, *by way of countervailing offense*, in that offensive weapons cannot disarm an enemy of his like weapons. In principle, though not necessarily in practice, two unstoppable strategic offensive instruments should have the same implications for statecraft as would a standoff between two impenetrable defenses.

## THE VITAL SYNERGISM

The best defense may be a good offense, provided the offense is good enough both to defeat the enemy's military power and to prevent him from punishing with a dying sting. The merit in this ancient aphorism depends on the environment for the combat in question and upon the specific tactical-technological and quantitative circumstances. In land warfare it has generally been the case that the strongest form of war was the operational offense functioning synergistically with the tactical defense. In other words, the traditional course of action was to invade the enemy's country—masking or avoiding his frontier fortresses—and then dig in on high ground (with flanks protected by a river, marsh, or wood), obliging the enemy to attack. An invasion can create this situation unintentionally when it achieves only an incomplete success. A classic example occurred in France during World War I. When the Schlieffen Plan failed on the Marne in the first week of September 1914, the German army withdrew to the best defensible high ground in its immediate rear and, sitting on occupied French territory, obliged the enemy to attack uphill. After consolidating the Western Front in mid-November (with the conclusion of the first Battle of Ypres), the Germans launched only two major offensives in the West during the next four years. The first was conducted in 1916 at Verdun to defeat the French by attrition. The second was an attempt in the spring of 1918 to separate the British and French armies at their boundary on the Somme and defeat the British before the Americans could field an army large and competent enough to ensure Allied victory.

Even a happy synergism of operational offense and tactical defense does not provide a magical elixir for success. Wise strategic philosophy and sound military method cannot compensate for gross deficiencies in material and manpower. After the summer of 1943—and the last major German offensive in Russia, at Kursk in July—it probably did not matter what blend of operational and tactical styles and methods the German army adopted in the East. Hitler has been vilified for his waste of scarce units with hopelessly inflexible stand-fast orders, but in 1943–1945 there was simply too little Wehrmacht attempting to defend too much territory against too materially strong a coalition of enemies.

Strategically, offense and defense are united when a military instrument can protect the country either by success in battle or by a reputation for such superior prowess in war that a would-be enemy dare not hazard a trial by arms. A naval blockade can have this synergistic character. Whether close or distant, a blockade invites the enemy to come out and fight, and pending acceptance of that invitation, the blockading navy protects the use of the sea for whatever purposes war leaders prefer.

Offensive attrition typically envisages three steps to military operations. An initial offensive blow is designed severely to impair the enemy's capability to strike; the enemy's weakened offensive capability then poses a more manageable tactical challenge for friendly defenses; residual friendly offensive forces subsequently should enjoy a marked military advantage over whatever reserve force the enemy has been able to withhold from combat. This stylized sequence of hypothetical campaign events aroused particular anxiety among many American arms control theorists in opposition to hypothetical SDI deployments. In other words, U.S. offensive forces would "set up" damaged and uncoordinated Soviet offensive forces for postlaunch defeat by U.S. strategic defenses. Defensive attrition is a classic idea, a time- and experience-hallowed formula for success in land warfare. The function of prepared defenses and associated tactics is not to hold indefinitely against any weight of assault, but so to weaken the enemy by attrition and perhaps disorganization that he is optimally vulnerable to a counterstroke.[11]

Offense and defense should work synergistically to reduce the performance required of either to a manageable level. This point is explained most easily with reference to the tactical synergism between sword and shield/body armor. A swordsman bereft of shield and armor is obliged either to take inordinate risks in quest of a quick kill or to devote himself almost totally to defensive swordplay. When there is no ability to resist or absorb punishment, even if offensive success is judged possible, knowledge that the outcome is uncertain will inhibit the freedom of action with which the offensive instrument would otherwise be used. When self-protection rests wholly upon the power to disarm the enemy, Pyrrhic victory is likely. Neglect of the principle of protection virtually invites the enemy to find a "knight's move" that evades the opponent's offensive strength (witness the U-boat campaigns of both world wars).[12]

States generally do not seek success in war as an end in itself. War must be worth the winning. A Pyrrhic victory, while preferable to defeat, is a victory achieved at a price seriously disproportionate to the gain. The ghost of Pyrrhus moves as a dire warning through the halls of nuclear-armed governments.

## THE APPEAL OF THE OFFENSIVE

An offensive strategy should feed upon its own success and allow maximum flexibility in the exercise and exploitation of the initiative. Whether one plans only for the initial clash of battle and intends to function strictly opportunistically thereafter or designs a grand battle that is to be synonymous with a campaign and with the whole of the war, an offensive style should secure control of the terms of the fighting. An offensive mode of operation, even if the overall policy and strategy are defensive in purpose, requires an activism of mind and behavior that has a strong appeal, for good reasons, to the military profession.[13] Fighting power and strategic effectiveness are both highly sensitive to morale. A defensive strategy can all too easily foster a passively defensive attitude towards tactical style and can permit the enemy to achieve moral ascendancy.

It is generally, but not universally, true that an offensive strategy requires larger forces than does a defensive strategy, but a defensive strategy at sea would require the deployment of much larger naval forces than would an offensive strategy. The local defense of sea lines of communication, even when the assets to be protected are herded in convoy, is far less efficient than defending them via a decisive battle against the concentrated naval strength of the enemy. Of course the enemy may decline to be accessible for climactic destruction or to permit itself to be blockaded.[14]

Contemporary strategic warfare could be characterized by weapon-exchange ratios that placed only relatively modest quantitative demands upon the offense. With warhead-to-launcher ratios as high as 10:1 and 8:1 (and they could be higher) and launcher-to-platform ratios as high as 24:1 or 20:1 (*Ohio* and *Typhoon* class SSBNs), cost-exchange arithmetic for an offense abundantly armed with accurate warheads is very favorable, provided the enemy's weapons can be located and denied the time to launch.

Offensive missions at the operational level of war—albeit in support of a defensive strategy—require larger and more militarily capable forces than defensive missions. If the United States was determined to assign extended deterrent tasks to its strategic nuclear forces, for example, it should build larger rather than smaller forces, that are highly lethal against well-protected military and political targets.[15] A minimum deterrent against nuclear attack upon the U.S. homeland probably need not be designed or sized to accomplish much more than the nuclear ruin of some large urban areas. For an extreme example, it is reliably reported that in the 1980s all sixty-four of Britain's submarine-launched ballistic missile (SLBM) force, with 192 warheads, were targeted upon the greater Moscow area.[16] In the context of a surprise attack, London could have relied on only one, at most two, of its four *Resolution* class ballistic missile submarines being safely out at sea (16–32 missiles with 48–96 warheads), but for a national weapon of "last resort," guaranteed penetration of Moscow's ABM system was deemed mandatory. In British eyes, *the* test of a minimally adequate national nuclear deterrent has been the ability to wreak conclusively massive damage upon the Moscow area.

By definition, offensive forces require the logistical reach to take war to the enemy, be they near or far, and must pay the transaction costs of projecting power over distance. Offensive military power—or, more strictly, military power capable of acting offensively—permits and encourages a more ambitious foreign policy. Given that threats to the United States can emanate from Europe and Asia, and that U.S. presidents—in common with most statesmen—would like to exercise extensive influence over their external security environment, it is not difficult to understand why a U.S. military reach confined to southern Canada and northern Mexico would lack both political appeal and strategic prudence.

Offensive striking power in whatever form—naval task forces, expeditionary forces, long range air and missile power—is appealing because of its ability to fight abroad rather than at home. From time to time, large countries in particular have had no choice other than to wage war at home and trust that the tyranny of distance and the operation of "friction" would drive the invader fatally beyond his "culminating point of victory."[17] But no country chooses to fight at home if there is any practicable alternative. The United States could not function significantly in the balance of power unless its armed forces had transoceanic reach. Germany, France, and Russia, however, could be more or less active players in the politics of European security regardless of the tilt between offense and defense in their military policies, merely because of their geographical position. This would not be true for a power located in the Americas. The overly tidy minds that read character of political purpose into the character of military capabilities often fail to appreciate that a United States pursuing a defensive strategy in support of a defensive policy in Europe and Asia requires armed forces capable of large-scale offensive action.

An offensive style in war expresses the sensible desire to exercise control over military, and hence probably political, events. If the enemy has his hands full attempting to thwart our initiatives, he will lack the freedom of action needed to conduct the war as he prefers. Of course, the defensive side hopes that "the paradoxical logic of conflict"[18] will cause the offensive side to bring about its own defeat through overextension or other forms of operational error. A basic appeal of an offensive mode of operation is the promise that it should carry to impose a favorable *decision*. Defense-heavy strategies for war necessarily have difficulty explaining "how we win." If the initiative is conceded to the enemy, he may choose to "take as much or as little of the war as he will."[19] A defensive posture is likely to deny us the ability to inflict intolerable pain on the enemy, and thus to defeat him. Most military machines decline voluntarily to batter themselves to destruction against powerful defenses. In the absence of offensive striking power, it is virtually impossible to craft a compelling theory of success in war. If the offense is eschewed, the full reward for successful defense will thereby be foregone also.

## THE APPEAL OF THE DEFENSIVE

At the policy level of conflict, the level where calculation of national interest determines why, whether, and how much war should be waged, there is a systemic "defender's advantage."[20] A state is generally more willing to fight to hold what it has than to fight to seize the assets of others. Assuming substantial military capability, a defender typically, but not invariably, can count on superior political determination as a force multiplier for deterrence or denial.

Tactically and operationally the defense may be regarded as purposely delayed offense. A defensive phase of operations can entice the enemy to commit to attack on particular axes, then utilize flank maneuvers to make the attack wrong-footed. Defensive operations can also encourage the creation of vulnerable salients that can be exploited for the attrition of the enemy force. Rival propositions on time contend for authority. On the one hand, an enemy on the move will generally provide information on his intentions that is critical for effective real-time battle and campaign planning. On the other hand, although conceding the initiative and adopting a defensive posture could yield a great advantage in intelligence, the enemy may move so swiftly or unexpectedly that the intelligence cannot be exploited for timely counterstrokes. Thus, the advantage of warning must be considered together with the ability to respond.[21]

A defensive cast to military plans and dispositions, whether real or feigned, may dampen foreign anxieties. There is scant historical evidence of countries going to war inadvertently as the result of military moves intended to be solely precautionary.[22] Nonetheless, there is much to be said for the prior interrogation by policy of national mobilization steps for the purpose of minimizing the risk that military professionals would unknowingly trip attack-warning indicators abroad.[23] One hardly need add that military action, or more likely inaction, intended to *reassure* an adversary that he is not about to be attacked could have the unfortunate consequence of reassuring him that his opponent is less than determined to oppose aggression. There is more tension than is readily apparent between the two words in the concepts of crisis management, limited war, escalation control, and even war termination.

Defensive plans and posture, or even just claims to that effect, have considerable value as political theater in influencing opinion in democratic polities. For example, in spite of conclusions about the character of "the next war" derived from careful analysis, the French government in the 1930s believed that it had to eschew offensive military planning if it was to secure another continental commitment from Britain. Unwisely, though understandably (given recent history: 1914–1918), the French saw more security in a full-scale military alliance with Britain than they did in national military planning crafted to cope with the actual evolving German threat. This is not to suggest that France knowingly pursued a defense policy and developed operational plans that were bound to fail. French strategic thought and military style in the 1930s were certainly defensive, or—at most—very deliberate. They were geared to the lessons of 1916–1918, not to the operational tempo of blitzkrieg. The wonders of blitzkrieg, however, were much plainer in 1940–1941 than they had been in 1938. Furthermore, it was the forward, arguably offensive, movement of the better French (and virtually all of the British) forces to the River Dyle to cover Brussels that almost literally opened the door into France at Sedan on the Meuse.[24] This French example was paralleled by NATO's political inability in the 1980s to conduct serious campaign planning for the defense of west-central Europe, which entailed more than the repelling of invading forces.[25]

Just as a defensive doctrine can help legitimize military preparation in democracies whose statecraft has only very modest ambitions, it can also have immediate political appeal to people who are convinced, or simply assume, that defense requires smaller forces than does offense. This conviction, though not wholly without merit, is only a half-truth at best. As Napoleon and his leading interpreters, Jomini and Clausewitz, emphasized, it is not necessarily (that is, not in a short war) overall force ratios that matter; much more important are the force ratios at the decisive points.[26] The German army was inferior in some key quantities to the combined armies of France and Britain in May 1940, but Allied folly and German tactical skill and operational artistry secured a massive superiority of force where it most mattered locally. Similarly, the U.S. Navy in the Pacific was distinctly inferior to the imperial Japanese navy in May and June of 1942, but through operational incompetence the Japanese contrived to be inferior at "the tip of the spear" in the critical battle of Midway.[27]

The tactical appeal of defense, and particularly of a passive style of defense, is all too easy to understand. Fortifications can enable mere garrison-quality troops to overperform, while first-class soldiers can be all but immovable, even in the face of exceedingly poor odds, when physical geography and engineering ingenuity are enlisted to multiply fighting power.

## SOME LESSONS OF HISTORY

There is limited validity to the thesis that the evolution of weapons technology has influenced the size of polities (one should not say states or nations, since these concepts have full meaning only for the modern world). It is certainly true that war, or at least force, has been the most important influence in shaping the political world. However, while it is valid to assert that in some important sense gunpowder gave us the modern unified state,[28] and that the oceangoing sailing ship (with broadside-firing artillery) permitted the acquisition of global maritime trading empires,[29] the proposition breaks down in this century. The railroad and the internal combustion engine have not guaranteed the consolidation, let alone the great expansion, of continental empire,[30] save in the very special case of the United States, nor have long-range ballistic missiles and spacecraft produced global empire. The logic and sentiment of national political affinities has more than offset any deterministic logic of "dominant" weaponry for the size of polities.[31] Indeed, as the twentieth century moves toward its close, the most powerful political force extant is that for the disaggregation of great multinational state-empires into their cultural or regional components, not for their consolidation or growth. The year 1991 witnessed the demise not only of the USSR, but also of the Russian empire. Similarly, the problem in Yugoslavia has more to do with minority nationality repudiation of what in effect has been the modern Serbian empire than with the rejection of communist rule.

Efforts to demonstrate historically how periods of military defensive advantage have alternated with periods of offensive advantage, *in aid of the thesis that an edge for the defense is benign for international peace and stability*, have been less than persuasive.[32] The problems are that decision in war has generally been achievable, albeit often at a very high price; that policymakers can never know reliably in advance the cost of the military decision they seek; and that success or failure in war is influenced by so many factors that a reductionist focus on weapons technology is seriously misleading. Military history is no more *essentially* about weapons technology than it is *essentially* about leadership, tactical and operational skill, strategic judgment, morale, or logistics. In short, reductionist claims of all kinds should be denied.

Interpreted sensibly, rather than driven to excessive lengths as Luttwak did in his *Strategy*, the idea of paradox is a key to understanding the relationship between offense and defense. Although there are times when a good offense is a good defense and vice versa, overly enthusiastic pursuit of either style of warfare tends to become self-defeating. As a general rule, war can only be won on the offensive, but it cannot be won by the offensive alone. There are limits to what can be achieved by either offensive or defensive operations alone. Undue devotion to one or the other mode of warfare poses severe problems of balance and thus detracts from overall strategic effectiveness. For example, even a magnificent strategic nuclear offensive capability is sharply limited in its strategic effectiveness by its inability reliably to deny all retaliatory options to the enemy.[33] Active and passive homeland defenses, if good enough, could transform the strategic offensive arsenal progressively from an instrument of retaliation into an instrument of coercion, and ultimately into an instrument of decision.

I believe that the quality of military personnel matters more than marginal advantages in weapons technology or weapon numbers. Provided the disparities are not monumental in size, human tactical and operational skills combined with a willingness to fight can often compensate for low numbers and technological deficiencies. This principle holds true at all levels of conflict, and whether an armed force is on the offensive or the defensive. Offensive success requires defensive cover lest victory in one theater, environment, or part of the battlefield be balanced (or overbalanced) by defeat elsewhere. Early in 1917, for example, there was ironic speculation in London on the subject of whether the British army could win the war before the Royal Navy lost it (at that time the navy was resisting the introduction of convoys in the face of the German renewal of unrestricted U-boat warfare).[34] In 1748, for a further example, Britain returned the key fortress of Louisbourg, located on Cape Breton Island and dominating the Gulf of the St. Lawrence, to France according to the terms of the Treaty of Aix-La-Chapelle, which concluded the War of Austrian Succession—a price worth paying for French evacuation of the Low Countries. The relevance of this synergism between operational defense and offense in the cold war era was almost painfully self-evident. The western alliance could not have succeeded in war on the Central Front in Europe if it had failed to defend its sea lines of communication across the Atlantic, or if the Soviet Union could have won a coercive strategic nuclear campaign and simply bypassed a theater stalemate.

The defense is most likely to succeed if the enemy can be denied the luxury of concentrating, unattrited and undistracted, on his offensive purpose. By the analogy employed above, an enemy swordsman will find his job much more difficult and dangerous if he is obliged not only to find a way of penetrating his opponent's protective armor, but also to avoid painful and weakening (if not fatal) strikes by his opponent's sword.

### EXTENDED DETERRENCE

For its defensive political purposes as a status quo power, the United States must prepare to wage operationally offensive operations at sea, in the air, and with its central strategic systems. The "transatlantic bargain" that cemented—as well as troubled—the NATO Alliance required a promise of U.S. nuclear action to punish the Soviet Union at home should it invade NATO territory. So long as the U.S. strategic posture was perceived as critical for the structure of the NATO deterrent, a primarily defensive orientation in that posture was ruled out a priori.

No matter which grand targeting design is preferred or is tactically and technically feasible, the idea of taking the war to the enemy is integral to the concept of extended deterrence. Rival opinions on the benefits and dangers of an offensively oriented strategic deterrent were simply ignored, while NATO willfully underprovided for direct regional defense in Europe. The U.S. strategic force posture was required by high policy to be able to reach and damage Soviet assets at home. The tactically offensive character of that posture may be judged to have arisen from technological circumstance (the relative incompetence of strategic defenses), but it was preeminently a reflection of the duties imposed by U.S. foreign policy.[35] To extend deterrence it is not sufficient simply to have the capability to reach the putative enemy. That enemy must believe that he runs an unacceptably large risk of suffering intolerable pain should the extended deterrent ever be unleashed against him. Credibility alone does not ensure a sufficiency of deterrent or strategic effect. Indeed, there is a fundamental tension between credibility and prospective pain. Because of sensible fear of retaliation, the more painful an action is, the less likely it is to be taken, and the less likely it is that anyone will believe it will be taken.

The quasi-official January 1988 report on *Discriminate Deterrence* made the commonsense point that an intelligent adversary will endeavor to negate the relevance of inherently indiscriminate deterrent threats by posing only very selective challenges.[36] That point may or may not be important as a prediction—as contrasted with a philosophical truth about strategy—but it inclined its authors to focus unduly on the adjective "discriminate" and insufficiently upon the noun "deterrence." Emerging technology certainly lends itself to adaptation in weaponry suitable for discriminate application, but the issue is whether the very discriminate threat or use of new weapons technology is compatible with theories of success in extended deterrence or in war itself. The United States is not particularly interested in the discriminate potential of weapons use as an end in itself; instead it requires that its weapons generate sufficient strategic effectiveness to achieve the goals set by policy. In the 1990s it is a U.S. strategic principle to apply force to decisive effect, as well as discriminately.

As noted above, an offensive style to U.S. military planning, which includes the ability to project and support power over great distances, is mandated by the logic of geostrategy. The United States happens to be buffered from Eurasia and from the local threats to the balance of power within that great bicontinent by oceans. To achieve a literally defensive deterrent, the United States would have to risk allowing the security of Eurasia to be reorganized by some bicontinental hegemonic state or coalition. However, by geopolitical principle, such a reorganization of security in Eurasia would pose severe threats to long-term American interests.[37] It is possible that Europe and Asia may achieve a new balance of power without the active participation of the United States, but American policymakers cannot assume such an outcome.

THE GREAT SDI DEBATE

The popularity of the appealing idea of nuclear "overkill" as well as an unmistakable nuclearphobia helped convince President Reagan in 1983 that the United States must shift the terms of the arms competition toward a new strategic defense initiative (SDI). Proponents of the SDI argued that the United States was dangerously hindered by a nuclear-aversive public (and Congress) from competing on even political terms with the Soviet Union in strategic offensive systems in general, and in ICBMs in particular.

Strategic analysis is an endangered species in the United States. Unfortunately, the SDI has been the kind of complex subject that cannot be treated competently outside an explicit framework of strategy assumptions, yet it lends itself to debate by a wide range of technicians and arms controllers whose modes of analysis rarely include the strategic. A central issue in the debate over SDI was whether the U.S. government really sought defensive forces in lieu of offensive forces, or favored defense and offense operating synergistically. At the level of naked concept or vision, strategic defense certainly was advertised politically as the functional replacement for offensive nuclear weaponry. In his March 23, 1983, speech, President Reagan both speculated about a condition wherein nuclear-armed, long-range missiles would be rendered "impotent and obsolete" and warned of the possible danger (in the currency of Soviet feelings of insecurity) of adding strategic defense to strategic offense.[38]

The years of renewed debate after 1983 on the subject of strategic defense have not seen much constructive public discussion of the SDI with reference to the means-ends issues of strategy. Strategic vision for new defenses cannot be restricted to the desirable terms of tactical engagement with offensive capabilities, or indeed with adversary defenses (if there should be two space-based defensive systems). Instead, the desirability of new defensive weapon deployments must be examined with reference to the policy ends and strategic objectives assigned to the U.S. armed forces as a whole. Before the U.S. government endorses the notion of a wholesale, or even a very substantial, transition to a defense-heavy strategic posture, it should have clearly in mind both what that posture must be able to do and what mix of offense and defense is desirable in the U.S. forces. As history marches into the disorderly 1990s, the arguments for and against active missile defenses need to be refocused and in many cases wholly rewritten to reflect the changing orientation in U.S. defense policy.[39]

Much has been made of the "moral imperative" to defend (the American) people, if such a defense is feasible. It would be morally superior, it is alleged, to deter a nuclear attack by plausible threats to intercept weapons in flight, than with the threat to punish an enemy's society. There is merit in this argument, there is enormous public-political value in it, and there is even strategic sense lurking there. Nonetheless, the U.S. government's "moral imperative" is not only to defend Americans physically, but also to defend the vital security interests of Americans in Eurasia. All combinations of strategic defense and offense are not equal in their ability to contribute strategic effectiveness in extending deterrence abroad.

In a strategically permissive context (when the adversary is bereft of convincing countermeasures), active missile defenses are a boon to regional security—as was demonstrated by *Patriot* in Desert Storm. As well as providing valuable antitactical ballistic missile (ATBM) protection, missile defenses added to competent offensive capabilities of all kinds would both help protect those capabilities and enhance the credibility of their contingent first use (for defensive policy purposes). For reasons of prevailing stability theory,[40] not to mention arms control complications, and with reference to superpower relations, the United States has explicitly denied that it seeks unilateral military advantage from the deployment of new strategic defenses. However, if regional conflicts and the ambitions of "rogue," would-be "rogue," or even "crazy,"[41] political leaders are to be the leading preoccupation for U.S. policymakers and defense planners in the decade ahead, then the United States as the leading protector of order must enjoy all manner of military advantage. If the United States lacks missile defense cover in parallel with air defense cover for its armed forces and for the assets of local friends, it will become less and less likely that Washington will judge the rising perils of forward deployment or actual intervention to be tolerably in balance with American regional interests. As missile technologies proliferate and weapons of mass destruction gain new owners, the SDI should be reconsidered and redefined, not as an "extra" likely to create dangerous instability in superpower strategic relations (it is not self-evident that there are superpower strategic relations anymore), but as a vital adjunct to more traditional military capabilities. The Bush Administration stepped up to this challenge when it redirected the SDI toward a system providing Global Protection against

Limited Strikes (GPALS).[42] Many of the traditional critics of ABM and later SDI have yet to revise their strategic arguments for the new era of the 1990s.

The argument in this chapter has emphasized the overriding importance of policy choice over military style at any level of activity—strategic, operational, or tactical. The complementarity of offense and defense is underwritten by all of military history. Defensive operations, when successful, serve to weaken the enemy and render him vulnerable to counteroffensive strokes. The defense may be *"the stronger form of waging war"* on land,[43] but rarely can war be won by defensive strategy alone. That judgment— how best to combine offense and defense— varies with the scale of ambition in war aims.

A status quo power, such as the United States, that is generally a defender of the existing order among states must be able to conduct offensive operations by the logic of policy, the grammar of war, and the facts of physical geography. In support of defensive policy goals a status quo state must be prepared to coerce, and if necessary defeat, disturbers of regional order. Virtually by definition, status quo and revolutionary or rogue polities find themselves locked into military styles of operation that are the reverse of their political orientation. A status quo power must design and execute, if necessary, an offensive strategy that will push back an aggressive rogue power from forcible acquisitions. In that case, the compelling need to coerce falls on the side endeavoring to restore order, and the rogue state is likely to switch to a defensive strategy in order to consolidate his gains.

Common sense is by far the best guide through the thicket of issues discussed here. The character of a state's leadership and that leadership's policy choices provide the context and guidance for grand and military strategy. The idea that offensive or defensive strategies can function as autonomous factors that make for war or for peace independent of policy choice is a plausible fallacy. Policy makes war, not types of weapons, character of strategy, or operational style.

# CHAPTER TWO

# Offensive and Defensive Weapons?

As the Arab use of antiaircraft missiles during the 1973 war against Israel has demonstrated once again, the distinction between "offensive" and "defensive" weapons is largely spurious.
—Martin van Creveld
*Technology and War*

## PURPOSE DETERMINES FUNCTION

The most important fact to know about a weapon is who owns it. Therein lies the most potent clue to its meaning for international security. ICBMs, tank forces, and nuclear attack submarines (SSNs) per se are not problems for U.S. national security; the problem is SSNs owned by potential enemies.

Most policymakers and defense analysts pay obeisance to Carl von Clausewitz's half-truth that "war is simply a continuation of political intercourse, with the addition of other means."[1] Clausewitz exaggerated the ease of fit between war and politics, even for his own day, but he did properly direct attention towards the policy world as the source of meaning for military preparation and action. The "materialist" approach to defense policy is ever prone to perpetrate the fallacy of equating threat with capability.[2] This is not to deny the importance of capabilities analysis, but rather to signal the inappropriateness of treating weapons as the disease rather than as the symptoms they are. The interpretation of intelligence information is often more difficult and error-prone than is its collection in the first place. It is harder to determine why, when, where, or whether a force will be used than it is to assess the quantity and qualities of that force. Prudence and concern over the options a military capability will give its political owners can encourage the mechanistic attribution of political intentions that match some reading of the apparent military facts. It is but a short step to equating threat with weapons.

Unfortunately for certainty in analysis, virtually all military capabilities lend themselves to alternative judgments about the motives of their owners. In 1939 Prime Minister Neville Chamberlain was convinced that Hitler neither wanted, nor was ready for, war.[3] At some time in the future, a U.S. president could be so convinced that "a nuclear war cannot be won and must never be fought"[4] that he would not believe intelligence warning indicators of a potential enemy's preparations for war. Political and cultural assumptions about the risk-taking propensities and determination of other states and societies are typically a more potent source of policy error than are mistakes in narrowly focused defense analysis. In July and very early August 1990, notwithstanding Defense Intelligence Agency warnings to the contrary, the U.S. Department of State simply did not believe that Iraq would invade Kuwait. Policy preconception overcame the evidence and powerful analysis that contradicted it.

Although weapons and the man-machine combinations known as weapon systems are, strictly speaking, only the instruments of policy, the fact remains that policy intentions can shift far more rapidly than the capabilities of armed forces. There is a standard presumption in the lore of international politics that for the purposes of order, if not immediately of peace, power is better balanced than unbalanced. The cold war, traceable ideologically to 1917 on the Soviet side and at least to the early 1920s on the U.S. side, erupted so rapidly in 1946–1947 because of what is best understood as capabilities analysis on the grand scale. World War II had completed the destruction of the European balance-of-power system, leaving the United States and the Soviet Union as the only two essential players in the security "game" in Europe and Asia. In the early part of the century, Britain assumed correctly that the new German High Seas Fleet—with a radius of effective action limited to the North Sea—was directed against her;[5] a similar assumption about the U.S. Navy was entertained as a possibility in London in the immediate aftermath of World War I.[6]

It is assumed, prudently if often erroneously, that long-range weapons will be used offensively—if there were no such intention, why build them at the high price long range typically exacts? The compatibility of long reach with offensive or defensive strategy and policy is a complication for threat assessors abroad. Also, sound policy judgment is complicated by the fact that superior war-fighting ability is virtually synonymous with superior deterrence. In fact, much of stability analysis in the West amounts to the exercise of a material-minded political, moral, and geostrategic equivalence most frequently expressed in the policy recommendations for, and policy products of, the arms control process (see Chapter 6). When applied to superpower nuclear arsenals, however, the parity principle could translate into effective geopolitical disparity. Weapons in the hands of a satisfied state or coalition have a strategic meaning different from weapons in the hands of a revolutionary, "super-rogue," or even "crazy" state. A blithely democratic approach to weapons can promote policy recommendations for parity between the weapon stocks of status quo and dissatisfied powers.

## INHERENT AMBIGUITIES

The matched ideas of offensive and defensive weapons seem to have taken root ineradicably in our strategic culture. In common usage, an offensive weapon is a weapon that has the reach to hurt an enemy at a distance. To be considered an offensive weapon in the so-called central strategic warfare between the superpowers, for example, a weapon must have the range to reach between continents. In ground warfare, however, all weapons, from bayonets to artillery pieces, can have direct offensive application. A defensive weapon, on the other hand, is typically understood to be a weapon of very limited reach. However, tactical context and operational purpose determine whether a weapon is used offensively, defensively, or indeed in both ways simultaneously. *Tactically viewed*, there is no valid distinction to be drawn between weapons on the basis of their allegedly offensive or defensive properties. This generalization holds whether the subject is knives or ICBMs. Policy determines whether they serve offensive or defensive functions.

The absurdity of the claimed offensive/defensive distinction at the tactical level may best be illustrated by the contrasting strategic functions of France's Maginot Line and Germany's Siegfried Line in 1939–1940.[7] Both were fixed fortifications, though the former was by far by the more formidable of the two. The Maginot Line was the servant of a comprehensively defensive strategy, notwithstanding the evolving plans to advance the left wing forward into central Belgium and southern Holland—otherwise known as "Plan D" and the "Breda Variant." The Siegfried Line, on the other hand, was the servant of an offensive strategy; a passive defense if ever there was one, the line was designed to close Germany's back door against the West and thereby free the Wehrmacht for operations in the East.

Soviet propagandists claimed that with its SDI the United States sought to develop "space strike weapons." Moscow argued both that strategic defense functioning synergistically with offense could have an overall offensive strategic purpose, and that long-range, space-based weaponry could operate in a tactically offensive as well as defensive mode. At the levels of philosophy and common sense, these Soviet points were correct—the real world of military hardware could lend itself to the interpretation that Moscow chose. The Soviets were not correct, however, in the strategic motives they attributed to most American promoters of SDI. The ICBM is another case of ambiguity. ICBMs are inherently neither offensive, nor even strategic, weapons. U.S. ICBMs are military instruments of a satisfied, status quo power and alliance; their function in peace is to deter and in war to restore deterrence. ICBMs are weapons like other weapons; the strategic effect of their tactical use could vary as widely as the policy goals they serve.

## INOFFENSIVE DEFENSE?

It is possible to design a national military force capable only of performing in defense of the home territory. Switzerland and Sweden are both heavily armed countries, but their arms lack reach and could not be employed effectively beyond the fortified, or at least very well surveyed, terrain of the national homeland. Any country can assume a militia-style military posture at the operational and strategic levels of analysis by utilizing the "nation in arms" concept. The result is an inoffensive defense.

Prominent among the problems with a militia-style defense (as indeed with a "strategic" posture consisting strictly of air and missile defense units) is its failure to provide the country's foreign-policy makers a military instrument with which they can project power. A militia-style defense can provide small numbers of soldiers for U.N. peacekeeping tasks (without the logistic assets to support them), but not much more. Even Japan, a country constitutionally prohibited from deploying offensive armaments, finds that its self-defense forces need an ever wider reach to protect maritime lines of communication and for air defense.

A serious strategic problem with the idea of inoffensive defense is that it sometimes offers only a distinctly third-rate promise of deterrent success. Territorial defenses of one kind or another—guerrilla (or partisan) warfare, fortification of difficult terrain, and so forth—may suffice for deterrence if the putative enemy is not strongly motivated to attack. Such a defense gives the enemy serious pause for thought, which may suffice, as it did for Switzerland in the two world wars. The most interesting case, however, is not Switzerland, but Germany. A politically significant body of opinion in Germany today favors a variant of strictly territorial defense—an "inoffensive deterrent." It is important to remember that the overriding purpose of defenses is seldom physical defense alone. It is to threaten the aggressor with a Pyrrhic victory—a price for aggression that is high enough to deter him. Unfortunately for a country such as Germany, the strategic and political value of her territory is likely to be so high in an enemy's estimation that territorial defenses could not even begin to impose a prohibitive scale of costs on an invader. Also, although inoffensive homeland defenses can be very credible, their lack of reach sharply limits the risks an aggressor would run.

Arguments for inoffensive defense take different forms according to the unique geostrategic circumstances of each country, but they share an underexamined premise pertaining to the systemic nature of international conflict. Proponents of inoffensive defense tend to espouse either strong or weak forms of the argument that "offensive" arms are, or can be, provocative. Indeed, offensive arms frequently have been defined as "aggressive."[8] According to this logic, whatever marginal benefit for deterrence may flow from weapons of greater reach would be more than offset by the enhanced motivation to plan for war they would encourage abroad. Although this belief contains a germ of truth, it has been irrelevant in the cases of most interest to Western countries in the twentieth century. For example, it was not at all likely that Soviet military policy during the cold war was fueled to any important degree by anxieties over the possibility of an attack by NATO. The Soviet general staff was deeply professional and realistic in its military analyses,[9] and one cannot even imagine a sixteen-member coalition agreeing secretly to a policy of aggression.[10] Although some in the West might have believed that mobile and long-range weapons in the hands of NATO forces in Central Europe would fuel deep anxieties in the East, it is more likely that Western forces created anxieties over the efficacy of Soviet plans for a successful theater offensive in the event of war (which Moscow did not want). NATO's armies were never scheduled to take the high road to Moscow in a great offensive; that fact must have been self-evident to Soviet political experts and defense professionals.

The concept of an inoffensive defense, in the form of a defense-dominant strategic posture, a territorial militia, "civilian defense" schemes, or a coastal defense navy can appeal to the popular yearning for a quiet life in international security affairs. For a country legally or traditionally neutral, such a defense makes sense—as the Swiss can attest. For members of NATO, for the coalition as a whole, and particularly for *the* superstate security guarantor, the concept makes no sense at all.

## GEOSTRATEGY AND THE UTILITY OF WEAPONS

The weapons most useful for defensive or offensive purposes vary dramatically with the geostrategic circumstances of each security community, as well as with the scale, scope, and direction of a state's foreign policy ambitions.[11] However, the changing technologies of transportation, including platforms for power projection, have had a continuing radical effect on the relative utility of weapons with different reaches. Local continental or close off-shore defense of the United States was not an unreasonable concept in the era when the threat was a transoceanic invasion from Europe.[12] In the nineteenth century America's first line of defense was not its local ability to repel an aggressor, but rather the workings of the European balance-of-power system. Military threats from abroad were better thwarted at the source than en route or on arrival. But even had that not been practicable, a strictly continental defense was still eminently feasible, though not infallible against a state or coalition endeavoring to project power across the ocean.[13] Active British military assistance to the Confederacy could have been an exception, though even in that hypothetical case continental European menaces would have had a major entropic impact on British effectiveness in North America.

Notwithstanding the high technical promise of SDI, robust defense of the United States against a full, superpower-scale nuclear threat is not possible at present.[14] In the absence of thoroughly reliable defenses, it is only by the development of a military posture with intercontinental reach that U.S. national security can be protected. A coastal-defense U.S. Navy had already been judged insufficient by the end of the nineteenth century; it is unthinkable today. Moreover, given the monumental problems of midcourse discrimination of warheads from decoys and "chaff," the United States SDI has been forced to attempt to develop "defensive" weapons with what amounts to a global reach. Only from orbiting platforms could U.S. missile defenses inflict a catastrophic rate of attrition upon attacking ICBMs (before the postboost vehicles had dispensed their warheads and decoys). Therefore, even with respect to unmistakably defensive missions, technology and geography mandate today that the respective strategic reach of defense and offense should be virtually identical.

Understandably, the American electorate appears to be as confused about the relationship between offense and defense as are many national security professionals. The dominant thread of Western strategic thought for a quarter century has paradoxically accorded defensive capability a uniquely offensive interpretation. A defense that defends *people* has great popular appeal, and hence political clout, but it challenges the intellectual bedrock of the dominant theory, perhaps the actual condition, of mutual nuclear deterrence.[15]

In the seemingly upside-down universe of modern strategy, the defense of society menaces the ability of the putative enemy to deter by the threat to punish *us*. Our safety, allegedly, requires that a superpower foe be unchallenged in his ability to devastate us. Stable deterrence mandates mutual vulnerability, in this mad logic. Notwithstanding President Reagan's vision of a reliable defense of U.S. society against ballistic missiles, neither his administration nor the one that succeeded it has overthrown the familiar, contingently murderous logic of mutual deterrence via fear of massive societal retaliation. That claim is easily supportable by reference to the attention paid to the awesome, if doubtfully defined, difficulty of effecting an orderly transition from a security condition of offense dominance to one of defense dominance.[16] Unsurprisingly, perhaps, the political condition behind superpower deterrence vanished before the doctrinal issues could be resolved.

Political perspective determines judgment on the offensive or defensive character of weaponry and military posture. For example, in the short-sighted French view at the turn of the century and again in the 1920s and 1930s, submarines were clearly defensive weapons for a second-class naval power like France.[17] But the British, with a great trading empire that needed freedom of maritime passage to survive, viewed submarines as offensive weapons. For a further example, throughout the cold war NATO viewed the Group of Soviet Forces in East Germany (GSFG) as plainly offensively armed and postured. GSFG was equipped and trained to seize (NATO) territory. But from the Soviet perspective (which was always political), until at least 1990, an offensive posture in land power was simply a matter of obeisance to sound military science and military art. The defense of socialism (or Soviet imperial interests) could not be construed as an offensive mission, either ideologically or in terms of realpolitik. The confusion caused by applying the terms offensive and defensive in situations like these illustrates the difficulty of making any intelligent use of them whatsoever.

## PROBLEMS OF DEFINITION

As with the abuse of the term "strategic" in strategic forces,[18] correcting the casual misuse of the adjectives "offensive" and "defensive" is a semantic lost cause. No useful purpose can be served by fighting the problem of imprecise language. Strategy is a practical subject; the language with which it is analyzed and described should be practical as well. Arbitrary use and abuse of the key value-charged terms "offense" and "defense" promotes confusion in thought, public debate, and even in policy. It matters when politicians fail to understand that offensive and defensive qualities can inhere in the same weapon or military unit. It is also important to remember that the political perspective of the owner is by far the most weighty influence on the designation of weapons as offensive or defensive. It is not a particularly complicated proposition to suggest that an offensive weapon can serve a defensive policy or that a defensive weapon can serve an offensive policy, yet people tend to resist the unsettling idea that there are no offensive or defensive weapons, only weapons.

Theorists and other commentators generally agree that mobility (obviously a variable) is the principal characteristic of an offensive weapon, closely followed by the capabilities of firepower and protection.[19] The ability to maneuver is virtually synonymous with, though certainly not confined to, offensive potential. Therefore it is not surprising that technical gains for tactical mobility tend to favor, though they do not mandate, offensive operational designs and strategic objectives. Tactical doctrine must be built around the potential effectiveness of man-machine weapon systems working in combined arms teams, rather than the strategic gleams in the eyes of generals and policymakers. But, the scope of operational and strategic ambition can expand as the tactical level of war *demonstrates* that it can deliver battlefield outcomes with operational and strategic implications.

The phenomenon of intellectual ossification, or hardening of the categories, has been nowhere more apparent than in the U.S. defense community's approach to strategic offense vis à vis strategic defense. The latter assumed positive and negative political symbolic status, on the Right and Left respectively, to the detriment of intelligent operational and strategic debate. Allegedly offensive and defensive technologies, tactics, operational schemes, strategies, and policies have been confused with each other, without recognition that weapons cannot be labeled as offensive or defensive outside operational, strategic, or policy contexts.[20] The world of the strategic thinker and high-level defense planner should be inclusive, not reductionist or exclusive. The idea that certain classes of weapon systems, certain tactics (prompt launch of ICBMs, for a classic case), and certain operational schemes can be identified as undesirably "destabilizing" (for which read "offensive" or even "aggressive"), regardless of the country employing them or the strategic context, is symptomatic of the Jominian fallacy of essentialist reasoning.[21] Reductionist thinking neglects, as it discards, the combined arms setting for weapons and fails to examine conflict as a whole.

## TECHNICIST FALLACIES

Weapons technology has played only a modest role at most in policies for war or peace and in the selection and subsequent amendment of war aims. This claim is somewhat counterintuitive, but is supported by a reasonable interpretation of the historical evidence. States and coalitions have demonstrated a remarkable proclivity to fight, and to fight on, in pursuit of perceived vital national interests, almost regardless of ever-manipulable technology-based tactical, operational, and strategic arguments.

The evolving nuclear facts of the current age have effected some significant changes in this situation, and politicians from very different political and strategic cultures have accepted some facsimile of a technological peace. Possibly because of an unprecedentedly powerful "crystal-ball effect,"[22] optimistic prognoses for the course and outcome of *great war* have met with far more policymaker skepticism than typically was the case prior to 1945. Nonetheless, the idea of a technological peace can easily be misinterpreted. The rivalry between states is not driven by an autonomous, ever-escalating technological arms race (see Chapter 3), and should war occur it is unlikely to be because of some technological trigger. (For example, the notion that some piece of space debris might impact a satellite, be mistaken for an antisatellite weapon and function as the mechanical equivalent of the assassinations in Sarajevo on June 28, 1914, is simply the stuff of which novels are made.)[23]

The technically minded arms control community is susceptible to the fallacy of reducing the rich complexities of arms competition to the simple model of a clockwork universe. The competition is viewed virtually as a perpetual motion machine, containing in its several parts all that is required for endless chains of actions and reactions. The task of the arms control technician is to tinker with the machinery and either shift it into a lower gear, or perhaps gracefully end its functioning altogether. The record of the past thirty years is littered with proposals for "technicist" arms race fixes, great and small. The ABM Treaty of 1972 is *the* monument to Western-style technical arms control, since the driving idea behind it was the speculative theory that fear of defenses fuels the offense.[24] Other examples range from proposed bans on all underground nuclear tests, through a prohibition against the testing of ballistic missiles in a depressed trajectory mode, to the CFE treaty providing for the asymmetrical thinning out of weapons in Europe from the Atlantic to the Urals (ATTU). All such ideas and regimes share a common willingness to discount Clausewitz's connection between arms and politics except, strangely, for the fragile assumption that the details of military posture, targeting doctrine, and plans can matter greatly in decisions on war or peace.[25]

There is no question that technology is important. Ask an Afghan or a Russian soldier what battlefield and campaign difference the *Stinger* personal air defense missile made. The problem is that technology has been examined for specific characteristics—offensive or defensive—that it does not have. Also, technological trends have been wrenched out of their social and political contexts and held unreasonably accountable for particular consequences in the bloody history of international relations.[26] Technology and its effective military application are dependent, not independent, variables.

A popular technicist fallacy is the notion that the utility, indeed the general consequences, of new weapon technologies can be predicted with confidence. People tend to think that the military world is a stationary one save for the new weapon under consideration. Arms control negotiations have a way of encouraging policymakers to prohibit or constrain future weapon technologies whose precise identity, let alone possible utility, they comprehend scarcely at all. In addition, questions of weapon utility cannot be divorced from broader issues of strategic theory. A weapon cannot contribute to deterrence if a prospective deterree does not know of its existence, but the greater the surprise that attends weapons employment, the more, and possibly the more long lasting, the utility of that weapon is likely to be.[27] In fact, some weapons will be useful only if the enemy is unaware of their existence, of their mode of operation, or of their precise capabilities.[28]

## WEAPONRY, HEGEMONY, AND THE BALANCE OF POWER

It is remarkable how frequently the general character of the inferable purposes of particular states is neglected in defense analysis and strategic discussion. Broadly speaking, a great power has three choices in policy at the highest level: to seek hegemony (domination, a leadership position based upon plainly superior power); to seek a balance of power; or to endeavor to join superior power. Virtually by definition, a (somewhat) dissatisfied state such as the Soviet Union of the cold war era will seek such hegemony as international conditions and its own resources and skills permit. People who commented negatively in the 1980s on the burden of defense for the United States drew simple historical analogies that could not be supported by the evidence. A cardinal error, for example, in Paul Kennedy's historical analysis of *The Rise and Fall of the Great Powers* was that he failed to distinguish between states which sought a hegemonic security and states which sought security through the working of the balance of power.[29] Because the United States was not seeking absolute security over any and all possible foes, U.S. defense requirements have not constituted a frighteningly open-ended draw upon national assets.

Professional defense planners are obliged to provide designs for military success: what else can they do? But it is a matter of budgetary and postural record that the United States and its allies sought a tolerable equilibrium in peace, not victory in (*East-West*) war, as the payoff for sustained defense allocation. Some policy commentators in the West were confused over the purposes of a so-called war-fighting approach to deterrence, but there was little possibility of a similar confusion on the part of West-watchers in the then-Soviet Union.

For reasons of geopolitics and the apparent permanence of antagonistic attitudes, Israel provides a rare example of a democratic and at least quasi-satisfied (if anything, territorially *over*-satisfied) country obliged to seek regional military dominance. Israel believes that there can be no safety in a rough equilibrium of power. Instead, she has to be able to wage successful war, simultaneously, against any or all of her Arab neighbors and near-neighbors. The Iran-Iraq War of the 1980s was a boon for Israel, because it precluded for a long period the possibility of the (re)construction of an Eastern Front bloc against her. Offensive operations must be synonymous with defensive operations for Israel, since her national territory is too small to permit any noteworthy trading of space for time.[30] Similarly, the offensive use of naval power has often been a necessary *defense* for a maritime power. There is, perhaps ironically, some strength in the analogy between contemporary Israel and the strategic condition of two-front war anxieties in imperial Germany, at least as German military planners at the time defined that condition.[31]

A generally fortunate national geography, long expressing a destiny made adequately manifest, has allowed the United States, aprés Britain, to seek security through the workings of the balance of power. Since 1945 that balance has not been flexible because the United States has been committed to one side of the balance, and has, in fact, comprised most of that side. However, it is probable that future security in Eurasia will require less and less active participation by the United States. This point is politically important for those who must explain the rationale for the U.S. defense effort and predict the future financial burden of defense. The most accurate way to characterize the high-level purpose of U.S. military power is that power is maintained and modernized *in defense of the balance of power in Eurasia* as a vital American national interest. Balance-of-power rationales for U.S. military participation in local and regional conflicts in Europe and Asia require translation into language domestically acceptable to American society. The U.S. capacity for collective action can be exercised effectively only if official power-balancing motives can be presented in ideologically appealing terms.

STABILITY: A MASTER CONCEPT?

The concept of stability has some precise, quantifiable, meanings in the worlds of the medical and engineering sciences. For good or ill, however, stability has assumed totemic significance in the social sciences and particularly in the multidiscipline of strategic studies. As employed widely by defense theorists, the concept of stability is without precise meaning—of course, this may be part of its attraction—though it would be inaccurate to claim that the concept is meaningless. The imprecision in the concept may be gauged by considering its polar opposite, instability. It is difficult to argue the benefits of instability,[32] though one person's stable balance may be another person's unstable balance.

Given that most people can agree on the blessings of stability, plainly the difficulty pertains to definition. Abstrusely academic though this topic may appear, it so happens that people's understanding of what is and what is not stabilizing can both assume a highly dogmatic character and have a major influence on their attitude toward the funding of particular weapon systems. The stabilizing/destabilizing dichotomy has partially replaced,[33] but certainly has not exiled, the older distinction between offensive and defensive. The problem with defining a stabilizing weapon is much the same as the problem with cosmological theories: there is always difficulty identifying the first cause. If, as orthodox wisdom will have it, a stabilizing weapon is one that diminishes incentives (both the owner's and the enemy's) to strike first in time of (or in anticipation of) crisis, what are those incentives and to what degree are they technical? Do they bear upon the details of military postures?

Broadly viewed, there are two dominant perspectives on stability and on how particular weapon systems should contribute to it. These perspectives may be termed the punitive and the war-fighting or denial. The former holds that stable deterrence is best secured by the ability to visit unacceptable punishment upon an adversary's society. The latter perspective argues that stable deterrence is best secured by the ability to deny military success to the enemy's armed forces. A state should decline to resort to arms either if it believes it will suffer intolerable damage as a consequence, or if it has sufficient reason to believe that it will lose the war on any reasonable military assessment. The war-fighting or denial approach to stable deterrence does not preclude the punitive perspective. Armed forces competent enough to engage directly the nuclear-equipped forces of the enemy must always have the ability to inflict massive societal damage. If one admits the relevance of genuinely strategic considerations, it rapidly becomes clear why the idea of a stable deterrence resting upon two societal-punitive striking forces enjoying great pre-launch survivability lacked appeal both in Moscow and in Washington. Stability is a condition that not only should apply to the tactical relationships among forces, but also—strategically—should obtain in the relationships between forces and foreign policy objectives. Arms control theory and a great deal of arms control malpractice since the 1920s have neglected this important application of the idea of stability.

In principle there is no particular reason why a tactical level of crisis stability between strategic forces cannot be maintained by offensive arms alone. However, in the cold war both superpowers recognize the value of a mixed offense-defense posture, though for political reasons the United States was able to pursue strategic defense only in the ASW realm in the 1970s and 1980s. The SDI was motivated from the outset by official pessimism over the willingness of U.S. society, and of the Congress in particular, to fund an adequately competitive, modern *offensive* arsenal. U.S. political victory in the cold war threatens to overtake policymaking on strategic-force modernization. A United States that had great difficulty thinking strategically about its so-called "strategic" forces in the 1980s (and before) is unlikely to perform more rationally in a period when perceptions of a superpower scale and quality of threat are absent.

There are several ways in which active strategic defenses could assist strategic stability, even as variously defined. A large and reliable strategic defensive addition to a first-class offensive force should lend important credibility of likely action to that force. Less expansively and expensively, strategic defense could function—as do fortification, mobility, proliferation of numbers, and launch tactics—to enhance the prelaunch survivability of strategic offensive forces and the endurance of their $C^3I$. More to the point for the 1990s, strategic defense—including regional air and missile defenses—should enhance stability by increasing the likelihood that the United States would actually intervene in some regional high-threat environments.

In practice, strategic defense has a grave constituency problem. If pursued on a large scale, such defense could threaten to drain money critically needed for offensive-force modernization, a modernization required to support such extended deterrence duties as there may be in the future. On a much smaller scale, strategic defense seems to many people to be an unusually politically controversial, technically uncertain, and possibly expensive way of providing a strategic effectiveness that could better be secured by more traditional means. A challenge for the 1990s and beyond is to rethink offense and defense and their implications for stability with reference to a regional, as contrasted with a superpower, level of conflict. The threat posed by weapons of mass destruction (nuclear, chemical, and biological) may become less and less a problem that can be answered appropriately by the stable deterrence of cautious Russian policymakers. Furthermore, a strategic defensive architecture that could serve, at best, only to add a probably redundant layer of uncertainty to superpower war planning should be able to defeat the small and technologically far less sophisticated offensive arsenals of "rogue" regional powers.[34]

## TECHNOLOGY AND TACTICS

The objectives of strategy are sheer vanity if the tactical instrument lacks fighting prowess or sufficient mass to succeed in combat. Political, strategic, and operational direction of the tactical instrument may be flawed, but sustained failure in combat must vitiate all higher level schemes. There can be "workarounds" for occasional and partial tactical failures or weaknesses,[35] but tactical ineffectiveness will be fatal if it pertains to the center of gravity of a state's war-making needs. If a maritime power cannot win naval battles or sea campaigns, or if a continental power cannot win land battles, then it is very likely to lose a war, barring compensatory excellence on the part of allies, gross incompetence by enemies, or sheer good luck on a heroic scale.

Weapons do not determine whether men will fight or how hard they will fight, but they always dictate *how* they will fight. There is no necessary and obvious tactical logic to all weapons. Only trial and error will reveal how weapons should be employed in combined-arms teams, but it has been a general rule that military organizations have sought to accommodate new weapons within an existing framework of tactics.[36] It has also been a general rule that through a dialectical process new weaponry is adopted and employed in ways both more daring than skeptics deemed wise, and less imaginative than true believers deemed possible and desirable.

The tactical effectiveness that generates operational possibilities is unique both to geographical environment and to the technology developed for a particular environment. Tactical level decision for great strategic effect would be particularly difficult to achieve in a central nuclear conflict because of the extensive distribution of high military value among a large number of vehicles widely dispersed in their deployment. Strategic nuclear delivery vehicles, unlike surface naval vessels and ground forces, need not be deployed in a concentrated fashion for protection. A high rate of attrition will affect the military utility of central strategic forces, but will have only a disproportionately modest effect on their deterrent value. Indeed, a would-be first striker must assume that the enemy would elect to retarget his much disrupted and reduced central nuclear forces in ways maximally damaging to societal values. Whether or not this response would, or technically could, occur, it would have to be assumed.

The potential strategic effectiveness of armed forces varies with technology. For example, in World War I the air arm was an important, though not crucial, adjunct to land and sea forces, but by World War II the air arm had to succeed with its war if the land and sea forces were to win theirs. Since 1945 the nuclear-equipped air arm has borne the contingent promise of being able to deliver victory by its own independent action. That promise was attenuated and then nullified by the appearance and development of countervailing nuclear-equipped forces abroad. War is always a matter of possibilities, not of certainties. Technology as an expander of strategic horizons can be limited in practice by problems of quantity, of geography and climate, of quality in the human dimension of weapon systems, and by the actions of the independent will of the enemy.[37]

It is tempting to argue that a Law of the Instrument applies comprehensively in war. In this context, such a law could mean that high policy, strategy, and operations will follow wherever tactical potential and achievement lead. However, the universe of statecraft and strategy is highly imperfect. The Law of the Instrument cost Germany defeat in both world wars. U-boats were available in 1917–1918 and hence were used in an unrestricted fashion—which is to say according to their nature, to the grammar of war that they had to obey to be tactically effective—thereby bringing the United States into the war. As a very dissatisfied power, the Nazi Germany of 1940–1941 had a military instrument in its Wehrmacht that could not be placed in a condition of rest—save vis à vis the invasion of Britain—given that it was expected and required to be capable of delivering decisive continental victory (in the East). Some of the public discussion of nuclear strategy of the past several decades has reflected acceptance of a Law of the Instrument. There has been a widespread expectation that nuclear weapons would be used in war—after all, they are available—even though the strategic rationale for such use was obscure.

## MORAL ISSUES, PUBLIC SUPPORT, AND THE CLASSIFICATION OF WEAPONS

Weapons widely understood to be offensive in character, which is to say weapons possessing high mobility, impressive firepower, and adequate protection, lend themselves to characterization as "aggressive" in nature. The point cannot be made too often than there has never been an aggressive weapon, only aggressive owners and operators of weapons. Moreover, an aggressive spirit in tactics and operations helps define military effectiveness and bears not at all upon aggressive strategy or predatory policy goals.

On the relatively rare but important occasions when moral questions are asked of defense professionals, their answers tend to be so defensive in both tone and content that they fuel rather than allay suspicion.[38] Two points should be registered firmly at the outset of any debate over nuclear weapons in strategy. First, if the United States is to have a defense policy worthy of the name, that policy must have a nuclear dimension. The United States could not retire unilaterally from nuclear-related security issues, even if it wanted to. Second, the United States is an open, pluralistic democracy wherein all of the policy-essential facts about nuclear strategy have been publicly available for decades. If the American people had wanted to repudiate nuclear weapons, or effect some other radical discontinuity in nuclear policy, they could have nominated and elected a person for president on such a platform.

A just nuclear defense is easy to explain in plausible moral terms as long as one confines discussion to the elevated ground of deterrence. The kernel of the problem lies in the recognition that deterrent effect requires a perception of contingent intent, of will as well as of capability. A popular democracy cannot bluff.[39] If it were truly U.S. policy to scuttle and run in the face of a nuclear danger perceived to be imminent, one may be certain that that fact could not be concealed for long from interested parties at home and abroad. Among the more relevant moral issues is not the old canard of "is anything worth 100 million (or 200 million) American lives?"—to which the answer has to be NO; but rather "is anything worth the taking of grave risks that might lead to an open-ended nuclear catastrophe?"—to which the answer should be YES, an answer that has been endorsed thus far by the American electorate. History has seen many endorsements of the proposition that peace is best maintained via awesome threats. Unfortunately, perhaps, the attractively economical argument that war can be rendered too terrible to be an act of policy has been denied by events, is unduly risk-prone (as a policy this theory would be "unsafe at any speed"), and fails the test of strategy. Even though military reality can make a mockery of the logic, force is basically an instrument, if sometimes a wayward instrument, of foreign policy. Monumental threats are at least as likely to paralyze the deterrer as to frighten the deterree, particularly in an age when a good offense can no longer double reliably as a good defense.

Strategic study can easily become the domain of narrow specialists who achieve expertise and authority through more and more intensive examination of a less and less broadly framed subject area. However, that recent history suggests that a clear strategic rationale for a weapon system is a necessary, if not reliably sufficient, condition for public support. When an administration discards a particular weapon plan for extrastrategic reasons, even though legislative support is reasonably firm—as appeared to be the case with MX/MPS (Multiple Protective Structures) in 1980–1981[40]—it is likely, unwittingly, to snatch defeat from the jaws of probable political victory.

# CHAPTER THREE

# The Arms Race Metaphor

The history of Europe since the close of the Middle Ages, with the possible exception of the period 1870–1914, gives little ground for supposing that the tensions produced by rival armaments-systems have been the sole, or even the principal cause of international conflicts; and the history of North America, whose greatest war arose between two communities which at its outset were virtually unarmed, gives even less.

—Michael Howard
*Studies in War and Peace*

The moral is obvious: it is that great armaments lead inevitably to war.

—Viscount Grey of Falloden
*Twenty-Five Years, 1892–1916*

## THE IDEA

An arms race may be defined qualitatively as a condition wherein two or more parties perceiving themselves to be in an adversary relationship increase or improve their armaments at a *rapid* rate and structure their respective military postures with a *general* attention to the past, current, and anticipated military and political behavior of the other parties.[1] This complex definition is of a soft, commonsense kind. It is not controversial to claim that an arms race must be set in a context of political antagonism, that some features of the rival military postures must be changing rapidly, and that each participant is "racing" in preparation for the possibility of fighting one or more of the other participants. However, neither careful scholarship nor more casual judgment provides algorithms reliably capable of distinguishing between an arms race and defense preparation or modernization "as usual."[2] A distinction is frequently drawn between quantitative and qualitative arms races,[3] though it is close to impossible to discover a race, or an alleged race, in modern times that did not accommodate both themes. Quantitative races commonly are held to be more dangerous to peace than are qualitative, or technological, races because the former can point to an advantage in numbers that may provide confidence in military victory, while in the latter the military postures of the rivals are in a state of perpetual anticipation, awaiting dramatic improvement.

Modern attitudes towards competitive armament were influenced decisively by the misreading of the events of the decade preceding 1914. According to this popular version of history, a spirit of militarism reinforced by the products of greedy, amoral munitions makers ("merchants of death") fueled interlocking arms races in both land and sea forces. Aided and abetted by the cynical machinations of secret diplomacy, these arms races *somehow* produced the Europe-wide explosion of July–August 1914.[4] This travesty of historical (mis)interpretation continues to have a powerful impact upon popular and even some scholarly attitudes. Myth and metaphor continue to attract adherents.[5] The relations of cause and effect are highly speculative in typically only lightly framed arms race models, while the notion of a *race* in armaments is a metaphor that is as misleading (a set distance? a winner? an agreed kind of course?) as it is prevalent. Since it would be burdensome and pedantic to qualify all references to arms "race" in this chapter, readers are advised that my use of "race," "racing," and similar metaphors does not constitute conceptual endorsement.

## ALLEGED EVILS

In popular usage, the concept of arms race, like crisis, is permeated with intimations of danger. This metaphor suggests rival states or coalitions competing in a track event that only one side can win, with victory presumably opening a window of opportunity for successful military action. One racer could decide to fight while he is still ahead, or while he is behind but still close, rather than waiting until the rival opens a long lead or actually "wins" the contest. What does victory mean in an arms race? How does a state know when it has won? How is the finishing line recognized? Some wars have been preceded by phenomena that could be described as arms races, but many have not. Moreover, some so-called arms races have not been followed by war at all. It is scarcely surprising that a process of competitive armament should precede hostilities, since pairs or groups of states that believe their strategic relationships are likely to lead to war will probably want to arm against that eventuality.[6]

In addition to suggesting danger, the concept of arms race also suggests futility and waste (the arms race "spiral" and the like). The most common theory of arms race dynamics posits an action-reaction mechanism that suggests futility and waste, virtually by definition.[7] If what state "A" does is offset by the actions of state "B," round by round (albeit in a time-lagged response), then neither state will enhance its national security. They will, however, waste their taxpayers' money in futile pursuit of unattainable major advantage.

It has been argued that an arms race makes extraordinary demands upon, indeed involves the political mobilization, of whole societies.[8] Maintaining popular support for extraordinary defense expenditure and acquiescence to the demands upon society for the provision of military personnel en masse require a constant drumbeat of vilification of the enemy and wholesale praise of the merit in the national cause. In short, this argument concludes, an arms race militarizes society. Although there is some truth in this claim, it is only a restatement of the occasional character of political life in a condition of inter-state anarchy. Threat analyses can feed upon each other in feedback loops, of course, but the democracies in the twentieth century have faced genuine external dangers from dissatisfied and "rogue" powers. To cite the danger of unmatched military might in the hands of an insecure, would-be hegemonic power is not to militarize American society foolishly. Military power derives its moral tone from the political purposes for which it is employed. A gun is morally neutral.

The metaphor of the arms *race* suggests a "mad (mindless and possibly precipitous) momentum" of competitive armament that has escaped political control. It suggests a system of arms competition that works by its own systemic logic or grammar, not by the policy logic of responsible statecraft. Threat analyses and arguments over the likely strategic effectiveness for deterrence of, say, an antisatellite weapon program, tend to be dismissed simply as political cover, rhetorical rationalizations for a competitive dynamic unmoved by political considerations. It follows from this reasoning that massive opportunity costs accrue from competitive armament. Indifferent to the unyielding nature of inter-state power politics (another object of easy ridicule despite the better part of three millennia of historical evidence), some people believe that happier and safer worlds than the world of arms races beckon to those prepared to take bold steps for peace.[9] How many hospitals in Africa could be built, staffed and equipped for the probable cost of a small ICBM program? Armament, particularly acutely competitive armament, is equated with political tension and war; disarmament, need one say, means peace in the language of idealism.

## HOW DOES AN ARMS RACE "WORK"?

Three families of explanation have been offered to explain arms race dynamics. They focus upon technological imperatives, action-reaction mechanisms, and domestic processes. Ignoring for the moment the non-trivial question of why an arms race begins (a question that none of the three families of explanation cited above can answer), it is important to recognize that any narrowly exclusive theory of arms race dynamics is likely to be unduly reductionist. First, it is argued that a race is fueled by rival, though probably largely parallel, technological imperatives. Like ripening plums, new weapon ideas are produced by the healthy tree of routinized innovation, which is high technology industry and official research and development establishments.[10] Constant communication among scientists, engineers, businessmen, military professionals, and legislators provides a closed loop wherein military requirements and technological possibilities are seldom usefully distinguishable. A requirement can be discovered after a technologist has conceived of the possibility; indeed this order of events has been typical of recent decades. Given that it is in the modern nature of human affairs to achieve progress through physical objects, defense-related industry—even if it were not motivated by very mundane considerations—can hardly help but invent a constant stream of new or improved military products. Therefore, there is an important sense in which the evolution of "the threat" is simply routine evidence of the rival's defense-industrial/scientific establishment conducting business as usual.

Second, the most popular family of models of arms race dynamics is of the action-reaction genus. One must beware of a lurking tautology.

There must be interaction between the parties; in other words, there must be a distinguishable *system* of stimulus and response for one to talk about an arms race or arms competition at all. Conceptually, at least, the idea of action-reaction is as unexceptionable as it is unenlightening. Of practical significance are the patterns, if any, of action and reaction. Are apparent actions really anticipatory reactions? Or are they severely time-lagged reactions to competitive events long past? Given the very different politics of weapon acquisition of the two superpowers, did they exhibit distinctive patterns of action and reaction? Since the Soviet Union typically had at least ten years advance knowledge of new U.S. weapons, it was known to field its "reaction" either before the triggering U.S. "action" or, indeed, even in the event that the U.S. "action" never took place at all (the Mig. 25 vis à vis the B-70, for example).

Third, a number of arms race models express the conviction that "we have seen the enemy and he is us." These may be termed domestic process models. Instead of positing two "black boxed" state arms racers rationally acting and reacting in a duel of competitive defense preparation, domestic process models argue that once a foreign enemy has been identified, the state arms racing system (not really subsystem) will probably function in an essentially self-sustaining manner in perpetuity. The technical dialectic between offense and defense can be adequately fueled by rival domestic teams. A pluralistic extended defense community does not need a foreign threat save as political rationale for its entire activity, or so the argument proceeds. The true criticality of that basic political rationale is being demonstrated in the 1990s.

The ideas introduced above matter deeply for national security. It is important to understand how national defense effort influences threat assessment and defense behavior abroad. Also, proponents of alternative models of arms race dynamics translate their favored speculative theory into precise policy recommendations. For example, an MX Rail Garrison (formally abandoned in 1991 by President Bush) or a strategic defense system Phase One (superseded in 1991 by the GPALS concept) will be opposed by people predicting specific adversary responses. In addition, particular arms control schemes will be advanced because they are believed to have a benign effect upon the pace and course of the arms competition. Since a state is presumably motivated to negate the utility of threats to its strategy, evidentially undisciplined public debate on arms race dynamics generates instant "back of the envelope" adversary reactions. Even notional threats can be a menace to defense acquisition programs if technical, tactical, or operational, imagination is allowed to triumph. "Red Teams" of extraofficial critics have given aid and comfort to the theme of U.S. restraint in arms competition. The problem is not with a "Red Team"—indeed quite the contrary. The problem is that undisciplined inventiveness concerning foreign technical choices and the bounds of foreign tactical and operational feasibility poses an endless series of unanswerable questions. If the burden of proof lies heavily and solely upon the program advocate, then there is a structural mismatch in the debate that is likely to be overlooked by legislators and opinion leaders functioning as judges. The challenge of careful study is to develop a theory of arms interaction sensitive both to the variety of interactions (time-lagged, anticipatory, possibly offsetting and asymmetrical) and to the distinctively national styles that shape patterns in behavior. An inter-state system of arms competition reflects national cultures, styles, assets, and political interests in contention.

## WHY "RACE" IN ARMS?

Arms race objectives are as variable as are the foreign policy goals they express.[11] At least five distinct objectives in an arms competition merit recognition. First, a state may race in arms with a view to achieving a window of opportunity for the military resolution of pressing political problems. In this age it is almost—but not quite—inconceivable that a nuclear-armed state would seriously aspire to gain a war-winning military advantage against nuclear-armed foes. It is important that at least a few defense professionals in the West should be willing to "think the unthinkable."[12] Orthodox, politically correct opinion can numb the imagination and thereby pave the way for strategic surprise by a state that declined to adhere to accepted truths about stability. An unduly firm conviction that nuclear war cannot be won tempts the fates and could become a self-negating prophecy. More to the point, as Robert Jervis has pointed out, "although *military* victory is impossible, victory is not: nuclear weapons can help reach many important political goals."[13]

Second, a state may compete vigorously in arms, not in quest of a fleeting opportunity of decisive advantage in war, but rather to construct a lasting hegemony. Logically, if unreliably, true major military advantage need not be exercised "in the field," except, perhaps, by way of token demonstration. By analogy, the credit of a multimillionaire is excellent; he seldom needs to demonstrate his ability to pay cash. In the words of Clausewitz: "The decision by arms is for all major and minor operations in war what cash payments is in commerce."[14] Foreign perception of a decisive military imbalance should incline the fearful to jump on the bandwagon of the rising (or risen) power rather than seek hopelessly to achieve some tolerable balance.

Third, as for the West in the cold war, success in an arms competition may mean simply the preservation of a balance of power. From this perspective, U.S. arms race behavior was motivated primarily by a determination to do enough to deny plausible theories of military victory to Soviet defense planners. One school of thought (minimum or even "existential"[15] deterrence) held that a steady jog can ensure success in the so-called arms race, because there is no finish line attainable even by the most energetic of arms sprinters. This argument founders on the rocks of geostrategic specificity. It is unlikely that a small, if survivable, deterrent force would be able to bear any extended-deterrent traffic. One may toy with Edward Rhodes's argument that the solution to extended-deterrence problems is not to seek rational nuclear use options—which he alleges is a hopeless quest—but rather to pursue rationally the ways in which the irrational can become more credible in the eyes of deterrer and deterree alike. It is a safe prediction that Professor Rhodes's "rationality of irrationality" solution to deterrence dilemmas has no promising political future, at least for the United States. No matter how clever, his formula affronts common sense, as he himself recognizes.[16]

After the late 1960s, the United States as arms competitor sought no more than a rough equivalence in the strategic balance.[17] Nonetheless, the precipitate dissolution of the political architecture and culture of Soviet state and imperial power since the late 1980s has shown beyond a reasonable doubt that Washington strained the tired Soviet system beyond its capacity to respond effectively. Admittedly this is a strong claim that exceeds the verifiable evidence. It is, frankly, a bold interpretation. Nonetheless, it is plausible to argue that the broad-fronted political-ideological and military-technical challenge posed to the USSR by Ronald Reagan's United States generated demands for commensurate competitive excellence that Soviet leaders knew their moribund system could not meet.[18] The American arms control community probably will fall on its collective pen rather than admit this possibility, but Ronald Reagan's SDI proposal in 1983 almost certainly should be registered as a triggering event in the ill-fated Soviet attempts to achieve significant domestic reform.

Fourth, arms race behavior may be motivated by a desire to acquire influence through alliance or stand-aside (neutral, non-belligerent) value. For example, for decades to come China may not aspire to "race" successfully against Russia or the United States, but a cumulatively substantial improvement in her relative military prowess would render her a third party worth acquiring as an ally, or—more likely—well worth bribing to stand aside from a conflict. Also, the course of any superpower military conflict should be dampened by joint recognition that even the victor would be severely weakened vis à vis a third party that had stood aside. Although the cold war finally died in 1989–1990, many American arms controllers remain locked in a mindset that recognizes just two principal players, each with an alliance chorus of security dependents of variable and different worth. Should a multipolar world emerge, arms race motives will be little different from those that became so familiar during the nearly half-century of cold war, but the motives will more likely be focused upon regional ambitions and anxieties than was the case with Soviet-American relations.

Finally, it is possible to contend, even if one does not acknowledge the point frontally, that states race in arms in order to control arms. Assertions and arguments over the value in arming to reduce arms was one of the more pervasive elements in the public debate over the modernization of strategic forces in the 1980s. There is one sense in which the claim "arming to parley, arming to reduce" is the last resort of the politically desperate. When all else fails, the argument that our negotiators must be armed with a visibly healthy intermediate-range ballistic missile, SDI, or other program if they are to succeed in promoting peace through arms control has been found to have steady domestic political merit. A major problem with the arms control rationale for weapons modernization is that it can prove difficult to claim simultaneously that the country must acquire "system X" and that "system X" is a critical bargaining chip.

## HOW DO ARMS RACES END?

Thus far, scholars have failed to develop a general theory of arms race behavior. Indeed, only very modest progress has been registered in developing the empirical historical base from which such an ambitious theory might be constructed. Notwithstanding, or perhaps because of, the poor state of theory and history bearing upon so-called arms races, policy advocates have brought forth claims that allege arms race wisdom for or against particular weapon developments. To enrich discussion and to disarm reductionist arguments, some alternative endings to arms races warrant consideration.

An arms race may conclude with one party retiring voluntarily from the contest, either because it loses motivation to race further or because it has learned that success is not practically attainable. A state is always more likely to "win" an arms race if the race pertains to its, but not to its rival's, principal environmental orientation for security. Maritime and insular Britain was always likely to beat imperial Germany in a naval race. Alfred Thayer Mahan was generally correct in his claims that a continental frontier was a fatal distraction for a country attempting to compete in maritime power with an insular adversary.[19] Britain demonstrated prior to 1914 that an arms race can be won.[20]

Contrary to the assertions of those who endorse a simplistic model of an "ever-escalating" arms race spiral, an arms race can be concluded by political reconciliation. The Anglo-French naval competition of the 1880s, 1890s, and very early 1900s faded away in the face of new German threats to France on land and to Britain at sea, and in 1904, in the perceived imminence of danger of a war that neither country wanted being catalyzed by their respective allies (Russia, for France; and Japan, for Britain).[21] Russian-American relations in the 1990s remain unfinished business, but there is no "arms race" between them. If there was a Soviet-American arms race from the late 1940s to the late 1980s, plainly it no longer exists—yet another example of a so-called arms race not ending in war. Even though an arms race can end in war, arms races do not cause wars. States do not fight because they are heavily armed; rather they are heavily armed because they judge war to be a serious possibility. I believe that *under*armament by satisfied powers has inadvertently contributed to the outbreak of war more often than reciprocal arms race behavior (*over*armament?) has fueled political tension to the flashpoint and ignited war.[22]

Arms races can be effectively concluded by negotiated agreement. The Washington Treaty of 1922 on naval arms limitation, notwithstanding its grievous weaknesses (particularly with respect to security in the western Pacific in the form of U.S. extended deterrence in protection of China),[23] had the signal virtue of providing the rationale and the instrument for heading off what appeared to be a burgeoning Anglo-American naval race. There was considerable political fuel for antagonism, since the United States in the 1920s, strengthened economically by the Great War, was behaving in international trade and finance much as Japan would do after 1970. However, Britain could not afford to race the United States in naval arms, and the United States sought wealth rather than empire. In that situation the treaty option suited both sides very well. (On balance, however, there is more to criticize than to praise about the Washington [1922]-London [1930, 1936] system of naval arms limitation.)[24] The political convenience of arms control praised in this instance pertains to Anglo-American political relations, or relations between two status quo countries. Writing with particular reference to the cruiser question (critical for convoy protection), which London and Washington settled by treaty in 1930, Bernard Brodie observed that "Great Britain and the United States, between whom no antagonism worth mentioning existed, proceeded to disarm each other in an unsettled world, relying completely, as Admiral Beamish put it, 'upon faith, hope, and parity, with parity said to be the most important of all.' "[25]

## WHAT IS DISTINCTIVE ABOUT AN ARMS RACE?

If the concept of arms race is to have integrity, it must refer to a rapid pace of change in rival military postures. The United States has been frequently criticized from the Left for being the technological leader in the competition. Those critics did not understand that technological leadership by a satisfied power is a useful support for peace (though British naval spokesmen prior to 1914 tended to argue that as the leading naval power, Britain should discourage innovation).[26] Rapid change in weapons technology unsettles near-term force planning and discourages military confidence in the readiness of forces for war.[27]

There cannot be an arms race, by any definition, if a rapid pace of change in military postures does not occur within a definable framework of intense political-military interaction. That interaction can assume many patterns, or perhaps even no regular pattern at all, but it must be present. Because arms races can occur only between states and coalitions of approximately equivalent technological competence, and because they are not "beauty contests" but competitions for leverage in diplomacy and readiness for war, a large measure of commonality will characterize rival military behavior. But for reasons of distinctive national geographies, military traditions, doctrines, and relations of relative influence among domestic organizations, each party to a competition will place a distinctive national signature expressing its strategic culture upon its competitive behavior.[28]

By definition, arms races mark strategic relationships that could deteriorate into a condition of war. It is political antagonism, however, that defines the risks of war. Military competition is merely a symptom. It can be argued persuasively that the arms race between the U.S. and the USSR was simply the modern way to maintain the balance of power. The competitive generation of national military power reflected the relative decline in importance of allies in securing and preserving a tolerable international order. The disparity in economic strength—or perhaps in militarily mobilizable economic strength—between the superpowers and all other states (*until recent years, at least*) resulted in the rivals competing more with unilaterally generated strength than with the strength that allies might bring to the contest.[29] There is much to be said in support of the proposition that the Soviet-American arms race was a modern version of balance-of-power politics.

It is useful to demythologize the concept of arms race by recognizing that there is nothing particularly remarkable or dangerous about it. The meaning of arms race is deemed to be so self-evident that people will campaign for its termination without bothering to define it, to find out where it came from, or how it might work. There is a great deal less to an arms race than the concept identifies.

## ARMS RACE, POLICY, AND GRAND STRATEGY

Arms races are about politics and the distribution of power. While there should be an internal rationality to an evolving military posture, defense analysis has to address questions of external rationality as well. The strategic effectiveness required of, say, ICBMs or special forces, cannot be derived from the narrow analysis of "strategic" or special forces issues. Technical and tactical considerations will suggest the suitability of more or less expansive operational objectives and hence of the outer bounds of prudent ambition for strategy, but one must look to politics to find the rationale for arms-competitive behavior.

The strategic geography of conflict plays a major role in shaping the structure and course of an arms competition. In the cold war, the United States was, for the third time this century, in conflict geopolitically with a country seeking some approximation of absolute security in and over Eurasia. So, for the third time this century the United States was obliged to provide for the projection of its power on a massive scale across intercontinental distances. If Soviet domination of Eurasia was to be avoided there was no alternative at that time (pending the rise of newly great, or the revival of, military powers in Europe and Asia) to the active pursuit by the United States of a balance-of-power policy. That policy had to find substantial expression in arms race behavior. Washington might have preferred to cease and desist from competitive armament for the first time since the 1880s, but if it did, it could not aspire to balance power in Eurasia or, indeed, anywhere else beyond North America. Such restraint would not have mattered had there been another agent for the balance of power willing and able to contain the Soviet Union.

The nature and location of the Soviet empire rendered the Soviet Union a threat to the security of peripheral Europe and Asia. Location and nature are intimately related, in that multinational continental empires can never be relaxed about possible threats, domestic or foreign. The Soviet Union, or Russia, could not endure if it were not a great military power. That claim can obscure the point that the true contrast is between great continental and great maritime powers, rather than between the Soviet Union and other great continental powers of times long past. From the U.S perspective, opposing Soviet power and influence in Eurasia committed the United States to arms competition. There was no other kind of competition for political influence that the Soviet Union could, or needed to, enter. Unlike the case of Anglo-American antagonism in the 1920s cited earlier (or Japanese-American antagonism today), Soviet-American rivalry was not about competition for the domination of world trade and could not take that form.

Critics may wax indignant over the "baroque arsenal" produced by high-technology industry,[30] but a rapid pace of technical change was characteristic of U.S. and Soviet defense preparation because it has been characteristic of modern societies. Of course the defense communities of the superpowers were motivated by mutual, reciprocated anxieties to seek technical advantage—witness the official U.S. interest during the late 1980s in so-called competitive strategies.[31] But those defense communities also struggle to make proper use of the technological advances that stem more from scientific enquiry and, in the West, commercial drive than from expansive or extravagant defense requirements.

There is always room for improvement in the detail and even in the structure of defense behavior, but the shallowness of generic criticism of "the arms race," or of U.S. participation in the alleged race, was readily uncovered. What were the alternatives? Given that the arms competition was about the politics of international security, a demand for an end to U.S. participation in the former translated inexorably into a demand for an end to U.S. participation in the latter. Mutual disarmament was by far the most popular claimed alternative to vigorous arms competitive behavior. The problem with the disarmament (or arms control, for the broader, more permissive term)[32] "alternative" to the arms race is that it tries to solve the problem by assuming it away. In other words, it would take the politics out of international politics. If the system of competitive armament and counterarmament called the arms race were the problem, disarmament would be the obvious solution. But the arms race is a symptom, not the root problem, as the political transformation of East-West relations since the mid-1980s has demonstrated.

## ARMS RACE AND ARMS CONTROL

Modern arms control theory is founded upon, and has been confounded by, two contrasting paradoxical propositions. First, it is argued that enemies need to cooperate in order to help manage the military expression of their antagonism in the interest of their common desire to avoid war.[33] The second, confounding, paradox holds that the political antagonism that renders arms control so desirable also renders it all but unattainable. The second paradox does not refer to arms control simply in a formal and descriptive sense. Negotiations on the control of arms and the occasional agreements and treaties they produce meet the criterion of arms control only if they reduce the risk of war. That is to say, only if they meet the test implicit in the overriding purpose of arms control. These two paradoxes provide important opposing insights: that enemies have interests in common as well as in conflict, indeed because they are in conflict, and that political enmity precludes significant cooperation for a common good. The public debate over arms control policy for the past two decades has been a debate about the relative force of these underacknowledged paradoxes.

A central problem for arms control policy as for the assessment of candidate agreements is that it is exceedingly difficult to operationalize the goals of arms control. Stated strategically, the classic ends of arms control are not in dispute. They are: to reduce the likelihood of war, to reduce the damage that could be suffered in war, and to reduce the burden of peacetime defense preparation. Not only is there tension among these worthy goals (for example, a likely consequence of a major reduction in the damage expected in war could be an unwanted reduction in deterrent effect); there also is a marked absence of consensus on the most suitable means for their accomplishment. If arms control worthy of the name must advance "stability" and reduce the risk of war, one has to know what does and does not advance stability in order to design a useful arms control agreement. In practice, this nontrivial difficulty is often ignored. If careful scholars cannot agree on a general theory of the causes of war or whether or not such a theory is even feasible, and if they cannot provide a generally acceptable explanation of arms race dynamics, arms control negotiations will assume the character either of a lottery or of an arm-wrestling match.

In a strategically literate universe wherein national security policy was contrived holistically, arms control and military force planning would be one and the same activity conducted by a single staff (or at least directed by a single intelligence). The Soviet Union traditionally took such a unified approach to arms control and force planning. More than two decades of SALT/START practice by the United States did not reveal a parallel organizational and strategic wisdom. Evidence in support of this judgment may be found in the fact that a flurry of official studies on the implications of the INF treaty for NATO's military posture and doctrine were conducted after the treaty had been negotiated, signed, and ratified; and in the fact that the military significance of START is still very much under review, even though that treaty has also been signed. The improvements in political relations that enabled the INF and START treaties to be signed in 1987 and 1991, respectively, render their strategic implications less urgent. That fact alone speaks volumes about the relative significance of arms control.

Americans are traditionally optimistic about future international security. Woodrow Wilson believed that he could effect a benign revolution and steer the country away from the evil practices of balance of power and secretive statecraft; Franklin Delano Roosevelt, though ruthlessly pragmatic in domestic politics, naively convinced himself that he could persuade "Uncle Joe" Stalin of America's good intentions; and a succession of recent presidents has seen value in arms control agreements and treaties, contrary to the historical evidence. The temptation to endorse the first arms control paradox in preference to the second has been irresistible, notwithstanding the contrary judgment that a review of the historical record would reveal.

### THE SOVIET-AMERICAN ARMS RACE

Notwithstanding a mutual distaste for each other's domestic political arrangements and habits, the United States and Russia enjoyed friendly relations through most of the nineteenth century.[34] Geopolitically, each found value in the occasional diplomatic support of the other against an overmighty Britain. Ideological antagonisms sharpened in the 1920s, but the Soviet-American arms competition, which may be dated loosely from the late 1940s (in the Soviet, though not the U.S. case), had almost nothing to do with ideological antipathy per se. The world is full of regimes that find each other ideologically repugnant, but they do not necessarily compete in armaments as a consequence. The origins of the Soviet-American arms competition were almost wholly geopolitical. By virtue of the defeat of Germany, the Soviet Union, though heavily damaged, became the principal menace to the Eurasian balance of power in 1945, a role last played by Russia in the mid-1850s.[35] The territorially bloated USSR of post-1945 Eurasia had become a continental superstate that could be contained only by the scale and quality of military power that *the* global superpower, the United States, could generate.

The relative and lonely preeminence on the scales of power of the United States and the Soviet Union had the effect of markedly restricting their grand-strategy options. In a previous era great powers could compete on the diplomatic plane for the purpose of bribing an adversary's allies to defect and acquiring new allies themselves. In the post-1945 world, even the loss (in 1949) and then the functional geostrategic reacquisition (in the early 1970s) of an ally as large and critically located as China had little impact upon the U.S. defense burden. For much of the postwar period, the loss or acquisition of allies was unimportant for the balance of power, *relative to the significance of unilateral superpower armament.*

Paradoxically, perhaps, the nuclear element in Soviet-American military competition both enhanced and reduced the political salience of arms competition. On the one hand, the sheer destructiveness of nuclear weapons sharply limited their policy utility. Prior to 1945, states competed in armaments that could be, and frequently were, used to win wars. On the other hand, nuclear deterrence discouraged military solutions to political problems and enhanced the almost ritualistic, or symbolic, importance of relative prowess in arms competition. There is a sense in which an arms race can function as a nonviolent surrogate for war.[36] That surrogate function, though by no means unique to the contemporary period, is more pronounced in a nuclear than a nonnuclear context. Popular literature is strewn with references to the *nuclear* arms race, and the concept of a *nuclear* arms race has the same potential for public misunderstanding as the concept of a *strategic* weapon. There has been no nuclear arms race; rather has there been a political competition wherein the military instrument of grand strategy contains a very significant nuclear element. Injudicious, indeed incorrectly reductionist, employment of the concept of a nuclear arms race is the kind of error that sets the political stage for the unwise, stand-alone arms-control treatment of different classes of arms. The U.S. defense community must think about deterring and, if need be, waging war as a whole—not about deterring or waging nuclear war in isolation.

The superpower arms competition was born out of the geopolitical circumstances created by the course and outcome of World War II, and it has been concluded as those circumstances—of effective political-military bipolarity—have registered cumulatively major change. The cold war ended in the late 1980s, but the distribution of military power remains structured much as it was during the four decades of that war-in-peace. Russian political intentions certainly have changed, but there are ample grounds for skepticism over the permanence of that development. The geopolitical and geostrategic circumstances that fueled Soviet-American political antagonism and its corollary, arms rivalry, have evolved into a new era of unknown character and duration. Notwithstanding "new thinking" in Moscow,[37] however, "geopolitics may come up trumps"[38] and ensure that traditional Russian security anxieties over the distribution of power, or correlation of forces, return to stimulate a drive for superior armament. When the only thing predictable about the successor polities to the USSR is change, no detailed

Western assumptions about the future course of Russian history should be presumed to have authority.

### ICBMs AND THE ARMS RACE

For sheer lethality, the ICBM has remained for thirty years the dominant, even ultimate, weapon in public perception. The unique combat qualities of ICBMs—or at least general perceptions of those qualities—have impressed themselves on the public mind as no other weapon has done in recent decades. ICBMs have attracted particular attention for their unsurpassed efficiency in the application of firepower over transoceanic distances. Despite the combined arms of the post-1960 strategic forces triad, missile gaps, both mythical (to the U.S. disadvantage in the early 1960s) and real (to the Soviet disadvantage in the mid to late 1960s), have meant ICBM missile gaps. From the late 1960s almost until the present day, a prospective disadvantage in the net combat prowess of ICBMs has been repeatedly judged intolerable.[39] A manifestation of this phenomenon was the criticism of the concept of the (now canceled) MX Rail Garrison in the late 1980s on the grounds that the missile was alleged to be survivable only with the benefit of strategic, as contrasted with tactical, warning.[40]

It was asserted time after time that an emerging "window of vulnerability" for U.S. ICBMs was likely to be debilitating to the net strategic effectiveness of the entire U.S. military posture. There are reasons—some plausible, others farfetched—why this might have been true. The allegations of impending ICBM vulnerability repeatedly achieved a political prominence unmatched by similar claims for other classes of weapons. Little analysis attempted to argue, as opposed to assert, that a perceived window of ICBM vulnerability, real or otherwise, would be a window of opportunity. Such an argument, had it been attempted in detail, would have required a shift of focus from tactical questions to matters of strategy.

It is interesting to note that the ICBM, the ultimate long-range artillery weapon, was developed by two superstates that shared strong traditions of excellence in artillery.[41] However, while the Soviet Strategic Rocket Forces were a direct manifestation of the Russian and Soviet artillery tradition, the U.S. ICBM program was an heir (bastard son, perhaps, in the view of air-minded people) to the tradition of excellence in strategic air power. The relevant U.S. tradition is the precise delivery of destructive energy over great distances against the war-making potential of an enemy. Soviet military theory on the proper employment of ICBMs reflected important elements of artillery thinking, while U.S. ideas on the military utility of ICBMs bore the signature of the ideas developed at the tactical school of the army air corps in the 1930s.[42]

The arms race country surveyed in this chapter has high policy as its unchallenged capital. Since I first began to research arms race and associated arms control questions more than twenty years ago, many tentative and speculative hypotheses about "the arms race phenomenon" have gained plausibility.[43] There has to be interaction between policy-guided arms programs, or one can hardly talk of an arms race or an arms-competitive system at all. However, the commonsense conviction of twenty years ago that a tight arms race spiral of action and reaction was inherently unlikely has changed from the status of near-maverick opinion to mainstream orthodoxy. Much remains to be explored and clarified.[44] Above all, the proposition that the concept of arms race is a thoroughly misleading metaphor should command more respect than is the case at present.

Weapons, which are the currency of arms competition, often lack persuasive strategic rationales in terms of means-ends relationships, but the commanding role of policy makes nonsense of the core of arms control theory and frustrates the more expansive ambitions for arms control practice. To endeavor to sidestep the inconvenience of political antagonism by depriving policymakers of their instruments of combat is an approach to peace that cannot possibly succeed. As Churchill said: "It is the greatest possible mistake to mix up disarmament with peace. When you have peace, you will have disarmament."[45]

# CHAPTER FOUR

# Policy Guidance and Weapons Acquisition

In fact, [policy] guidance provided by political appointees had typically been seen by the targeteers as so out of sync with reality, or so vague, that there was little to be done but to ignore it.
—Janne E. Nolan
*Guardians of the Arsenal*

## THE FOUR CORNERS

The weapons acquisition process is deeply influenced by public mood, by perception of threat, and by beliefs about what weapons are affordable. But, in its internal rationality that acquisition process must relate properly to strategy, to policy, and to the technology base. Policy decides what should be achieved; strategy explains how means can be applied to secure ends; weapons acquisition provides the military means; and technology is the process of scientific discovery and engineering improvement that yields choices for new weapons programs.

One may refer to "the four corners" of *policy*, *strategy*, *acquisition*, and *technology*. Each corner supports the others; indeed, they often appear in practice to overlap, even though four distinctive functions are identified. A weakness at any of the four corners affects the value of the whole enterprise. For example:

- If *policy* is unset or unclear, then strategic guidance for weapon acquisition becomes guesswork, because planners will not know what they are to accomplish.

- If *strategy* is missing or incompetent, then policy goals will not be achieved and the weapons acquisition process will lack authoritative direction.
- If the *weapons acquisition process* is grossly inefficient, then what should be attainable policy goals and sensible strategy will be vitiated by a lack of ready and suitable weaponry. In addition, the country's technology base will not be exploited to anywhere near its optimum potential.
- If the *technology base* is neglected or is subjected to foolish investment decisions, the weapons acquisition process will lack the technological qualities to exploit in timely and effective support of national military strategy and policy.

Ever-shifting political currents over strategic desiderata have a negative impact upon what could be an orderly and policy-responsive weapons acquisition process. The impact of domestic democratic and demagogic politics upon a defense community that is none too expert in strategy anyway is predictably unfriendly to rational argument. Of course, this condition can advance military programs or retard them. I do not suggest that these four corners comprise the framework of the real political world of weapons acquisition, but the slings and arrows of that real political world are far more readily thwarted when the corners are in good shape, with mutually interdependent rationales that would-be program terminators have difficulty penetrating.

## PROBLEMS WITH POLICY GUIDANCE

Policy may be defined as the purposes of a state as chosen by the government of the day. Policy should not specify means—that is the function of grand and military strategy. National security policymaking is in the business of identifying goals, not of picking or managing instruments. If policymakers affirm the value of arms control negotiations per se, or of a particular weapon system unrelated to its strategic utility, they confuse means with ends. In the face of adversity, some statesmen seek to escape from political and strategic conundra by immersing themselves in detail at the operational, tactical, and technical levels of war. Adolf Hitler embodied an ever more extreme case of this flight into detail as he lost the initiative on all fronts in 1943 and after.[1]

Without strategy, policy is merely idle vision, and strategy without suitable tactical instruments is simply a set of ideas. If it is policy to deter attack upon distant friends, strategy must specify *what* is to be deterred, and *how* and *with what instruments* deterrence is to be achieved. If the means for deterrence will not be available for several years, then policymakers must decide whether to risk a bluff or redefine policy. The so-called Carter Doctrine of 1980, which committed the United States to defend the Persian Gulf area against Soviet attack or seizure, was a classic case (subsequently admitted to have been such by its authors) of the announcement of policy purpose prior to the acquisition of policy means. A decade of enhanced military investment, the disappearance of the Soviet Union as a politically active threat and then its disappearance altogether, and the consequent focus upon regional disturbers of order rather than a nuclear-armed superpower, all rendered feasible in the 1990s what would have been a desperate gamble a decade earlier.

Policy is not comprised solely of the declarations of policymakers, no matter how senior they are or how often they repeat a point. Instead, policy comprises the capabilities, declarations, and actions of government. If a government either cannot, or chooses not to, do something, then that "something" cannot be policy, no matter what the president or others may have said. For example, the Reagan Administration consistently affirmed zero tolerance for Soviet cheating on arms control agreements, but since there were no punitive sanctions applied over the course of eight years, or even any safeguards implemented, it is reasonable to conclude that zero tolerance of Soviet cheating was not really U.S. policy.[2] A less exclusive view of policy would accommodate the frequent phenomenon of policy as aspiration. Given that political leaders are hired to lead, one should not expect the rhetorical expression of leadership mechanically to follow provision of policy means. Indeed, in the absence of political leadership means will likely prove unobtainable. Without a working political consensus, a U.S. president's policy guidance is almost certain to be irrelevant. In a pluralistic democracy where the executive and legislative branches of government are separate and generally equal, the military means of national security policy are obtained by the varied arts of leadership, not by command (or by the power of strategic reason alone, or even significantly). The very different histories of the MX ICBM and *Trident* II D-5 SLBM illustrate the contrast between weapons acquisition with and without a stable political consensus.

Notwithstanding the high value typically accorded planning in the

U.S. defense community, the basis for sound planning frequently is absent. Governments can, and in some senses should, muddle through in a flexible manner, responding creatively to changing circumstances. But, if there is a serious deficiency in the understanding of the principles and purposes behind policy and strategy, then muddling through can approximate pure pragmatism, wherein anything that appears to work well enough for today is confused with effective government.

## THE UTILITY OF "MAGIC NUMBERS"

For understandable political reasons, both the executive and the legislative branches of government pretend that there are right numbers in the defense area. Those who speak on the record as participants in national security debate must argue that the number of weapons—the force levels—recommended for procurement are neither too few nor too many. The history of war says that the all-important issue of victory or defeat is the product of many interacting, and in many cases unpredictable, factors. Numbers certainly matter,[3] but victories have been won with force ratios of all kinds. For their mental health, perhaps, some officials and politicians need to believe that there are "magic numbers" (of ships, ICBMs, maneuver battalions, rates of real defense budgetary increase, and the like) that would all but *guarantee* the national safety.

It is a great analytical and political convenience if an allegedly "right number"—a force *ratio* or an absolute (typically enemy-independent) figure—can be established in the public mind. At the turn of the century it was axiomatic in Britain to assume that the Royal Navy should be built to a two-power standard in capital ships.[4] This meant that acrimonious political debate about "the threat" could be circumvented, since it was settled policy that the Royal Navy's battleline should be equal to the battlelines of the next two strongest navies in the world (this standard was a carry-over from Britain's eighteenth century security problem of coping with the French and Spanish fleets combined).[5] The kind of totemic significance attached in Britain to the two-power standard came to be invested in the U.S. Navy's bid to achieve a 600-ship fleet in the 1980s.[6] The point is not that the two-power standard, or the 600-ship navy, was arbitrary, but rather that it had gained a widespread acceptance as the "right number." Acceptance of such a number is conducive to a politically permissive context for orderly weapons acquisition.

There are many ways the weapon acquisition problems of the ICBM force may be described, but one important problem was the official inability to invest sufficient magic in the *minimum* number (1,500) of high-quality warheads deemed essential to support national security policy through the 1980s.[7] There were good reasons why a working consensus failed to grow around the 1,500 number: the MX was retailed as armament for arms control; simpleminded analyses of prelaunch survivability overshadowed public consideration of its tactical utility in action (and hence, to track back, of its utility for deterrence); and the system was assumed, falsely, to have several genuine functional competitors elsewhere in the strategic triad. By its deeds the Congress showed itself more concerned about avoiding the procurement of a weapon in numbers whose aggregate lethality might be too high than about procuring a weapon in numbers plainly adequate to provide the strategic effectiveness demanded by policy. It was no fault of the air force that the MX program suffered traumatic political shock when the Reagan Administration casually discarded the 200-missile MPS basing scheme inherited from President Carter. The Scowcroft Commission Report of 1983 rescued the MX ICBM[8]—after the Congress had rejected superhard-silo and closely spaced basing in 1981 and 1982, respectively—but near fatal political damage already had been wrought on the "magic number" front. Congress would not take the procurement of 100 MX ICBMs seriously when that number was an arbitrary 50 percent cut from the previous number and the leading argument offered for procurement was the need to show Moscow that the United States was committed to ICBM modernization. If the MX ICBM procurement battle was about the demonstration of political will and not really about providing the "right number" and kind of weapons for deterrence, then perhaps the deployment of 50 missiles would be sufficient.

Specific numbers acquire authority with time—a sad commentary upon the quality of strategic rationality in debates over weapon procurement and force levels. Repetition, familiarity, and the perception that the armed services believe in particular numbers lend a priceless—if spurious—authority to the answers to questions that defy conclusive analytical resolution.

## WHERE DOES POLICY COME FROM?

Policy guidance, understood broadly rather than with reference to particular official documents, flows from the dynamic interaction between well-established principles (e.g., there shall be a triad of strategic offensive forces which must include an ICBM element) and the shifting climate of opinion (e.g., ICBM modernization is or is not very important as a support to arms control policy). The wellspring of policy guidance for defense organizations may be separated for consideration into five sources of nourishment, each of which interacts with the others.

First, inertia from the past, the legacy of history, can be well-nigh overwhelming. Notwithstanding the thousands of decisions and votes that compose the history of the U.S. ICBM program, *the* decision for the United States to move with maximum speed to acquire an ICBM force was made in 1954.[9] Not only has that decision never been repealed, it has never been challenged in a politically noteworthy way. It is an important consideration for the future of the ICBM program that the program already has a continuous history of more than three and a half decades. Similarly, it matters greatly that people—whatever the detail of their program preferences—are familiar and comfortable with the idea and the long-established reality of ICBMs in the strategic posture. In protracted peacetime defense establishments tend to avoid radical shifts in military posture, even when they effect a transition from the war-in-peace of the cold war to a possibly less stressful, but also more chaotic, era. To abandon ICBMs altogether would be a radical postural change, and would—or would appear to—risk unsettling a strategic balance that has performed well enough on the U.S. end. Speaking in Aspen on August 2, 1990, President Bush said, "We can defer final decisions on our land-based ICBMs—as we see how the START talks proceed—but we must keep our options open. And that means completing the development of the small ICBM and the rail-based Peacekeeper."[10]

One year later, President Bush was still affirming a need to "continue the development of land-based, mobile ICBMs in order to keep our deployment options open."[11] By late September 1991, he had canceled *Peacekeeper* Rail Garrison and "the mobile portions of the small ICBM," but he remained committed to strategic modernization with a small, silo-housed single-warhead ICBM.[12] In its turn, the small ICBM was canceled by President Bush in January 1992. To date, however, the United States remains faithful to its nearly four-decade-long commitment to deploy an ICBM force.

Second, policy guidance flows from, and in response to, the course of events in security politics. Popular and congressional attitudes toward new weapons and force size, which are expressed in a greater or smaller scale of budgetary provision, are shaped at the margin by a volatile climate of opinion. People's beliefs concerning how much deterring Moscow, or others, is likely to need are ever liable to influence by extrastrategic rational factors. Indeed, there is a historical pattern of "surge and coast" in the U.S. defense effort that defies explanation in terms of reasonable threat evaluation.

Third, in common with all security communities, the United States provides policy guidance that reflects its geographically conditioned strategic culture. For reasons that may be traced in part to eighteenth- and nineteenth-century experience, U.S. policymakers are prone to ask more of the technology of war than it can deliver.[13] Moreover, the tactical application of force is liable to be confused with strategic effectiveness. One of the most successful soldiers in U.S. history, Ulysses S. Grant, unfortunately inspired several generations of soldiers with the strong belief that war, properly approached, was about hard fighting and that strategy was really un-American.[14]

Fourth, the quality of policy guidance is influenced by the fact that the baggage of strategic ideas carried by many policymakers, executive and legislative, is both light in weight and simple in content. Many people make a lifetime choice, as they do with their religious beliefs, and avoid the potential discomfiture that could flow from an open-minded attitude towards the possibility of new revelations. This phenomenon should be neutral in its implications for policy guidance. In practice, however, arms control ideas-become-ideology (a case of strategic dogmatics) have exercised a pervasive, if unsteady, influence upon the U.S. weapons acquisition process. For example, the idea that particular weapons, regardless of ownership or political context, are inherently stabilizing or destabilizing has become holy writ.

Finally, American policymakers and commentators are predisposed to look with favor or disfavor upon new weapon technologies without understanding, or even being very interested in, their strategic implications. In the realm of technological debates over weaponry, strategy innocence (or indifference) unites Left and Right. A substantially autonomous technology push is an ever-present danger, as is its mirror image, a substantially autonomous technology disavowal. U.S. strategic debates often resemble in-house squabbles among engineers.

At least two kinds of uncertainty hinder the design and execution of an effective connection between policy guidance and military posture. On the one hand the policymaker can never be certain which bets to cover with military preparation. After all, the future is unknowable. On the other hand, the defense planner can never be certain just how much strategic effectiveness his chosen military forces can generate in support of policy choices. Perennial difficulties, discussed persuasively in books by Janne E. Nolan, Scott D. Sagan, and Robert Jervis,[15] include the paucity of two-way communication between policymakers and their military executive agents; lack of empathy and understanding between Washington and the "field" (even when formal two-way communication is satisfactory) stemming from the different worldviews traceable to very different functions; a tendency for policy (guidance) and critiques of policy to place impracticable demands upon the military instrument; and a proclivity for changes in policy guidance to have unintended and unforeseen consequences at the "sharp end." Examples abound of practical problems with strategic philosophy or political vision masquerading as policy.

I will cite but one area of difficulty: the Reagan and Bush administrations' commitment to a "defensive transition." President Bush has said that "a defensive strategic deterrent makes more sense in the '90s than ever before,"[16] but, in his *National Security Strategy* report in March 1990 he wrote, "We continue to seek with the Soviet Union a *cooperative transition* to deployed defenses and reductions in strategic offensive arms."[17] What kind of guidance can sentiments such as these provide for the actual direction of practical activity by professional defense planners? Does the United States intend to shift some of the burden of deterrence from strategic offensive to strategic (and theater) defensive arms? Is a *cooperative* transition mandatory—and if so, for political or for strategic and economic reasons—or only strongly desirable? In October 1991, authoritative (though ambiguous) signals of Soviet interest in a cooperative move towards ballistic missile defenses, particularly for early warning of accidental or third party attack, were received in Washington at long last. Subsequently President Boris Yeltsin has stated a willingness to join with the United States in providing a joint ballistic missile defense, but the practical implications of that historic policy reversal remain obscure. Matters such as these have the ability to kill the effectiveness of defense bureaucracies that must take their cues from policy and strategy guidance.

## STRATEGIC IDEAS AND WEAPONS ACQUISITION

This discussion is not a cynical review of the ways in which a weapon program—good, bad, or indifferent—can be "packaged" and retailed to the gullible. Two concerns are the threads for this analysis: first, that the United States should spend its scarce resources in ways that are strategically efficient,[18] and second, that strategically superior programs be recognized as such.

A persuasive strategic rationale will always help a weapon program, but it cannot reliably help enough. Attitudes toward particular programs are rarely framed by strategic calculations. Cogent strategic reasoning will not sway staunch political opponents of the program in question, but at the very least a robust strategic rationale will neutralize hostile strategic rationales. When an administration enjoys broad, if prospectively ephemeral, support for improving the national defense, it is seldom tempted to muddy the political waters by introducing strategy arguments that are politically redundant. The relative neglect of strategic explanation, however, will prove detrimental to the future of the program when hard budgetary times return, as they always do.

The periodic surges in defense effort characteristic of American peacetime defense preparation are never launched on the basis of a popular strategic conviction any more detailed than a powerful belief that the country should be doing *more*. In that situation (most recently in 1981–1983), the executive branch is generally trusted to get on with the job. The marketplace for strategic ideas becomes active as the surge falters and the defense effort moves into coasting and then descent phases. Legislators demand that executive-branch policymakers make choices among expensive programs. In particular they demand that programs that are relatively unpopular (for a wide variety of reasons, most of which probably have nothing to do with strategy) be justified time after time after time in excruciating detail.

For reasons of responsible practice and in the interests of political effectiveness, policymakers should view the multilevel (grand strategic, military strategic, operational, and tactical) realities of means-ends (hence generically, strategic) issues as "boxes within boxes." A particular weapon program should lend itself to truthful, simple explanation both at the level of "bumper sticker" assertion ("The B-2 Deters!"; "MX for Peace!" and the like), and under close legislative scrutiny on an issue such as why 20 rather than 15 bombers are more likely to provide the quantity and quality of strategic effectiveness required for the support of policy. The United States has always adhered to some variant of what is known pejoratively as the "war-fighting" theory of deterrence.[19] However, there are no popular votes for expected effectiveness in "war-fighting," only for deterrence, and the public and many legislators seem confused about the complementary relationship that binds the two. The same point long applied to opinion in cold-war Europe over NATO's military effectiveness. Military modernization programs won political approval only if they could be described as contributing to the deterrence of war in Europe, not to the defense of Europe. NATO-Europe did not actually want to be defended, even successfully. NATO has been about war prevention, not military victory.

Ideas about the strategic effectiveness of a weapon system must be nested in an inclusive theory of deterrence and war. If strategic imagination is at a premium, critical commentators can be trusted to find an abundance of "what ifs." But one is much more likely to persuade skeptics and to lend strength to supporters if the B-2 bomber, or a GPALS missile defense system, *or whatever*, is explained in a framework of deterrence in the context of political assumptions, of all arms, and of the hypothetical course of war as a whole.

## SOMETIMES IT IS NECESSARY TO TAKE THE ENEMY INTO ACCOUNT

The fact that deterrence is a cross-cultural phenomenon is as readily admitted in principle as it is neglected in practice. War is war, and a nuclear-armed ICBM lends itself to easy comprehension in any language. But when a country will choose to fight, how its leaders will calculate risks, what level of risks will be deemed tolerable, and how much war it will be prepared to wage, are questions unanswerable by any general theory of strategy and undetectable by intelligence-gathering platforms in orbit. The audience that matters most for the contingent threats implicit in U.S. military posture resides abroad. The opinion of key American legislators on the stabilizing or destabilizing characteristics of particular U.S. weapons may be critical for the budgetary history of those weapons, but the judgments that matter most will be made by America's foes and allies.

The principal enemy against which U.S. forces must be optimized is an adversary's *strategy*. The U.S. military purpose—for deterrence or for success in war—should be to enforce the disintegration of the means-ends nexus which is that strategy. However, it is particularly important in an era of shrinking defense budgets not to depend unduly on strategy as a way of economizing on tactical means. Great powers can rarely, and never reliably, be outmaneuvered into defeat. Hard fighting typically must be done somewhere by someone. It has become fashionable to assert the importance of "fighting smarter" and of exploiting technological advantages when available.[20] These sensible admonitions can slip into the errors of "strategism" and "technicism."[21] The former posits superior strategy as a cure-all for national security ills while the latter finds its wonder drug in new military technologies. Strategists and operational artists must remember that simplicity is a principle of war. To be clever is not necessarily to be wise. Civilian strategists in particular may exaggerate the importance of the planning phase of strategy (which J. C. Wylie notes "is the connection between the theoretical consideration of war and the conduct of war"),[22] implicitly discounting the problems that can arise in execution. On the technicist fallacy, Admiral Wylie again offers words of enduring merit: "The ultimate determinant in war is the man on the scene with a gun."[23] Since Wylie retired as a rear admiral in the U.S. Navy, that judgment carries particular weight because it is somewhat antipathetic to his service culture.[24]

Military requirements can be stated with reference to tactical, operational, strategic and even policy-political goals (such as the two-power standard cited earlier, a U.S. Navy "second to none," a strategic-forces posture "essentially equivalent" [in what and *how* essentially?]). In this century the United States in practice has not required of its armed forces that they be able, acting alone, to defeat foreign enemies (though some war plans have been directed at bilateral cases, U.S.-Japan, preeminently). The United States has required that its armed forces develop and apply the strength to wage and win coalition war. Nuclear facts have contributed a vast indeterminacy to military requirements, in part because they have delegitimized the concept of victory.[25] What should a government require of its strategic nuclear forces if (or rather when) those forces, regardless of their size or quality, are judged incapable of delivering anything better than a distinctly Pyrrhic victory, and if major military success and advantage are deemed politically impermissible for fear they will trigger an intolerable level of punitive retaliation?

The perils of enemy-independent strategy were revealed to the Allies' disfavor in 1914 and again in 1939–1940. Although there is everything to be said for imposing a preferred character of conflict on an enemy, that privilege must be won; it cannot simply be assumed for convenience in planning. The United States and its NATO allies still need to recognize that a future Russian enemy would be a very determined foe, not easily discouraged from seeking its definition of victory (since it would have chosen to go to war). Such an enemy would be waging war in a manner, and for operational objectives, inseparable from its continentalist political character and strategic culture.[26] At the present time NATO is struggling to come to grips with a post–cold war context and has announced what amounts to an enemy-independent strategic concept. NATO's strategy henceforth is to be directed towards the support of regional stability in Europe. As a newly enemy-independent alliance, NATO has understandable problems focusing its defense planning for the 1990s. It is commonplace today to claim that NATO is changing its nature from being a collective defense to being a collective security organization. Whether this is a timely adjustment or merely wishful thinking, only time will tell. From the perspective of today, it is more likely that the next problem for security in Europe will be posed by Germany than by Russia.

Narrow systems analysis can encourage the acquisition of weapons too specialized in function or limited in scale to provide the flexibility needed in an uncertain future against a real enemy with an independent will. For example, policymakers cannot possibly be certain exactly what operational effectiveness they, or their successors, might need to ask of the B-2 bomber force. However, unless one subscribes to the theory that war termination (that is, "how we win," or at least do not lose) is a subject best left unexplored, military requirements should be informed by an end-to-end theory of war that functions also as a theory of deterrence.[27] In the absence of such a theory, how can any particular kind or size of strategic force posture be *required*? What could the posture be asked to accomplish—and why? Nonetheless, because war is permeated with uncertainties, unknowns (even unknown unknowns), statesmen and strategists have to be prepared to change game plans and substitute a new theory of war under the pressure of unexpected events. If short-war plans for military success fail to deliver success, plans for long-war victory must be considered, along with ideas for a negotiated settlement.

THE QUEST FOR THE PERFECT WEAPON

From time to time a class of weapon system proceeds beyond imminent obsolescence to the point where it is obsolete (or where it is obsolete against a major foe). Operation in combined arms teams may offset particular weaknesses for a while, but most weapons eventually reach a zone beyond which they can no longer function in the changed techno-logical-tactical conditions of the day. There are limits to how much a particular weapon can be improved. For example, the cavalryman and the line-of-battle ship were overtaken by technology, and the solution to their crises was not their further improvement as cavalry or as capital ship. This situation, a true crisis of technical-tactical relevance, has yet to appear for any of the legs of the strategic forces triad, though that prospect has been much discussed.

Technology can neither deter wars nor wage and win wars. Instead, technology applied in *large numbers* of man-machine weapon systems and generally functioning in the sense of a combined-arms team (naval task force, strategic triad, armored battle group) does deter and can win. Speaking of fleet engagements between line-of-battle ships in the age of fighting sail, Vice Admiral Horatio Nelson observed that "num-bers only can annihilate."[28] Superior weapons generally are worth striving for, but superior weapons can only be as effective in battle as tactics or numbers permit. Ship for ship, the German High Seas Fleet of 1916 was a superior fighting instrument to the British Grand Fleet.[29] The trouble for Germany was that she could deploy only sixteen first-line battleships at Jutland to oppose Britain's twenty-eight. Unless the arsenals of two countries are a generation or more apart in their levels of applied technology (say, Germany and Poland in September 1939), better weapons will be useful but not critical. Moreover, a navy will not find in marginal technical advantages adequate compensation for defi-ciencies in its personnel. Appraising the overall performance and effec-tiveness of the German navy in World War I, Arthur Marder judged that "The German Navy collapsed in part because it overlooked the fundamental truth that the human factor is always the decisive one. That their lower-deck personnel proved unequal to the strain of war is obvious. The real weakness of the German naval system lay in the gulf that divided officer from rating."[30]

The tactical utility of a new or much improved weapon cannot be grasped with assurance until it is tested in battle. Also, tactical utility will fluctuate with operational context, terrain, weather, and skill and determination in employment. Reliable and late-model weapons will enhance the effectiveness of a good army, but they will not transform a rabble-in-arms led by ignorant amateurs into a first-class fighting force. Without the authority of trial by battle, all elements of the armed services in peacetime will focus on improving the weapon systems central to their doctrines of war.[31] The professional vested interest in existing weapon types is so strong that a quest for perfection, type by type rather than in combined-arms perspective, is built into the defense preparatory system.

Unless there are unusually powerful offsetting factors, it is generally true that weapons technology molds tactics and suggests operational style. The combination of ceramic and "reactive" (explosive) armor on modern tanks, for example, might enable those tanks to execute a classic deep battle:[32] they could brush aside infantry equipped with ineffective antitank guided weapons (ATGWs). For a further example, the novel threats posed by mines and submarines drove the British Royal Navy in 1912 finally to abandon plans for the close blockade of German ports and naval bases.[33] This technology-driven change in operational concept and plans (from close to very distant blockade) meant that, in theory at least, the German High Seas Fleet could venture far into the North Sea without the necessity of doing battle against heavy odds.[34] If the United States were to deploy a strategic defense system far more extensive than that envisaged in the GPALS concept, or Russia were to deploy nontoken missile defense or both, the tactics, operational objectives, and conceivably even the strategic missions for offensive missile forces would have to adapt.

It is an ubiquitous and inescapable fact that war-winning "super weapons" are either figments of the imagination or can be "super" only if the enemy is remarkably foolish or unlucky. Bulletproof soldiers, thoroughly reliable defenses, perfectly accurate strategic offensive weapons that can find their targets (or be told where those targets are), unsinkable ships—this is the stuff of which dreams and popular novels are made, not tactical doctrines and defense plans. It is in the very nature of responsible armed services and modern technology-based industry to press for product improvements (more accurate, faster, harder to locate, easier to maintain, and so forth) in the tools of deterrence and war. Although there is security against technological surprise *effect* in the sheer quantity and diversity of military equipment, it is important to acknowledge that true technical shortfalls can occur (such as thoroughly unreliable torpedoes, very hard to kill tanks, all-but-invisible-to-radar "stealthy" aircraft). Such shortfalls may be only temporary, but they could yield major military disadvantage should war occur prior to their correction. More to the point, as often as not the identity and severity of true technical shortfalls will not be known and understood until they are discovered in the field.

The Persian Gulf War of 1991 illustrates very well the arguments advanced in this chapter. The interim report on the war provided to Congress by the Department of Defense was an unusually balanced document, given the pressures of time, the perils of hasty composition, and the pressures of strongly vested interests. The report argued that "a revolutionary new generation of high-technology weapons, combined with innovative and effective doctrine, gave our forces the edge."[35] It proceeded to laud the high quality of U.S. military personnel deployed to the Gulf. In addition to citing a technological edge and the superior prowess of U.S. military personnel, the report cited as "general lessons" of the war the significance of "decisive presidential leadership," "sound planning," and appreciation of "how long it takes to build a high-quality military force." Notwithstanding the prominence commentators accorded the new weapon systems employed for the first time against Iraq, this was not a victory achieved by wonder weapons. As General Schwartzkopf observed, the Coalition could have won the war even if it had been equipped with Iraqi weaponry. The key advantages for the Coalition were the military competence of its personnel and the coherence of its system of war. The nominal advantages conferred by superior military technology were realized in massive strategic effect through the skill with which they were used.

## STRATEGY AND MILITARY REQUIREMENTS

There are many historical examples of policymakers who did not understand that the policy, and particularly the strategy, they chose made impracticable demands upon the tactical instrument available. In 1692 and again in 1805, French admirals were ordered to fight battles they knew they could not win;[36] from 1914 to 1918, both coalitions asked far more of their armies than they were capable of achieving. There is always a danger that strategic ideas will outrun possible tactical performance. For example, an important thread in U.S. (and NATO) maritime strategy in the 1980s might have been confounded by the increasing elusiveness of Russian submarines,[37] while in the same period the impenetrability and agility of some Russian strategic targets challenged the integrity of the theory of deterrence that informed U.S. central war strategy.[38]

Questions of military force planning are much more difficult to answer than is often assumed.[39] Critically important aspects of such questions do not lend themselves to mathematical modelling. This is not to deny that most tactical problems do lend themselves to quantitative assault, as the allied experience with operations analysis in World War II showed. For example, there are correct answers (classic staff solutions) to such questions as the proper size of a convoy (larger convoys are more defensible than smaller convoys) and the weight and character of air or missile attack necessary to achieve a particular level of damage against a target set of specified character. Unfortunately, important though solvable tactical problems are, one cannot aggregate tactical solutions to arrive at grand strategic answers. Strategy, duly educated as to tactical feasibility, must choose which mix of tactical means it intends to employ. Unless the strategy indicates exactly what naval and air forces will be required to do—broad judgments that do not lend themselves to support via mathematical demonstration—mere multiplication of the military requirements for handling discrete tactical problems cannot show how much is enough. A condition in which the tactical can become quasi-strategic is the case of the pure-attrition approach to conflict. If the concept of operations consists of nothing more elevated than the unit by unit subtraction of an enemy's total military power, then strategy is indeed reduced to "brute arithmetic." But even if attrition is favorably asymmetrical, it is always mutual, and it can come with heavy transaction costs.

An East-West military conflict in the cold war era could have been short, both because escalation could be rapid and because the fear of explosive escalation might have persuaded the combatants to seek a cease-fire very expeditiously. However, there were also powerful reasons of logic and geopolitics not to assume that any general conflict would be short in duration. The military requirements for a long war (lasting for months and perhaps more), let alone for a very long war (lasting for several years), are always dramatically different from the requirements for a short war. There are understandable political and bureaucratic reasons why the requirements for long war tend not to be addressed seriously.[40] The difficulties of surviving a short war can seem so overwhelming that long-war questions appear to be an irrelevant luxury. Also, consideration of long-war issues implies failure in prewar deterrence and in the short war that extends to become a condition of protracted hostilities.

In recent decades, official spokesmen were fond of arguing that U.S. military requirements were dictated by a dynamic external threat and that they were not, or should not be, treated as matters for great U.S.

policy discretion. As often stated, this argument was misleading. In a very general sense the United States must determine its military requirements in the light of intelligence information about the military power of possible enemies. Technological, tactical, operational, strategic, and political choices, however, intervene between "the threat" and the determination of U.S. military requirements. Two geographically different superpowers, with different political and strategic cultures and distinctive, if intimately related, security problems do not compete (or "race") in armaments in a simple, or simple-minded, way.[41]

U.S. strategic-force requirements could be driven honestly and competently, though necessarily imperfectly, by targeting analysis. In order to meet some fair reading of policy guidance, the U.S. Strategic Command could work backward from the damage that must be inflicted upon specified targets with known or estimated characteristics to the ideal force posture needed to maintain the required degree of lethality against those targets.[42] Targeting analysis for weapon selection and attack planning must be performed, but the choice of targets to be struck and the priorities among them are not self-evident for all likely circumstances. Targeting analysis as a basis for deriving force requirements plainly loses authority when, as at present, it is not self-evident who the enemy will be. Policy guidance, theories of deterrence, and doctrines of war help establish targeting priorities (priorities in importance and priorities in time-urgency for attack), but operational circumstances could vary extensively (if, for example, the United States was taking the initiative on a compellent or coercive mission, or if it was striking back with much-reduced and damaged forces).[43] In addition, a military logic pertaining to some strongly believed, as well as demonstrated, grammar of war could be in a condition of tension with a policy logic discerned by statesmen.[44]

## THE WEAPONS ACQUISITION PROCESS: SELF-INFLICTED WOUNDS

Several prefatory remarks are in order. First, the Department of Defense generally performs well in the acquisition of new weapon systems, but good performance is rarely newsworthy. Second, an important source of the pathologies that do beset the weapons acquisition process is legislation that does not have the timely production in adequate numbers of first-class fighting equipment as its overriding objective, whatever its worthy motives. Third, much of the public discussion of the weapons acquisition process is adversarial in tone: defensive, accusatory, or both. The purpose of this brief discussion is not to make a case for or against any group, branch of government, or proposals for reform (such as the Carlucci initiatives early in the first Reagan Administration, the subsequent Packard Commission Report, and so forth). Of course the process could stand improvement, and undoubtedly there is more than enough error to be allocated among all participants. The purpose here is simply to register some of the more gratuitous, damaging features of the process by which the United States acquires its major weapon systems.

Traditionally, engineering excellence (broadly understood) has been the military-competitive long suit of the United States, and applied technology has been the cutting edge of U.S. military effectiveness. But in recent years, "little and late" is a fit characterization of the application by U.S. science-based industry of new, or radically improved, technologies to defense. By far the most important competitive strategy for the U.S. in the technological area would be a revised acquisition process that allowed expedition in the transition from technology to weapon when such expedition is necessary. The United States devalues the currency of technological advantage by acquiring too few systems, and by acquiring them much later than they could have and therefore at a much higher cost. The U.S. success in the cold war was achieved despite the flawed procurement practices criticized here. French errors in military procurement had a noticeable negative impact upon military performance in 1940; German procurement errors in the 1939–1941 period had a similar negative effect upon performance in the crisis years of 1943–1944. Soviet-American strategic relations were permissive of American pathologies in weapons procurement, or late procurement, or nonprocurement. The appropriate lesson to draw from U.S. success in the cold war is not that the weapons acquisition process does not matter, but that the United States simply dodged a bullet in recent decades. It would be imprudent to assume that Dame Fortune will bless the irresponsible with perpetual immunity to serious harm from procurement malperformance.

This argument may pose difficulties for some readers. After all, has not grande guerre been deterred? Did not the USSR all but sue for peace before its demise? Was not Iraq humbled by a Desert Storm of awesome effectiveness? How can one argue with success? I maintain that the quality of the U.S. strategic forces as a factor for deterrence has never been severely tested. Procurement, efficient or otherwise, plainly was adequate for its real-world tasks, but what if some newly great power should prove to be beyond deterrence? Future strategic historians would identify the dilatory pace of the SDI as the source of dire consequences. It is important not to lose a sense of proportion and empathy for the dilemmas of policymakers and force planners, though empathy should be in short supply for politicians who decline to recognize strategic arguments for major weapon programs.

A good part of what passes for "waste, fraud, and mismanagement" is in fact behavior guided by recognition of the special character of defense preparation and the unique nature of war.[45] If an efficient defense is measured by evidence of an appropriate supply of strategic effectiveness to meet the demands of policymakers (national, in need of military support for policy, and foreign, in need of deterrence or of discipline by action), the salience of deterrence poses obvious problems. The Department of Defense is by far the largest single economic enterprise in the United States, but its business is not business, and it cannot be judged intelligently by standard business criteria of efficiency such as profitability. (What is the return on investment—peace?) To cite just one example, it is "efficient," in peacetime, for Defense Department supply officers and for U.S. weapon contractors and subcontractors to purchase many capital goods, such as computer-controlled machine tools, offshore. But heavy reliance on offshore procurement is unwise because of the prospect of a massive disruption in global trading patterns in the event of some kinds of war.

Without condoning fraud or mismanagement, there is still no escaping recognition that some of the problems besetting the U.S. weapons acquisition system arise from fundamental flaws in the system. Procurement practices and styles that work well for the acquisition of technically undemanding products at the lowest cost are almost wholly inappropriate for the purchase of major weapons, and weapon support systems that are literally beyond the state of the art at the time of contract award. Toilet seats can be bought on a competitive, least-cost basis on the open market; ICBMs, "stealthy" bombers, and nuclear powered attack submarines cannot.

American weapons procurement characteristically moves infrequently, by step-level jumps between or even over generations in technology. Furthermore, it is the American tradition to seek maximum flexibility via multipurpose platforms, rather than by the development of a family of more specialized items. This American preference may be seen in the design of main battle tanks, submarines, and in ICBMs. Complementary to this approach is a production philosophy not authoritatively geared to the proposition that the country's scarce national defense-industrial assets should be kept healthy by steady exercise. In the context of the politics of weapons procurement in a pluralistic democracy, the consequences of the American step-level jump preference are that too much of importance for the national security rides on the performance of too few programs, that too much too soon tends to be asked of the latest model (or beyond) of weapons and support systems, and that vital continuities in technological-industrial expertise are imperiled in the "down years" of a surge-coast-surge-coast defense budget "wave train."

Many legislators and commentators on national defense appear to believe that masterpieces of the weapon-maker's art can be produced to order, on time, and at the predicted and agreed price. With few exceptions, though, the American system of weapons acquisition virtually guarantees that most major weapon programs will be high-risk enterprises with reference to technical performance, dollar cost, and delivery time. As noted above, the U.S. weapons acquisition process places a premium on innovation and all but requires prospective prime contractors to overpromise on performance, cost, and delivery schedule. There are reactions of shock and allegations of error, incompetence, and venality when radically new weapons appear with substantial "shakedown" problems. Critics of the B-1B and the B-2, for example, could gain useful historical perspective on the teething troubles of new weapons were they to acquaint themselves with the initial difficulties with the B-29 (the largest U.S. weapon program of World War II), B-36, B-47, and B-52. Also, the U.S. Army has been known to acquire a new generation of rifles that for a while did not work well under rugged field conditions, and some ballistic missile systems have been produced and operated with technical problems that dwarf those of the B-1B (or of the Inertial Measurement Unit [IMU] for the MX ICBM). Innovation cannot help but be a high-risk exercise.

The obvious virtues of the open, pluralist democracy of the United States cease to be virtues if carried to excess. There is everything to be said in favor of informed debate about controversial technical choices that have tactical and some operational implications for strategic choices, but decisions must be made if a prudent national defense posture is to be crafted. Furthermore, the acquisition of weapons requires that parametric decisions both be made and *remain made* through the procurement cycle. The U.S. body politic sometimes seems to function more as a debating society in permanent session on major defense issues than as a national security community recognizing that capability-in-being, imperfect though it is, is the touchstone of physical safety.

## THE INSTRUCTIVE CASE OF THE MX ICBM

The MX ICBM provides a classic example of the U.S. defense community functioning both at its best and its worst. The program was an engineering triumph, with only minor reservations, all but ruined by almost willful mishandling at the levels of policy and strategy.

It was a minor miracle that the MX program achieved its December 1986 initial operating capability (IOC) on schedule, given the ambushes it had survived over the course of a decade. In strategic terms the program was late, which is to say that the United States needed the putative strategic effectiveness of the *Peacekeeper* ICBM force before it was available. Although the MX's availability in the field was paced to a noteworthy degree by the difficulties attendant upon the transition from prototype to production-model IMUs, delay was attributable also to basic policy reviews in 1977 and 1981 as administrations changed. MX IOC should have been achievable by 1983. It so happens that the United States did not have crisis need of this ICBM's strategic effectiveness in the early or mid 1980s, but the Carter and Reagan Administrations would not know that.

The early and mid 1980s saw the full-scale eruption of disagreements over the strategic desirability of MX deployments of alternative sizes and basing character.[46] These disagreements among politically influential players in the politics of ICBM modernization could not have been evaded in their entirety, no matter how the program had proceeded in its early years (say, from 1974 to 1981). It was a political fact of enormous significance, however, that MX had been presented throughout the 1970s in a rather mindless engineering sense as a system invulnerable to attack.[47] The distaste felt by many legislators for the sheer firepower of an MX ICBM force was relatively inactive politically in the 1970s, both because the weapon was a weapon for the future and because officials appeared resolutely committed to the search for a robust, survivable basing mode. Previously submerged disagreements surfaced with a vengeance when missile procurement decision time arrived, and when officials failed to discover a basing mode *capable of attracting and holding widespread political support.*

Probably the greatest political damage to the consensus necessary for an orderly MX program was inflicted unwittingly by the Reagan Administration in 1981. Paradoxically, then, the most potent damage to the MX program was wrought by the strongest proponents of ICBM modernization and not by liberal critics; such critics had little political clout in 1980–1981. Some influential conservative, generically prodefense commentators waged guerrilla warfare against MX/MPS. This conservative critique began by labeling the MX/MPS "Carter's program." In addition, although the program was admitted to have some merit, it was judged not to be as good as it could and should be in a narrow defense-analytical sense (for example, on the issue of vertical as contrasted with horizontal shelters for the shell game of ICBM hide and seek). This was plainly a case of "the best" functioning as the foe of the "good enough," and the effect was extremely damaging. Given that many liberal commentators had always been uneasy about the counterforce potency of a 10-MIRV MX ICBM force, the Reagan Administration's 1981 reopening of the Pandora's box of basing-mode debate proved to be a predictably fateful, and all but fatal, political development.

The MX ICBM program suffered gratuitously from what has been called the "chuckle" or ridicule factor. The sensible, if unduly emphasized, search for a survivable basing mode was permitted to degenerate into a politically undisciplined hobby-shop enterprise that attracted public disdain and laughter rather than respect and support. Too many basing options were considered too publicly, and too many technically or tactically ingenious engineering solutions appeared to be absurd (deployment on dirigibles, for example).[48] Further unwarranted political damage was wrought upon the program by the belated choice of *Peacekeeper* as the weapon name at a time when the lethality of the system, in the absence of an agreed survivable basing mode, was fueling charges of strategic destabilization. Earlier, certainly before MX had secured such a firm grip on the language of public discourse, *Peacekeeper* might have been an admirable name. But in the political climate of the early 1980s, it appeared to be ironic, and its net effect was to generate more damaging chuckles.

From time to time, generically antimilitary as well as more responsible pro–arms control forces coalesce in spirited and sustained opposition to a particular weapon system or capability. The MX, in company with BMD/SDI and the B-2, suffered politically from the apparently unshakable labels "controversial" and "troubled." Whether or not there are good reasons to regard a system as controversial and politically troubled, repeated labeling as such by commentators and news anchorpersons (as in the case of the MX ICBM, the SDI, and the B-2 program) rapidly becomes self-validating.

## THE POLITICS OF WEAPONS ACQUISITION

The significance of strategic weapon systems for national security renders them magnets for public attention, but the complexity and variety of strategic issues restricts the attainment of expertise in their regard to a few full-time defense professionals, legislators and commentators must be selective in their focus. They tend to focus upon a mix of high-end and low-end issues, such as ICBMs and coffeemakers. The former is obviously important in all senses, while the latter brings a $300 billion per annum subject down to a scale easily comprehended by the average voter. Since time is always scarce, and since nonexperts find it much easier to grasp one subject rather than the intricate connections between and among subjects, it is frequently the case that the misfortune of one weapon system in attracting noisy, controversial attention is the good fortune of other weapon systems or defense items that cannot be accommodated on an already crowded political agenda.

The connection between an ICBM modernization program, for example, and a condition of peace (or nonwar, at least) is one that many people in different cultures find counterintuitive. People not educated in strategic history are vulnerable to the assertion that an ICBM (or a war elephant, or a crossbow)[49] is a "weapon of war" rather than a "peacekeeper." The realization that threats to wage war can help to keep the peace cannot inoculate people reliably against the urge to assign guilt by association to the asserted peacekeepers. Wars certainly have occurred despite the operation of intended "deterrents." The merits of democracy are not at issue here, but the problems that Alexis de Tocqueville noted for the conduct of a prudent foreign policy are apparent, for example, in the unreasonably steady appeal that arms control processes have held for electors in democracies.[50]

The very success of the international security order of the cold war in preventing war between the great powers provided the seeds of possible future failure. In the absence of recent experience of a sense of acute danger, particularly when governments affirm and reaffirm the commonsense claim that a nuclear war cannot be won, it is difficult for democratic polities to take military preparation seriously for very long. The British "Ten Year Rule," which operated from 1919 until 1931[51]— the formal policy guidance for defense planners to the effect that a major conflict was assumed to be all but impossible for the next ten years (a moving horizon)—has its functional equivalent in the United States today. The time frames judged tolerable for the solution or major alleviation of U.S. defense problems are exceedingly relaxed, and becoming more so as peace is declared to have arrived.

Since the late 1960s a permanent and semiorganized opposition to new weapon programs has emerged. The focus of the assault shifts over time, but Western legislators in search of budget economies and members of the general public who harbor an inchoate distaste for the weapons *of war* enjoy easy access to legitimate, or legitimate-looking, strategic argument from groups and individuals whose often full-time activity it is to craft arguments in opposition to the weapon villain of the moment. As was noted earlier, the master concept of stability is sufficiently slippery that opposition to, or defense of, virtually any new weapon development can be mounted with reference to allegedly objective criteria. Richard K. Betts made a related point when he argued that "both the success and the failure of the concept of deterrence as a guide to action is that, over time, it has become synonymous with whatever military objectives of any sort are pursued."[52]

Civics textbooks tell us that rule by ignorance can be prevented only by the education, including the self-education, of the electorate. To date, American (and, in earlier times, British) performance in the national security sphere has been good enough to ensure the survival, or better, of core national values and of a tolerably compatible international order. However, investigations into the quality and quantity of education in strategy at U.S. colleges of higher military education have found much to criticize;[53] while studies of nuclear-age education in America's high schools have revealed that the overwhelming weight of such "education" feeds naive antiwar sentiments.[54] Over the long run a popular democracy and its values cannot survive without a strategically literate, attentive public. Strategically ill-directed and ill-managed national security communities can muddle through for long periods as a consequence of the weight of their material assets (brute force), the structural flaws in their foreign foes, and sheer good luck. Eventually, however, a polity that persists in strategy malperformance is certain to find that unfriendly historical circumstances render a negative judgment on its fitness to prosper and perhaps even to survive.

# CHAPTER FIVE

# Defense Planning for Uncertainty

> . . . plans are worthless, but planning is everything.
>
> —Dwight D. Eisenhower

## TRENDS, COUNTERTRENDS, AND THE PERILS OF PREDICTION

The future is always uncertain, but contemporary defense planners confront a challenge to their self-assurance and the plausibility of their arguments much more severe than those faced by their recent predecessors. For more than forty years, threat analysis and assertion in Washington, D.C., could confine itself, by and large, to military details, because there was a working consensus on the political dimension (threat = capability × *intentions*). There is no truly scientific way to conduct force planning, but that ongoing exercise can be performed well enough when differences over the threat pertain to details rather than fundamentals. There is no Soviet Union threatening to attack NATO-Europe or to launch a surprise attack upon U.S. strategic nuclear forces. On what basis and to what ends can U.S. defense professionals ply their trade in the 1990s? This chapter addresses the problem of prudent defense planning in a world that is effectively new, a world stripped of familiar, anchoring assumptions, but not governed by any "new order."[1]

How should statesmen and defense planners think about the future?

Everything relates to everything else, often in ways that are obscure. It is a common error to identify and attempt to analyze the significance of trends *serially*. As the military world is a world of combined arms, so the quality of national security is the product of the interaction of many trends. A trend in military technology favoring precise over-the-horizon attack enables the United States to consider an all-conventional defense, albeit with nuclear cover for counterdeterrence. However, it is easy to forget that a trend in one direction often generates a countertrend. Not only is there a law of diminishing marginal returns to effort, which suggests why activities do not continue without limit, but people observe trends, or events that threaten to become trends, and purposefully take action to thwart them. For that reason, an exponentially rising unit cost for major weapon platforms will not lead to a U.S. Air Force with one fighter plane. Some years from now the U.S. defense budget will assuredly rise again in real terms, partly as a result of the insecurity consequences of what will eventually be recognized as an imprudent trend in reductions.

Trend analysis is dominated by strategic culture as well as being influenced by less basic attitudes, beliefs, and settled procedures. Unfolding sequences of events, trends, and candidate trends are related to a familiar and generally approved universe; *mindsets* shape perceptions and judgments. For more than forty years the U.S. defense community thought in terms of a primary mission to oppose Soviet power, and each environmentally specific armed service crafted doctrines keyed to dominant scenarios.[2] In peacetime, when the authority of field experience is lacking, the new tends to be accommodated within the familiar, rather than permitted to challenge its continuing validity. Much educated prediction, or futurology, is little more than laundry-list trend spotting. It is relatively easy to spot trends in politics, social mores, technology, and so forth, but it is difficult to conduct holistic analysis explaining what the identified trends mean. It is one thing to know what appears to be happening; it is quite another to provide sound judgment on the implications of several interrelated streams of activity. "Experts" know a great deal about relatively little.

It is only human for our reach to exceed our grasp. Governments seek the impossible: they want to know what will happen. By definition, the future has not happened. No quantity of research dollars and no degree of sophistication in research methodology can overcome that frustrating fact. Scholarship is often helpful, but in political affairs it cannot discover that which has yet to occur.

TREND ANALYSIS: PIERCING THE VEIL

If a trend is understood as a persisting tendency, it should be identifiable as it happens. Successful politicians and strategists are those who work with, rather than against, the trends that bear upon their activities, which can be a matter of luck as well as forethought. However, there is everything to be said for the proposition that suitably educated statesmen or strategists will make much of their own good fortune. An assassin's bullet or a storm at sea can undo years of careful preparation, but overall, the statesman or military leader who enjoys a superior understanding of *the structure of his situation*, always assuming that his material assets are adequate, will find that fortune tends to smile on him. For example, he will have the ability to learn what is, and what is not, possible and will adjust his strategy and his objectives accordingly. A primary condition for success in statecraft in general, and in military matters in particular, is recognition of the bounds of the possible. Disdain for this principle leads to ruin. As Ronald Lewin wrote of Adolf Hitler, his "vision of a Great Teutonic Empire was a fantasy. . . . An Empire is a very large proposition. By making the Thousand Year Reich his prime objective without evolving even the most insignificant means of making it a success, except by the use of force, Hitler committed his greatest mistake. All his other errors were in matters ancillary to this main and fatal project."[3]

A prominent error among futurologists is discounting what may be termed self-negating trends (or self-negating prophecies). Often people and institutions interested in ensuring that particular events adverse to their interests do not become a trend or in turning back an unwelcome trend are able to take effective counteractions. One should never underestimate the human potential for folly,[4] but survival instincts apply to individuals, institutions, and polities. No military platform is of permanent value, for example, but the continuing utility of classes of weapon platforms is somewhat routinely ensured by adjustments at the levels of technology, tactics, operations, military strategy, and even grand strategy. Whether or not there is a trend favoring the effectiveness of the strategic defense over the strategic offense is connected to the level of effort expended to negate such a trend.

Of course some trends are truly irreversible: trends toward higher unit costs and lower numbers of major combat platforms (from one weapon generation to another); trends toward better tactical intelligence and rapid integration of that information with military assets capable of exploiting it ("information age warfare"); and in more dis-crete historical cases, trends from sail to steam, from coal to oil, or from the horse to the internal combustion engine. However, many trends carry within themselves the seeds of their own negation. For example, some elements of the contemporary U.S. defense community have sol-emnly debated the prospects for a defensive transition in strategic ca-pabilities without appreciating that an offensive transition would be all but immanent in such a transition.[5]

I do not claim that there will be an equal reaction to every action in a mechanistic sense, but many trends run aground on the phenomenon of sharply diminishing, even negative, returns to effort. Military his-tory is littered with the wreckage of operational designs whose degree of failure was very much the measure and consequence of prior success. For example, the sheer geographical scope of the German successes in 1939–1942 and the Japanese successes in 1941–1942 helped guarantee the enormity of their final disasters. The surge-and-coast pattern in U.S. defense expenditure since World War II is an example of a trend that ensures its own demise.[6] Periods of irresponsible economizing are recurrent features of the U.S. and British experience in the peacetime practice of national security provision. The steeper the budgetary and capabilities decline, the more marked the surge that will be required to effect a rapid course correction.

It is common for people to confuse causes and consequences and to rest satisfied with recognition of inputs rather than attempt to under-stand outputs and the downstream implications of events. One should beware of analyses that simply list trends or factors because they can express the taxonomic fallacy. Listings of new trends, possible new trends, factors that might intervene, and so on, are indigestible as well as speculative, profoundly unhelpful, and inconclusive. This is not to demean the value of timely "heads-up" notice that "radar is coming," "AIDS really matters," or "global warming may be a history redirect-ing phenomenon." Still, it is easy to identify trends and factors; the dif-ficulty lies in providing a plausible explanation of what those trends and factors will mean and how they will interact.

The claim that causes and consequences pose very different chal-lenges to understanding can be augmented by discussion of the idea that surprise and surprise effect can differ markedly. Statesmen and defense planners must worry, to some extent, about future events that they cannot possibly identify in advance. The more pertinent chal-lenge, however, is to understand the possible and probable effects of trends and even of "acts of God" that cannot really be called surprises. The unexpected consequences of known elements performing in possibly surprising combinations is a realm worthy of study.

Notwithstanding the impression that detailed histories can give, great events or major trends with wide and deep implications do tend to have great, wide, and deep causes (roots, origins, and so forth). One should not confuse precipitating events with causes. For example, the details of the brief crisis of July 1914 and of the protracted crises of 1938–1939 are bizarre and fascinating, but, all that could be called surprising (and even this is debatable) about the outbreak of the two World Wars were the actual dates of their irruption. Without succumbing to a deterministic philosophy, one must recognize, as did many people at the time, that there were many roads to war in the 1900s and 1910s, and again in the 1930s and 1940s. Because history provided but one unique course of events, it does not follow that a particular outcome could only have resulted from that unique set of events.

It is true, but not particularly helpful, to say that defense planners already know most of what they need to know about the future in order to perform creditably. The trouble is, they do not understand potentially key elements of what they "know." (Note that a focus on detail ensures that few *small* errors will be committed).[7] To see, and even to count, is not necessarily to understand. Paradoxically, the very breadth, depth, and general sophistication of U.S. intelligence activities provides a sense of confidence that can mislead. Intelligence communities can inadvertently train themselves, inch by inch as it were, not to be surprised by sequences of events (candidate trends) that should surprise them. Also, an adversary "intelligence and watch" community may be deceived purposefully. One can cite apparent counterexamples (such as convoy in World War I),[8] but the strategic culture of an armed service has historically provided a potent source of misunderstanding of the future. Obviously, an armed service is shaped by its interpretation of its past, and as Carl Builder has suggested, World War II was the dominant experience of success for each of the U.S. armed services—their finest hour.[9]

Strategic culture can intrude to impede understanding of changing circumstances. In the first half of the seventeenth century the Dutch Republic was taught by hard-earned experience what it had to do to defeat Spanish power at sea. But in the first of their three trade wars with England (1652–1654), the Dutch discovered that the amateurish and makeshift naval power that had performed admirably against Spain was hopelessly inadequate against the disciplined and heavily armed ships of Oliver Cromwell's English Commonwealth.[10] In the 1690s and after, the English statesmen and admirals who had been trained in the battle against the Dutch in the proper ways to wage war at sea and to use seapower for the ends of policy, required retraining themselves in order to cope with the naval problems posed by war with France. They discovered that a great continental state could not easily be brought to accept unfavorable terms of peace, even as a consequence of severe damage to its seaborne trade.[11]

### SUPER THREATS

Individuals and institutions are always liable to misinterpret emerging contemporary phenomena in terms of apparently relevant past experience. The Dutch knew how to fight at sea *against Spain*, and the English knew how to fight at sea *against the Dutch*. In both cases, the countries, and the maritime establishments in particular, allowed themselves to mistake an extraordinary challenge for a familiar threat. From time to time extraordinary security challenges do appear. It is not surprising that the true severity of such challenges tends to be appreciated only belatedly.

There is some merit in distinguishing between what may be categorized as routine, as contrasted with extraordinary, threats. Extraordinary security danger fails the important test of contemporary plausibility. All defense communities interpret the present in terms of the past, so genuine novelty in scale of menace is much clearer in retrospect than in prospect. Democracies have a way of responding, perhaps overresponding, only to clear and present dangers. It can be difficult to convey the idea that the very implausibility of extraordinary security dangers contributes substantially to the severity of the dangers they pose. No country could afford to purchase the armaments that would be suggested by the worst fears of speculative theorists. However, general prudence suggests the inadvisability of designing a national defense establishment so that it would not offend political enemies. That can be a prescription for disaster.[12] It is useful to anchor this point in amplification of the two historical cases previously cited. The Dutch Republic entered the second half of the seventeenth century comprehensively unprepared to protect its sea-based prosperity against a country blessed with the geostrategic and maritime advantages of England under the Commonwealth. For reason of their geographical location, the Dutch were unable to ensure national survival between 1650 and 1700, let alone prosperity, except through subordination to England (against the new threat from Louis XIV's France). By way of contrast, in the eighteenth century England was able to identify and pursue a course in statecraft and a system of war that enabled her statesmen to cope very well indeed with the fact that France—unlike the Netherlands— could not be beaten as a direct consequence of defeat at sea.[13]

For further illustrations of this argument, consider how well or how badly potential victims coped with the extraordinary security problems posed by Attila the Hun, Mohammed and the Arabs, Genghis Khan's Mongols, and Adolf Hitler. What unites these cases is the fact that key victim states, actual and potential, had been predisposed by their historical experience and strategic cultures not to recognize the novel scale of the dangers that threatened them.

First, Attila and his Huns were no surprise. Although they terrified other barbarian tribes, they were long known to Roman statesmen and for several decades had appeared to be potential tools of Roman policy. Prior to the 420s A.D., the Huns were not viewed as "just another" barbarian horde, but neither were they regarded by Roman policy as a radically novel or unprecedentedly large security challenge. The great classical scholar, J. B. Bury, observed that "at the time of the death of Theodosius [395 A.D.] they [the Huns] were probably regarded as one more barbarian enemy, neither more nor less formidable than the Germans who threatened the Danubian barrier . . . No one could foresee that after a generation had passed Rome would be confronted by a large and aggressive Hunnic empire."[14]

In practice, by the late 420s the Roman Empire in the East had realized that the Huns were no routine threat. In long retrospect, it is easy to exaggerate the menace posed by the Huns. The demise of the Hunnic empire upon the death of Attila in 453, not to mention his lack of strategic skill, shows that there was less of enduring lethality about this peril than seemed to be true at the close of the 440s and in much subsequent historiography.[15] Nonetheless, for twenty years (434–453) Attila's Huns were easily the most powerful military force in Europe, eclipsing any barbarian perils the Romans had confronted up to that time. The Olympian judgment that the Huns under Attila were "for a few years more than a nuisance to the Romans, though at no time a real danger"[16] should be treated with caution. In fact, beginning in 422 the

Eastern Roman Empire was obliged to purchase some facsimile of peace at the price of 350 pounds of gold per year; by 443 the price had risen substantially to the annual level of 2,100 pounds.[17] The Western Empire was able to withstand Attila's invasion of 451 only because of a very hasty alliance of grim necessity with the Visigoths.

Second, the rise of militant Islam in Arabia in the 630s and 640s was utterly unanticipated by the neighboring great powers. The civilizations and superpolities of Byzantium (East Rome) and Persia, who had just waged their final round of exhausting warfare that concluded with Byzantine victory in 628, were not anticipating the emergence of an extraordinary threat from the desert to the South. Romilly Jenkins wrote:

> The great majority of the population [of the Arabian peninsula] consisted of nomadic tribes at feud with one another and scarcely conscious of ethnic or religious relationship. Islam realized the economic need for expansion by providing religious and thus national unity. A few early successes in the field were sufficient to rally the nomadic Beduin by thousands to the standard. The exhaustion of both Byzantine and Persian empires did the rest.[18]

Benjamin Isaac concluded that

> there is no evidence at all that either power [Byzantium or Persia] thought a serious danger threatened from the south. . . . There was no obvious reason to fear destruction by the Arabs, as no one could predict the rise of Islam. In the end it was a wholly unexpected war of ideas and religion that brought down the existing order.[19]

Third, Kievan and other Russian polities had coped more or less adequately for more than three centuries with armies of raiders from the steppes. In the early thirteenth century there seemed to be no particular reason why the Mongols, in their turn, would not prove to be a manageable menace.[20] "Russian" national security policy proved unequal to the extraordinary challenge and the "Mongol Yoke" descended for two and a half centuries.

Fourth, although World War II was really round two of a single conflict and was fueled preeminently by a German bid to reverse the outcome of round one, Adolf Hitler proved to be a political phenomenon that Western statesmen found all but impossible to anticipate or comprehend. There was nothing inevitable about Hitler's rise to power, though the kind of war he unleashed was probably unstoppable. No matter who had ruled Germany in the 1930s, both the balance of power problems (created in part by an overpowerful but perilously fearful Germany)[21] that generated World War I and the legacies of that war would have promoted instability. In other words, prudent French and British statesmen in the early 1930s should have anticipated, as some did, the political recovery of Germany and German demands for the formal unravelling of many of the provisions of the Treaty of Versailles (1919). Indeed the 1920s had already witnessed considerable movement in those regards, promoted competently enough by Gustav Stresemann.[22] But it was not until the winter of 1938–1939 that the full dimension of the Nazi threat to international order began to be appreciated (which is not to deny that there were a few voices crying accurately in the wilderness). At the time, it was not self-evident that Adolf Hitler was a reckless gambler in a hurry, a gambler who would double his bets in the face of adversity.[23] As late as spring 1939, Britain and France sought by diplomatic means to deter Hitler from moving on Poland. History has witnessed relatively very few utterly reckless bids for continental (eventually world) empire by a leader who is truly beyond deterrence. Reasonable people in satisfied polities are hindered by a conditioned incapacity to recognize massive unreason, or very alien reason, in others in pursuit of heroic, if wicked, goals.[24] Thanks to geography, Britain, the USSR, and the United States survived the extraordinary challenge posed by Hitler's Germany, though the Third French Republic did not.

These cases of unusual challenges to national security carry six important implications for coping with uncertainty. First, extraordinary security dangers do arise, albeit rarely and unpredictably. Second, greater-than-expected dangers are treated as matters of routine until the necessity for a nonroutine response is demonstrated by events. Third, some polities adapt rapidly to a condition of unusual menace (the [East] Roman Empire and Attila in the late 440s) or are granted time to adapt by a favorable geography (Byzantium and the Arabs, England and France, the United States and Nazi Germany), while others are less flexible or capable (Kiev and the Mongols, the Dutch Republic versus England and then France). Fourth, strategic foresight and adaptability are priceless assets, but they are not necessarily sufficient for coping with unwelcome change on a major scale. Security dangers can arise that require a certain quantity of material response, just as dangers can arise that must be met in combat—they cannot be prevented, deterred, or otherwise finessed. Not all dangers can be deflected. Fifth, prior success as a security community can encourage excessive confidence in the face of unknown and unknowable future dangers.[25] Sixth, nonlinear, act-of-God, bolt-from-the-blue events are so extraordinary that for excellent reasons any intelligence system will discount them thoroughly—and very occasionally they will be wrong. Even if an intelligence system is persuaded that extraordinary, perhaps counterintuitive, danger threatens, persuading political leaders that systemic menace is approaching is no easy task. After all, extraordinary danger implies the necessity for extraordinary response—and what if the danger has been misidentified?

To observe that trends, unlike acts of God, come in bunches is to notice little more than the natural complexity of affairs. Events, great and not so great, may have a simple detonator, but they tend not to have a simple or single cause. As one contemplates the remainder of the 1990s and the early 2000s, wondering if some further discontinuities (beyond the demise of the cold war and the crash of the Soviet state) in objective conditions will erupt to unsettle the relevant political, social, economic, and military universe for defense planning, one must avoid the temptation to consider possible changes *seriatim*, in isolation. Historians have identified dozens of possible "causes" of the decline and fall of the Roman Empire,[26] but if one had been a Roman strategic planner in the mid-fourth century A.D., which trends should one have watched most closely? Today it is obvious that the military demands upon an ailing Soviet economy, the ability of that economy to produce on demand, the burdens of inflexible bureaucracy, the political legitimacy of the Soviet state and extended empire, and the authority of the Communist Party and so on were intimately interrelated. There are no laws in social science. A condition of free wheeling "possibilism"[27] means that although many past and current trends can be identified and a list of possible nonlinear changes in conditions can be provided, specific changes cannot be predicted with authority. However, that does not mean that the long-range planner is left naked to confront the unknown.

## DISTRIBUTION OF POWER: THE ROOTS OF
## DEFENSE PLANNING

The American way in war and defense planning is shaped by American strategic culture, but what the United States attempts to achieve in war and peace as well as the roles it seeks to play depend on American perceptions of the international distribution of power. Budgetary and bureaucratic processes, weapons acquisition, civil-military relations, technological promise and performance, doctrine, tactics, operational art, and strategy are ultimately driven or shaped by the broad course, the general line, set in statecraft by the country's leaders. The true test of state performance is how well it provides national security in an essentially anarchic system of inter-state relations.[28] By far the greatest threat to national security is that of an unfavorable international distribution of power.[29] If policy, which is synonymous with statecraft at this elevated level, is inadequate, no amount of efficiency in weapon procurement practices will protect the country's interests. In searching for a basis for defense planning in the face of great uncertainty, this section reviews briefly the general architecture of international power to which U.S. high policy must relate.

## 1900–1916: THE OLD REGIME

Throughout the nineteenth century Britain's Royal Navy effectively insulated the United States from unwanted involvement in European quarrels and from the possibility of serious and sustained European intervention in the Americas. The Royal Navy rendered the North Atlantic a secure defensive moat for the United States, with Canada functioning as a convenient hostage for British good behavior. Residual U.S. distrust of British imperialism was reflected in the typically friendly character of Russo-American relations. An important principle of the balance of power is that the enemy of my enemy is my friend. In the same way that, in Russian eyes, the United States provided a healthy outflanking distraction for Britain's Europe-based seapower, so, in U.S. eyes, imperial Russia distracted British power in Europe and Central Asia. The United States entered the twentieth century distrustful of entangling alliances and the machinations of Old World statesmen.[30]

By the first decade of this century it was tacitly understood that war between Britain and the United States was all but impossible: such a war was planned for, but not taken very seriously. Rising U.S. seapower outflanked Britain's naval stranglehold on peninsular Europe and, in principle, could invalidate British strategy altogether. In practice, the Royal Navy concentrated in the North Sea after 1905 for the day of reckoning with Germany's new High Seas Fleet, politically untroubled by the existence of the U.S. fleet to the West.[31]

Until 1916–1917, the United States was not an active participant in the balance of power, notwithstanding her enormous economic resources for fighting a war. Indeed, until early 1917 there did not seem to be any very pressing need for the United States to play an active role. The Western Allies valued U.S. productive assets for the generation of war material, but they did not believe that a host of undertrained and ill-equipped American soldiers were needed in the field. Furthermore, the military events of 1914 to (very early) 1917 indicated that there was a healthy military imbalance in Europe in favor of the Allies.[32] In 1916 Russia was still in the field, the extent of damage to the French army's fighting ability was not fully apparent, Britain had only begun to make her full weight felt with her new armies, Germany had been very seriously bloodied, and Allied credit in the United States was still adequate, (if barely).

### 1917–1990: TO REDRESS THE BALANCE

In World War I the German war machine (only belatedly fully mobilized after 1916)[33] defeated imperial Russia, fought France to a standstill, bankrupted Britain and threatened her with defeat, and nearly won before U.S. military power could exert itself properly. In short, after 1916 there was no balance of power in Europe (or Asia) without full U.S. participation. In the 1920s and early 1930s the balance of power in Europe was not challenged. Britain and France proved they could not beat Nazi Germany in 1939–1940;[34] there is good reason to believe that Britain and the USSR likewise would have failed in 1941–1943. It is all too obvious that once the British Royal Navy was fully committed to the containment of Germany in Europe (after 1905 and again after 1938), there was no balance to Japanese power in East Asia if the United States chose not to provide it. In the early decades of this century the statesmen and defense planners for a world-girdling British Empire faced the possibility of simultaneous threats in three regions: in home waters, in the Mediterranean, and in the Far East. The Anglo-Japanese Alliance of 1902–1922, general amity in Anglo-American political relations, and, after 1922, the Washington system of naval arms limitation served to postpone the day of strategic reckoning when imperial military overstretch could no longer be concealed or finessed by a superior statecraft and diplomacy. In the twentieth century Britain could concentrate its fleet in home waters to limit the maritime action of a Northern European enemy (Germany), but it could not simultaneously maintain in, or dispatch to, the Pacific a fleet capable of deterring and defeating burgeoning Japanese naval power.[35]

Of necessity, the United States was *the* Western end of the balance of power from 1945 until sometime in the 1960s. The so-called Western Alliance truly was a U.S.-led and guarded client-states system—a benign version of the Delian League led by Athens after the Persian Wars. Furthermore, technological accident, economic considerations, and geopolitics all coalesced to ensure that the centerpiece of the U.S. custodial role would be the extended nuclear deterrent.

From the mid-1960s until the close of the 1980s little changed in the formal structure of the Western end of the balance of power. Physically, Europe and Asia recovered fully from World War II and modernized their economies, while U.S. economic and financial hegemony all but vanished. Nonetheless, as in a time warp, the Western Alliance of 1990 was arranged very much as it had been in the mid-1950s (following the 1954 agreement on the terms and conditions for German rearmament). In the 1970s and 1980s it was evident that the United States must continue to play the leading role as a net security producer in the face of Soviet military power that was growing in quality and quantity through the mid-1980s. But it was also evident that many of the enduring features of Western security architecture were as much a product of inertia as cogent reason.

## 1991–2000: TRANSITION—BUT TO WHAT?

The familiar postwar world with its cold war features is a thing of the past, but will the immediate future see radical improvement in the quality of international security? That remains to be determined. The French Revolution led to Napoleon's coup d'état (18th Brumaire, November 9, 1798); the real Russian Revolution that toppled the Romanovs led to the coup by Lenin (November 6, 1917); the second Russian revolution, inadvertently triggered and "ridden" by Gorbachev, has led, so far, to an abortive left-wing (not right-wing, as the media claimed) coup, and may yet lead to almost anything. For the time being, the erstwhile Soviet empire is in the throes of a severe "time of troubles," but the case for the United States remaining locally engaged in the structure of security in Eurasia is overwhelming. Events in the

East have proceeded with scant regard to encouragement or discouragement from the West. It should not be "back to basics" on both sides of what used to be the East-West balance.

An important purpose of alliance is the influencing, even the control, of allies.[36] The United States cannot, and should not seek to, control security events in Europe, but the continuing, if atrophying, U.S. leadership role in NATO and the large local U.S. military presence license Washington as a major, unique player in the politics of what, after all, is not her continent. Behind the excitement about a "common European home," a newly reunited Germany, a Carolingian revival, and so forth, is widespread recognition that the U.S.-guided coalition of the West is extant, is familiar (no surprises), and has a track record of working well enough (albeit under yesterday's conditions). Also, as a sometimes conveniently distant protecting power, the United States is as benign a guardian as guardians can be.[37]

There is a great deal to be said for the United States passing an updated model of its security-production baton to some successor political-military entity, but to what or which? A Franco-German "West" would not work for long and would certainly offend most other European countries, while a greater Germany-led "West" would scarcely be a superior alternative to the old U.S.-led NATO. Many statesmen, or would-be statesmen, in Europe, both East and West, are hoping that the Conference on Security and Cooperation in Europe (CSCE), which began so inauspiciously in Helsinki in 1975, may develop into a general new Concert of Europe (plus North America). The "German problem," which has driven European security politics all through this century, may finally be laid to rest within a security framework that changes the terms of competition and debate. Unfortunately it is not certain that the CSCE has the potential to function as a new superregional security framework. It carries more promise of working like a down-sized League of Nations than an up-sized NATO.

U.S. defense planners are understandably more than a little puzzled about what they should be planning for, or against, in the 1990s. It is reasonably plain already, however, that the end of the cold war cannot be equated with the outbreak of some general condition of peace. The breakup of the Soviet hegemonic and territorial empire has been effected by national, ethnic, and even in some modest measure religious and historical forces that are rebalkanizing Eastern Europe. Whatever is happening in East-Central Europe at the present time certainly cannot be called a process of peace. The current violence in what used to be Yugoslavia is a microcosm of much more extensive phenomena.

## 2001–2020: BACK TO THE FUTURE?

Theoretically, looking forward to the next century, it is distantly possible that the balance of power in Eurasia, which thrice in this century has summoned massive assistance from the United States (1917–1918, 1941–1945, 1947–1990), might be returned to management and control by local players. The first decade of the twenty-first century could see Russia share Eurasia with a superstate West-Central Europe, a regional great power China, and a near-superstate Japan—with a prosperous United States on the sidelines of regular active involvement in security affairs. It is unlikely that the United States will be able safely and smoothly to devolve all of its erstwhile guardianship duties to capable Europeans, Chinese, and Japanese. Indeed, it is likely that Russia will recover in important respects from its low point in the 1990s; that the German revival will proceed out of hand, given the power vacuum in Eastern Europe; and that some "Balkan trigger" will revive more than memories of the last decades of the Ottoman and Austro-Hungarian empires.

The overriding virtue of NATO has been its benignly entangling consequences for the United States vis à vis the balance of power *in* Europe. A United States either expelled or self-excluded from most of the security "transition" activity of the 1990s would probably attempt to aid Europe in time of dire need, but with too little and too late to help prevent a further catastrophe. The many cogent theoretical reasons for U.S. withdrawal from security arrangements in Europe are overwhelmed by pragmatically grounded fears that a new, post–U.S.-dependent, post-NATO structure for European security could well provide no security at all. Americans are prone to expect happy endings as the reward for virtue. The end of what was called the cold war and the U.S. defeat of the USSR of the 1970s and 1980s does not mean the "end of history" in Fukuyama's sense of a close to ideological struggles over political philosophy and practice.[38] Power politics is an enduring tale, even though players change, technology evolves, and new world orders come and go.

### KNOWNS AND UNKNOWNS

By definition one cannot know that which has yet to occur, but unless history, or one form of history, truly has just ended, one in fact knows a great deal about the future. For example, no one today can pen an accurate word portrait of the Russia of 2020, but the ingredients that must constitute that Russia flow from a thousand years of fairly accessible historical record and are well known indeed.[39] This is not to claim deterministically that Russia is condemned to repeat its grimly tyrannical history. It is merely to say that Russian and Soviet history and culture have conditioned Russians to believe, think, and act in certain ways. Western observers of a culture as alien as that of Russia are prone to see what they expect or want to see, particularly if their contacts are urban, Western-oriented intellectuals. At the present time, the jury is out on whether Russia has the resources to transform herself into a robust, functioning democracy. The failure of the inept left-wing coup of August 19, 1991, said little about the true strength of the Russian popular will to achieve a working democracy, but there is not much in Russian political culture to fuel democratic processes. Everything is possible, given time, but time may be in short supply, considering the critical domestic problems that press for resolution in the near term.

Given that little can be known about the future, the interesting question remains: what is known that is important for statesmen and defense planners to know? First, bad times follow good. The political dimension of a superpower-level threat to U.S. interests is in recess at present, but history has witnessed many a "new world order." They never last. Several new world orders are possible, but the only such order that would be reliably U.S.-friendly would be U.S.-imposed. The most enduring of new world orders recorded in history was that of the Pax Romana from the accession of Augustus (27 B.C.) to the death of Marcus Aurelius (180 A.D.).[40] It seems unlikely—against the odds, so to speak—that the U.S. national security condition in the future will even approach the generally happy example set by Rome in the century and a half cited. International security is primarily about the distribution of power (actual, perceived, anticipated). Unless in some meaningful sense history has ended, anxieties over the distribution of power must beset U.S. statecraft in the future. The cold war is over, but does it really matter? A condition of cold war, of war-in-peace, is quite common in international relations. The threat to U.S. security was never the USSR per se, but rather the threat of unbalanced power in Europe and Asia. Although the specific future character of that threat is speculative at this point, to assume it has been removed is to dismiss the entire history of international relations as valueless in planning for the future. Since the sixteenth century, Britain, and later the United States, opposed a succession of would-be continental hegemons: Spain, France, Germany, the USSR. There is no evidence to suggest an end to this historical pattern.

Second, power needs to be balanced in, not with, Eurasia. Preferably, as prior to 1917, it would not be the United States that did most of the balancing. Exactly who will need what quantity of balancing in the future cannot be known, but the need to balance power endures.

Third, enmities and alliances are not eternal. The U.S. government today cannot know for certain which acts or threatened acts by which states should occasion alarm in the United States over the next two decades, but it is a certainty that new security alarms will be sounded in the future. Many of the surprises to which the United States will be subject over the next several decades will scarcely matter at all for national security.

Fourth, arms control is merely an instrument of policy (it should be an instrument of defense planning, though too often it is merely a process of diplomacy), entirely subordinate to the tenor of political relations. Only countries that might plausibly fight each other require arms control—which is precisely why worthwhile arms control measures cannot be secured between them. The arms control paradox is rather like the credit paradox: to secure a large loan one has first to prove that one does not need it. Similarly, arms control worthy of note is achievable only between states that do not need it.

Fifth, the Soviet threat, along with the Soviet Union itself has evaporated, but no order has yet emerged for the new, politically disturbed Europe. There are no designs for a new security order in Europe that promise to be effective. Such designs as there are should be labeled visions, not policy constructs. There is no political status quo in the former Soviet Union at present, and the United States cannot predict with high confidence who will rule, or attempt to rule, even six months from now. History does not repeat itself in detail, but it would be foolish to proclaim the process of liberalization in the former Soviet Union irreversible because of the failure of the 1991 coup. Western political values have no roots in Russia. A return to firm, even despotic, government would be in the Russian and the Soviet tradition. Russia will remain a great nuclear-armed power with understandable security concerns about political turmoil in the new and old countries of Eastern Europe, about an emerging (possible) superstate in Western Europe, about an emerging Chinese superstate to the East, and about peripheral or some quasi-autonomous regions within what remains of the territorial empire at home. Probably most difficult of all will be Russia's security relationship with the independent Ukraine—a relationship that could generate very dangerous tensions.

Sixth, there will be an increase in regional disorder. Bipolar "bloc" management and global conflict created some mutual dependencies between super and local states which, on balance, helped restrain open military conflict regionally and locally. Post–cold war super or great powers have been freed strategically to intervene in regional disputes, but are less motivated, or domestically permitted, to do so. The fact of regional disorder does not translate mechanistically into an imperative calling for U.S. intervention.

Seventh, strategic forces and military space assets, maritime power, and then landpower—in descending order—are the geostrategically ordained priorities among U.S. military instruments. This will be as true in 2020 as it is today, or indeed, as it was in 1980, 1970, 1960, and 1950. One cannot plan not to be surprised, but one can and should plan against many of the grave dangers that could arise from surprise effect. If, for example, the United States maintains a first-class strategic offensive posture, deploys modest strategic defenses to counter undeterrable threats, and retains a large and balanced navy, there is little that could menace the vital or *survival* interests of Americans. It is sensible to be aware of, but not to worry uselessly about, the possibility of genuinely unknown unknowns. History can deliver almost totally unanticipated "super threats," as described above. Fortunately, this happens very rarely. Most statesmen in most generations do not have to cope with an Attila the Hun, a Genghis Khan, a Napoleon, or an Adolf Hitler.

The detail of new security arrangements is sufficiently uncertain that precise implications for U.S. policy cannot be drawn as yet. From time to time the old order changes and while modes of conduct are plain enough, policy objectives can shift (balance Russia, keep Constantinople out of Russian hands, balance France, balance France and Russia, and so forth).

I believe that the historical experience of coalitions advises that only continuous and locally important players are in the game of helping to shape coalition policy. If the United States aspires to a leading policy-shaping role in the West, it needs a military presence in the territory of most concern. Continental allies and their foes respect only those commitments they can see. U.S. association with a successor body to NATO, more Europe-inclusive, would certainly be preferable to no formal association at all with European security arrangements, but association would not be a very effective form of participation. It is American to be optimistic, to expect progress, and to feel frustrated and even angry when confronted with significant setbacks. Notwithstanding a political culture that pulls in the opposite direction, it is important to be patient and tolerate with what promises to be a very messy period in the evolution of Central and Eastern Europe. A united Germany's most extensive experiment to date with popular democracy ended with Adolf Hitler, while the Russian experiment with popular sovereignty ended with Stalin. An economically successful Germany in the 1990s, ideally well-embedded in European-plus organizations, should bear little resemblance to its unhappy forbear of the 1920s and 1930s. Nonetheless, question marks surround the political maturity of virtually all of the societies East of the Rhine in an era when their destiny is largely their own to shape.

It is uncertain where priorities among policy objectives will end up. For example, will the United States be more concerned for the time being to help guide allies than to discourage adventure on the part of declining former foes? It is certain that the terminal Soviet crisis-of-empire has left the United States alone as *the* first-class superpower. It is also certain that circumstances are shaping policy and strategy more than vice versa.[41] Those who want America to "come home, now" fail to appreciate that hegemonic or near-hegemonic power, and perhaps authority, carries great responsibilities and can function as the essential engine for a tolerable order. The United States cannot direct the political traffic of security throughout Europe, but by remaining an important regional, if foreign, player with a global reach, it can help minimize the prospect of a third twentieth-century slide from crisis to conflagration. This general point has been true of superpowers a millennium apart. Secretary of Defense Dick Cheney has said: "America's global military posture and leadership promotes an international environment in which free peoples and those seeking freedom can prosper. . . . not only does our presence deter Soviet influence, it also can dampen regional arms competition and discourage local powers from seeking to dominate their neighbors."[42]

Describing the goodwill with which traders and pilgrims were treated in the Eastern Mediterranean in the middle of the eleventh century, Sir Steven Runciman wrote that "this goodwill was guaranteed by the power of Byzantium."[43] Runciman and Cheney register the same point: international civility prospers in the presence of a well-armed guardian.

## LONG-RANGE PLANNING

There is nourishing food for thought in the following judgment by Samuel P. Huntington: "Gorbachev may be able to discard communism, but he cannot discard geography and the geopolitical imperatives that have shaped Russian and Soviet behavior for centuries."[44]

Radical changes, even major discontinuities—the sudden regime change, the reversal of an alliance, the technological breakthrough, the unpredicted asteroid strike,[45] and so on—can have implications for U.S. national security policy ranging from the traumatic to the trivial. Even discontinuities that seem dramatic and fraught with dire implications often have less dramatic an impact than is expected at the time. But nightmares can come true, as the Shi'ite Islamic revival that followed Shah Reza Pahlavi's Iran illustrated so grotesquely. Huntington suggests an important reason why the effect of unexpected discontinuity upon the course of events is frequently dampened. The geopolitical factors that generally work for continuity in policy can be powerful indeed. It matters who rules in Moscow, but the objective geopolitical conditions for such rule may matter even more. Mikhail Gorbachev's policy maneuvers from 1985 to 1990 represented a radical shift in course from that pursued by Leonid Brezhnev, but both Brezhnev and Gorbachev were sincere believers in the Soviet system and its legitimizing ideology. The only serious measures of imperial devolution sanctioned by Soviet leaders were those conceded under the pressure of events in 1918–1919 and 1989–1991. Gorbachev endeavored unsuccessfully to save his Soviet inheritance, not to speed its dissolution.

The study of history should alert the long-range planner to the ways in which elements of discontinuity can have their effects reduced by enduring factors as well as by the sheer complexity of affairs. Technologically comparable states, for example, will register a military advantage here or there, but potential superiority in one or even several weapons is not the stuff from which victory can be crafted. Military effectiveness, let alone strategic effectiveness, is a composite of weaponized technologies, material and human quantity and quality (skill, discipline, morale), plans, tactics, operational art and strategy—and for *net* effectiveness, of the performance of the enemy.[46]

Notwithstanding uncertainty over what the future will bring, political and military leaders must know whither they would like to go. A U.S. president should hold firmly to what may be called a *theory of statecraft*. This theory would identify a broadly desirable, dynamic security condition for the United States and explain how that condition could be attained and sustained. A theory of statecraft has policy, grand strategy, and military strategy sections. The U.S. government cannot plan the future, but it can be ready to cope well enough with many plausible threats to vital national interests and even with some highly implausible threats as well. The need is not to predict the future. Instead, the need is to be ready to adjust to demands and opportunities the details of which are unexpected but may be anticipated generically.

A rush of discontinuities can overwhelm a state beyond its ability to act; then it can only react after the unexpected event as best it can. But it is no conceit on the part of policymakers to believe that much of the future environment that will determine national security requirements comprises material and attitudes that can be shaped by U.S. policy. Even Marxist theorists, with their concept of "objective conditions," long acknowledged that history helps those who help themselves (or what was an elite party of dedicated revolutionaries for?). It is true that little effort was required to overthrow Kerensky's provisional government in 1917, but it is not true to claim that objective historical forces somehow handed the baton of progress to an obedient and submissive Lenin. The Bolshevik coup, otherwise known as the October Revolution, was brought about by a dedicated elite who regarded themselves as the sharpest instrument of contemporary history.

It is important to be alert to the certainty of surprise and surprise effect and to the fact that discontinuities can pose awesome, nonroutine challenges. It is scarcely less important to recognize the measure of influence that a great power can exert over its own security circumstances. The Third French Republic, for example, could do very little after 1871 to inhibit the immoderate growth in power and influence of the new imperial Germany, but Paris did succeed in effecting a security condition wherein she fought *with* Russia, *with* Britain, and eventually *with* the United States as allies when she was finally obliged to fight Germany in self-defense. That was no small achievement.[47] Because of the lack of evidence, there can never be an unambiguous audit trail from military preparation intended to deter to the failure of the undesired events to occur. However, it is reasonable to postulate that U.S.

grand strategy has had a positive influence on the country's security environment. It is always possible for a state inadvertently to promote its own insecurity, but there is as little danger of a U.S. administration proceeding oblivious to the workings of the classical "security dilemma"[48] as there is of the United States triggering that dilemma by overzealously leading posses for peace in the name of some dimly conceived new world order.

The policymakers of a superstate are not simply cast in a reactive mode, required to attempt to respond to whatever the future may bring. By its choices of policy, grand strategy, and military strategy, the United States will assuredly influence its external security condition. The United States needs an overarching theory of statecraft; it must know in what direction it should head in policy, grand strategy, and military strategy. Identification of destination, that is, policy goals, is important not so much because their attainment is important, but because in the permanent "here and now" one needs robust, rather than fleeting or expedient, algorithms for guidance. For example, is the INF treaty, the treaty on Conventional Forces in Europe (CFE), or the START treaty of net benefit to U.S. and, more generally, Western security? The U.S. government must be flexible in coping with unexpected problems and opportunities, unanticipated resource constraints, and so on. However, flexibility should not be reduced to mere opportunism, which may be defined as expedient exploitation of an immediately attractive or simply available option. If pursued without disciplined reference to a sense of medium- or long-term direction, opportunistic action can produce a net loss in whatever currency is at issue.

The INF treaty provided a healthy imbalance in favor of NATO in numbers of nuclear delivery systems to be destroyed. But did the NATO of 1987 want to promote the denuclearization of non-Soviet Europe? The START treaty should effect a 30 percent reduction in central strategic arsenals, but why is that of net benefit to U.S. security? Again, where is the United States headed? Political opportunities, not to mention demands, for the reduction of U.S. forces in Europe are growing rapidly. What is the U.S. and NATO policy goal in this regard? The CFE treaty must be appraised in light of the road it represents for NATO as well as its internal merits and limitations.[49] Arms control agreements have been known to do the wrong things quite effectively.

The United States continuously constructs and reconstructs the future to the limited degree that it can be shaped by U.S. policy choices. The future begins now. Whether or not Washington will have the ser-

vices of balanced armed forces of appropriate size to cope with the unpredictable strategic demands that will be imposed by policy in 2000 or
2010 depends upon the incremental choices made in the ever-moving
present. The long-range planner must balance the prospective delights
of new capability the day after tomorrow against the tangible benefits
of ready capability today. Unfortunately, the U.S. armed forces have no
guarantee that strategic demand for their services in acute crisis or
major war will not be issued sooner rather than later. Desert Shield
and Desert Storm in 1990–1991 illustrated with unusual clarity just
how rich is the menu of surprises history can serve up to policymakers
and defense planners.

## SEVEN PRINCIPLES FOR DEFENSE PLANNING

The political sustainability of defense effort is not an independent variable; it is dependent in part on the quality of strategic rationale provided. In planning it is always important to ask the question "what is
true?" For example, will Russia need deterring? But since confident
identification of truth is unlikely, the relevant question becomes what
to plan for or against in a period wherein old certainties appear to ex-
pire on a weekly basis. The 1990s are shaping up as a very uncomfort-
able decade for defense professionals.

It is helpful to approach the tasks of defense planning in the 1990s
by drawing a distinction between defense activity that is *threat-driven*
and defense activity that is *uncertainty-pulled*. Specific threat-driven
defense preparation is the only strategic condition with which contemporary Americans are familiar. Defense life without an overshadowing
and multifaceted Soviet threat has been all but unthinkable. However,
the endurance, stability, simplicity, and intensity of the Soviet military
threat stands out as a historical aberration among the strategic histories of great powers. The post-cold-war world is emerging for U.S. defense planners as a dynamic context characterized by great uncertainty over the leading threats. U.S. defense planning is being *pulled*
by prudence towards preparation for generic kinds of challenges (witness the idea of the "base force" organized to meet strategic, Atlantic,
Pacific, and contingency needs)—intervention in regional conflicts an
ocean away, for example.[50] No longer is U.S. defense planning *driven* by
the needs to neutralize specifically detailed threats that are confidently recognized.

More common historically than the bipolar military standoff is a situation wherein rival polities bear watching and just might emerge as enemies in surprising combinations. Of course defense planners must define threats as they conduct regular defense planning and military training activities. Nonetheless, an uncertainty-pulled, though disciplined, approach to defense planning is more likely to serve the nation well in the 1990s, than an endeavor to fight the declining political credibility of major threat.

The section that follows identifies broad principles for the guidance of defense planning through a period of radical change. It is my contention that uncertainty-pull should inform contemporary planning.

### 1: Face Facts, Recognize Ignorance

Much that the professional defense planner would like to know is unknowable. Ignorance of the details of the future is not a problem for, or a weakness in, planning; it is a permanent condition for which no apology is necessary. Particular events can rarely be predicted. Wisdom begins with frank recognition that detailed "future history" is beyond research.

Good defense planning, therefore, cannot be a quest for the unattainable. The challenge is to plan intelligently and rationally in the face of massive uncertainties. Historically, not even the crises and wars that were planned and then launched deliberately (at times, places, and with a character carefully preselected) have tended to be conducted successfully. Witness the disastrous consequences of German, Italian, and Japanese grand-strategic choices in the period 1939–1942. No less important than realizing what cannot be known about future history is appreciating what is known about future security environments. Regardless of who is up or down in the domestic politics of important foreign countries, the United States requires a military framework for the rapid generation of deterrent or actual war-fighting effect. The defense planner is able to proceed prudently and usefully from the enduring fact that his glass of relevant knowledge will always be half, or more, full. What he knows about the structure, or probable structure, of future U.S. defense needs will typically be more than adequate as a basis for the framing of recommendations.

The defense planner confronting the awesome and potentially paralyzing fact of his ignorance of the future should be encouraged to develop the two lists introduced earlier in this chapter: the knowns and the unknowns (and unknowables). Even in a context of seismic-scale political shock, à la 1989–1991, the planner will find that he knows a great deal both about the kinds of demands that foreign policy is likely to lay upon the military establishment and about the quantity and quality of strategic effectiveness that particular military threats or use options should generate.

### 2: Apply Geostrategic Priorities for Fault-Tolerant Planning

The U.S. defense planner does not need a crystal ball; that is fortunate, since crystal balls are out of stock. Instead, he needs a gold-embossed plaque on his desk that reads as follows:

*First Priority*:     Strategic (nuclear) and space forces.
*Second Priority*:  Long-range maritime and air forces.
*Third Priority*:    Ground and tactical air forces.

These priorities are not a matter for choice. They are, in my view, objectively true for the United States, given the national geography and the state of the art of modern technology. Various politicians and defense planners may deny these priorities by ill-considered actions, but that possibility does not alter the objective nature of the truth they represent.

It would be agreeable if there were some way to be absolutely certain that what one planned in the defense realm was "right," but there is not. Strategy is not a science. Recognizing the unpredictability of events, however, and being dutiful students of Carl von Clausewitz[51] and of Murphy and his Law, defense planners must ask what the negative consequences would be of a range of different errors in U.S. military policy. For an effectively insular, if continental-scale, country in a nuclear age, the priorities specified above should appeal to common sense because they incorporate, in toto, a unified vision of military policy and, logically and practically, a descending critical dependence. In order, the three priorities pertain to the protection of the United States in the most basic of ways vis à vis the most awesome of dangers, the ability to wage war at long distances abroad, and the ability to conduct large-scale regional military campaigns.

### 3: Recognize that the Long Term Is a Succession of Short Terms

Long-term hopes for a less bellicose world, in common with visions of a truly all-Eurasian balance of power for those continents, are exactly that—hopes and visions. In the long term most things are possible, if not equally likely, but in the meantime, the U.S. defense planner must attempt to cope with a far more disorderly world than has been familiar since the late 1940s.

The fuel for international (and intercommunal, interethnic, interreligious) conflict is increasingly abundant, but the forces for order and discipline are in retreat. The bizarre notion that the 1990s and beyond will somehow see the elevation in significance of the politics of international economics without the commensurate elevation of military force to support or advance asserted economic interests should not be accorded much respect.[52] Even though the canonical major threats of the cold war have lost credibility, the world is becoming a more dangerous place.

The ability of the United States to shape its future security environment is real but incomplete. A long-term future goal could be the development of a new security order in Europe and Asia wherein local polities would ensure a bicontinental balance and the United States could play the classic "balancer" role that sometimes was available to Britain in centuries past. For the time being, however, such a future condition is strictly a matter for speculative enquiry; it will have to be constructed brick by brick, short run by short run. It is at least as likely as not that out of the current turmoil in European politics there will emerge a superpolity that will menace the balance of power in Europe and Asia yet again.

The United States should have learned from its three twentieth-century interventions in European security politics that the time to shape the future is *as that future unfolds*. Should the United States elect in the 1990s to bring its forces home and stand down much of its military posture, it will risk repeating past errors and may be choosing to minimize its impact upon the course of Eurasian political history.

### 4: Sustain or Acquire the Flexibility to Adjust to Changing Circumstances

U.S. defense planners cannot know today what demands policy will place upon the armed forces five to ten years hence, but they do know both the kinds of demands that could be forthcoming and the character of military capabilities the country will require. For the briefest of possible sets of examples, the U.S. defense planner knows that his country must be able to deter and preferably defend (with offensive and/or defensive counterforce—nuclear, conventional or unconventional) against threats of attack by weapons of mass destruction; to wage and sustain war over very great distances; to fight alongside friends and allies, and unilaterally effect a forced regional entry; and so forth.

Of course it is difficult to size forces for a world wherein plausible and semiplausible threats are diffuse, but the marked increase in uncertainty over future dangers (the absence of self-evident dominant scenarios for force planning), as noted already, means that defense planning has to be uncertainty-pulled rather than driven by specific threats. Thus it is not so much the identified or readily predictable military capabilities of particular states that should discipline the process of defense planning and budgeting in the 1990s, but rather a more general prudence. From the geography of inter-state security relationships, the character of U.S. foreign policy, and a history-derived prudential wisdom, it is not particularly difficult to specify, interrelate, and prioritize among the kinds of military capabilities that the United States should maintain and modernize. Above all, the United States needs the ability to adjust flexibly to circumstances that are unexpected in detail though not in kind.

Flexibility has many components, including an openness of mind, an excellence in doctrine (or in provision for doctrinal revision), and a suitable elasticity of organizational framework.[53] Also, however, flexibility is a matter of money and time. Just as the basis for flexibility in strategic nuclear employment can be said to reside in meticulously detailed mission planning (for the SIOP[54] that is already in the computer and has been trained for, so flexibility tomorrow in the use of military power of all kinds must depend upon decisions made today. Decisions on military investment made in the early 1990s will determine the military capabilities of 2000 and, at the level of technology base and human resources, how quickly the United States could implement different kinds of defense mobilization in the late 1990s. It was for that reason that the Bush Administration identified "reconstitution" as one of the fundamentals of its defense planning.[55]

### 5: Learn from the Past

History cannot tell us what will happen in the 1990s, but it can tell us what could happen. The past is the repository of experience that should alert us to the questions we need to ask. History is unique. It will not be repeated in detail, but the same kinds of problems and opportunities recur, regardless of changing state players, political leaders, and levels of technology. Moreover, statesmen and defense planners are prone to commit old errors in new ways. It so happens, for example, that the principal lessons that stand out from the extensive experience of the 1920s and 1930s on negotiated strategic arms limitation fit the history of SALT in the 1970s and 1980s almost perfectly.[56]

In some ways, the challenge of the 1990s is unique for the U.S. defense planner as well as his country: a context wherein the military forces of yesterday's enemy are still in the field. But even settled certainties have a way of being suddenly overturned. Speaking in the House of Commons just a year before Britain was obliged to embark upon a twenty-year war with France, Prime Minister William Pitt (The Younger) observed, without contradiction from the floor, that "unquestionably there never was a time in the history of this country when, from the situation of Europe, we might more reasonably expect fifteen years of peace, than we may at the present moment."[57] Pitt was unlucky, not foolish.

Defense planners throughout history have faced uncertainties on the scale that confronts Americans in the 1990s. Today's details are unique; the situation is not. The absence of a dominant, specific external threat is far from an unusual state of affairs. The past is there for the education of those statesmen and defense planners wise enough to use it.

### 6: Play to American Strengths

Self-knowledge, as Sun Tzu advised, is critical for success in strategy and statecraft.[58] Freedom of choice among means and methods in national security policy is somewhat constrained. Nationally preferred approaches to security problems may fail to deliver the requisite strategic effectiveness. Nonetheless, reflection upon American (or indeed, any country's) history yields the insight that Americans and their polity are better at some kinds of military tasks than at others. This situation should be expected since, for good and for ill, each country's armed forces are an expression of the society and political system that produced them and which they serve. For example, following the military disasters of 1940–1942, the British Chief of the Imperial General Staff, General Alan Brooke, believed that "we [British] are undoubtedly softer as a nation than any of our enemies except the Italians."[59] Typical German evaluation of the physical and moral resilience of the

American soldier in 1942 and later was similarly unflattering.[60] Nazi German society in the 1930s, not to mention the years of combat experience (in Poland, France, Russia, North Africa), had provided hard schools for the German soldier of 1942–1943.

National geography and historical experience forge what is known as a strategic culture. From this culture one can talk of an "American way" in defense preparation and in war. Of necessity, Americans have been excellent at conquering great distances—though mobility can translate into mere motion rather than effective fighting power at the sharp end—and at substituting machines of all kinds for scarce or militarily inefficient manpower.[61] As U.S. defense planners consider their options for the remainder of the 1990s, they should reflect honestly upon which activities the American armed forces tend to conduct well or poorly. Countries specialize militarily. The priorities specified in the second principle match, tolerably accurately and in descending order, the kinds of military activity at which Americans excel.

### 7: Reexamine Assumptions, Reshape Rationales

The size and character of the U.S. defense posture as late as 1990–1991 was the product of strategic assumptions and beliefs that were then between thirty and forty years old—the age of the foreign policy and grand strategy that U.S. military power served. Policy and strategy assumptions are not invalid because they are old. Indeed, it can be useful to remember that nothing ages as rapidly as this morning's news headlines. U.S. defense policy cannot and should not be remade in accordance with instant judgments about the ebb and flow of current events (or of "trends" that are only days, months, or perhaps a year old). Policy and strategy that in their basic elements were set in the 1950s, but then accommodated many changes at the margin over subsequent decades, eventually came to assume an existential dignity and authority. There may still be excellent reasons for maintaining a strategic forces triad, for example, albeit one notably stood down from very high readiness, and for approaching nuclear targeting via the big-war framework of SIOP planning. But a period assuredly arrives wherein fine tuning of the extant concept or approach imposes an unwise burden of opportunity costs. In accordance with the paradoxical logic of strategy, success breeds failure and, following Clausewitz, there is a "culminating point of victory" beyond which lies entropy.[62] Quantitative change eventually compels qualitative change.

Some U.S. military planning from the past thirty years remains relevant for the 1990s, but the political framework for those contingent actions has changed. Both the rationales understood for planning purposes and those advanced for the garnering of necessary public support must change as well. In a democracy, strategic wisdom bereft of public support is just a set of ideas.

If followed in practice, the seven broad principles advanced here should reduce the burden of anxiety that flows from uncertainty. They can serve as a rough and ready compass, invaluable in foggy conditions. On many matters of detail statesmen and defense planners will be more or less wrong. That is a given. The challenge is to find an approach to defense planning that provides a useful level of insurance against the bad consequences of unpleasant surprises.

### JUDGMENT AND CALCULATION

In an excellent analysis of the underappreciated challenges of force planning, Colonel Robert P. Haffa, Jr., correctly declares that "a rational framework for planning military forces based on tests of their adequacy—threat assessment, campaign analysis and quantitative modeling—exists and has been used effectively."[63] At least, he is correct up to a point. There is a "rational framework" for force planning, even if it is typically overridden in practice by arbitrary budgetary factors and strategically irrelevant political factors. Some caveats are in order, however.

First, even though a process of analysis may be reasonably defined as rational, it will not necessarily encourage wise judgments. One can plan rationally to accomplish the wrong goals.[64] Second, like the superequation in the cartoon that has a mysterious, miraculous, but alas invisible term, there is a missing formula to rational defense planning for strategic nuclear forces. Not only is the outcome of war not mathematically calculable, but the broad prewar and wartime tasks assigned to strategic forces do not lend themselves to numerically exact analysis. The issue is not one of tactical analysis, of weapons placed on targets, but rather of strategic effect. How much threatened or applied force will achieve the desired deterrent effect? Third, what can it mean to claim that "a rational framework for planning military forces . . . exists *and has been used effectively*?" Should one infer from the absence of *grande guerre* between the superpowers that the United States planned and effected the "right" strategic forces? Is it possible that war was deterred despite the United States having acquired the "wrong" forces? Or, perhaps, one should infer nothing in particular, since there is no reliable way of knowing either whether Moscow needed deterring or whether, if deterrence did function, the details of the U.S. strategic forces were salient or not.

Notwithstanding these caveats, Haffa's plea for a strategically rational approach to force planning is important and should be heeded. The difficulty lies in what his method omits. Probably the beginning of wisdom is recognition that there is no magical solution to the perennial difficulties of connecting most effectively foreign policy needs, force planning, and the sharp end of employment policy (war plans).

While recognizing the merit in Napoleon's belief about the key to successful generalship—applying superior force at the "decisive" point[65]—it must be acknowledged that military victories have been won with a wide range of favorable and unfavorable force ratios.[66] Unless there is good reason to anticipate a purely attritional struggle, one must always allow for the possibility that excellence in technology, tactics, operational art, or strategy can provide some substitution value for brute arithmetic. Former Defense Under Secretary Fred Charles Iklé suggested that

> The confrontation of these U.S. and Soviet missile forces has evoked a morbid fascination among many defense technicians. By a banal and unrealistically abstract calculation—the so-called "missile exchange"—these technicians pretend to measure the "stability" of deterrence.[67]

For forty years some of Iklé's former colleagues at Rand have encouraged, deliberately or inadvertently, the false belief that (nuclear) war is a mathematically calculable event. The first of the Rand basing studies, R-266, *Selection and Use of Strategic Air Bases*,[68]

> was among the first attempts to abstract the "nuclear exchange," to place it, like one of Wohlstetter's exercises in mathematical logic from earlier days, in a rarefied universe all its own, apart from the world of political leaders and their appreciation of horrible risk, apart from the broader issues of how nuclear weapons fit into an overall strategy. . . . Wohlstetter made the issue of calcu-

lated vulnerability the central focus of strategic analysis generally.[69]

A Rand study of April 1989 was admirably open about its central analytical premise.

> According to our definition, crisis stability rests on the correlation
> of nuclear forces and, in particular, on the hypothetical outcomes
> of nuclear attacks. Consequently, to analyze crisis stability, we
> must make assumptions about the U.S. and the Soviet offensive
> and defensive force postures and about the relevant scenario for
> calculating the outcome of strategic exchanges.[70]

One hesitates to call this approach to stability entirely worthless. There is, after all, some value in the improvement of one's information about the expected tactical performance of U.S. (strategic) forces, even if the information is gleaned from stylized, hypothetical nuclear wars. However, the analysis is thoroughly misconceived if it is valued for the insights it might yield about crisis stability or any other kind of stability. In a sense, it is foolish to argue with a definition of crisis stability that can be neither true nor false, but only more or less useful. Nonetheless, it can be claimed with high confidence that "the correlation of nuclear forces" and "in particular, the hypothetical outcomes of nuclear attacks," though important for decisions on war or peace, are trivial in significance compared with the political urges to fight. As former Commander in Chief of the Strategic Air Command (CINCSAC) General Russell E. Dougherty has written, "there are no 'experts' in waging nuclear conflict."[71] Profoundly inexpert statesmen are unmoved by the variability of the mathematically calculable outcomes to hypothetical nuclear wars save to anticipate a generic catastrophe. Arsenal exchange models and the "wars" they direct may have some value at the tactical and operational levels, but contrary to Haffa's claim, they cannot function "as a tool with which to judge strategic stability."[72] Wars do not erupt because military balances are unstable, by some definitions. The causes of war are as complex as they are overwhelmingly political.[73]

# CHAPTER SIX

# Technological Peace
# and Political Peace:
# The Case of Arms Control

A tendency arises to seek the solution of difficulties in artificial
and sometimes complicated international arrangements, contem-
plating an indefinite future, instead of in simple national proce-
dure meeting each new situation as it develops, governed by a settled general national policy.

—Alfred Thayer Mahan
*Retrospect and Prospect*

## THEORY AND PRACTICE

It was no accident that the founding fathers of modern, and largely
American, arms control theory specified broad goals that were all but
indistinguishable from the goals one could set for a wise defense policy
writ large.[1] Specifically, arms control was proclaimed to be about reduction in the risks of war, reduction in the damage that might otherwise
be suffered in war, and reduction in the burden of peacetime military
preparation. More elaborate objectives than these have been derived
from time to time, but these three command general acceptance as the
canonical trinity of arms control purposes.

Mere recital of the broad American goals in arms control, however,
tells one nothing about the practicability of the enterprise. Furthermore, goals are neither theory nor strategy. It is necessary, indeed essential, for policymakers to know why they should pursue arms control, but ends without specified means or methods and not tied together
with plausible theory promote frustration and disillusionment. I be-

lieve it can be argued that the history of the past thirty, indeed seventy, years has shown both that the dominant theory has been deficient and even that the very idea of arms control theory lacks integrity.[2] The attempted practice of arms control has demonstrated that the problem is not only, if at all, that of managing an arms race system. Instead, or in addition, the problem is the political rivalry that drives programs of competitive armament. Since arms control was reinvented in the United States in the late 1950s as a way of coping pragmatically with military dangers *in the context of acute political antagonism,*[3] the thesis that the latter dominates the former is a fundamental challenge to the logic of arms control. The basic problem for U.S. policy on arms control during the cold war era was not Soviet armaments; it was the political interests defined by the Soviet leaders as requiring military support. While there was certainly some connection between the scale and nature of Western armament and Soviet military effort, there were closer links between that effort and the very nature of the Soviet state of that period, particularly its political interests.

Politicians and commentators seeking to influence opinion can have a severe crisis of conscience over the central truth-in-advertising problem of arms control. It is always tempting to seek maximum blessing-by-association for the particular arms control product of the day. The general goals of arms control are so self-evidently desirable that questionable or trivial agreements can be enhanced in their perceived merit by formal association with arms control in general.

## RIVAL PARADOXES

The idea of limited cooperation between enemies is not the invention of modern arms control theory. A Byzantine-Persian treaty of 562 reaffirmed an agreement dating back to 441–442 that required both parties to refrain from fortifying cities or other installations near their border.[4] For another example, the high-medieval papacy succeeded in imposing rules of warfare upon Christians fighting fellow Christians.[5] In this century the Geneva Convention regarding the treatment of prisoners of war has generally been obeyed by signatory-combatants.[6] However, the idea that states in a condition defined by policy as one of enmity—or perhaps just of mutual watchfulness—should regulate their military preparations by tacit or formal agreement, is paradoxical.

The political enmity that theoretically renders arms control relevant, *of necessity* inhibits or precludes substantive cooperation. Modern arms control theory recognizes this salient fact, but argues that a common interest in the avoidance of war, particularly in the avoidance of nuclear war, is so pressing that political rivalry actually facilitates endeavors to provide technical regulation of competitive armaments. The central thrust of arms control is neither the search for peace through disarmament (the idea that states cannot fight if they are not armed), nor a backdoor quest for political reconciliation. Instead, the purpose of arms control is minimizing the danger that the competitive military instruments themselves could be a significant or critical cause of war.[7]

It is a commonsense proposition that arms and policy are mutually reinforcing. While the roots of Soviet-American antagonism lay in geopolitics, ideological incompatibilities, and anxieties over the balance of power,[8] day-by-day threat perception was certainly influenced by competitive armaments and military behavior in general (allegedly "provocative" naval exercises, worrisome antisatellite and ICBM tests, and the like). The hypothesis, therefore, is that limited cooperative management of military behavior can dampen anxieties, reduce tensions, and prevent the misreading of political intentions. The relationship between capabilities and intentions is notoriously difficult to read. The ancient maxim, If you wish for peace, prepare for war, is always liable to produce in practice some misinterpretation of purpose. Precautionary armament to deter is also competitive armament for waging war, depending upon which end of the gun barrel is your location. It is a thesis of the arms control movement that the partial joint management of military competition can help prevent situations wherein precautions for peace are misread as settled intentions for war.

On the fringes of the arms control debate are sundry psychiatrists, psychologists, and anthropologists who take the view that competitive armaments and war (the two tend to be confused) are the products of variably diseased minds or atavistic cultural traits.[9] Expressing this perspective the UNESCO charter claims that the fences of peace are constructed in the minds of children, or mankind in general. In its less classical form, this notion held that the collective insanity of the nuclear arms race was the cybernetic product of mutual misunderstanding and misperception. Since no reasonable person wants nuclear war (or any kind of war), proponents of this position argue, the problems of insecurity must flow from an absence of accurate communication between candidate adversaries. Variants of this theme may be found in the myriad people-to-people exchanges, in the heartland of arms control country—as with the Pugwash conferences—as well, for example, as when the U.S. and Soviet ministers of defense and chiefs of staff met to exchange views on military doctrine in 1988, 1989, and 1990. Misunderstandings and misperceptions do characterize international politics, but it is not obvious that such misunderstandings and misperceptions are very important, that they lend themselves to nonmarginal alleviation, or that they ought to be an important focus of an arms control process, broadly conceived and practiced.[10]

## STRATEGY COMES FIRST

In a founding text of modern arms-control theory, Thomas C. Schelling and Morton H. Halperin wrote: "We believe that arms control is a promising, but still only dimly perceived, enlargement of the scope of our military strategy."[11] Later they advised that "there is hardly an objective of arms control to be described in this study that is not equally a continuing urgent objective of national military strategy—of our unilateral military plans and policies."[12] It should follow, in the orderly universe of Schelling and Halperin—and as repeated in a host of *pro forma* claims since that time—that arms control, tacit or negotiated, is an alternative path to the same national security that could only be secured more expensively and more dangerously by unilateral military effort.

Three potential sources of difficulty could upset the arms control enterprise as described above. First, national military strategy might be indeterminate, meaning that there is too little strategy guidance for arms control policy. Second, even if military strategy is well established and internally coherent, arms control policymaking still might go its own way. Third, military strategy and arms control policy may be admirably congruent, but the adversary might decide that he can advance his interests better by unilateral effort than by limited cooperation. The historical record of the past two decades—the SALT-START period—supports the view that the first difficulty cited is probably the most prevalent and ultimately debilitating. As the old saying has it, if you do not know where you are going, any road will take you there.

Both policy process and individuals can determine policy content. The relative political power actually exercised by the Defense Department, the State Department, and the White House—modified by the degree to which the Congress is determined to interfere—shapes U.S.

arms control policy. The Defense Department is inclined to view arms control as a branch of force planning; the State Department is inclined to approach it as just another stream of diplomacy; and the White House is apt to regard it as a vehicle for visible "statesmanship" (the president as historic peacemaker, and the like). More often than not, given the baronial character of the U.S. federal government, arms control policy activity encompasses all of these perspectives—force planning, diplomacy, and political leadership—with the distinctive perspectives pulling the players in different directions.

It may be argued that arms control is too important to be left to the generals, the diplomats, or the president's political handlers, but a fundamental question lurks here unresolved. What is arms control really about? The lingua franca of arms control is armaments, but to most people, including politicians, the details of armaments are as meaningless and boring as they are secondary in significance relative to the political importance of the arms control process.[13] This popular view is tolerably well founded in historical experience. It also happens to be convenient. It provides a plausible excuse for the typically only very modest achievements registered in arms control agreements. Lip service is paid to the proposition that arms control should serve military-strategic goals, but in practice the United States has seldom succeeded in designing, adhering to, negotiating, or enforcing arms control policies that pass muster as strategically worthwhile. This is not a narrow defense-analytical judgment. The means-ends nexus of strategy that must be used as the strategic measure of merit in arms control could accommodate the proposition that arms control serves political ends in an effective manner, were it only true.

For reasons that speak to the political culture of the United States as well as its particular form of central government (which is weak relative to that of, say, Britain or France), the United States has inordinate difficulty designing, and then adhering to, arms control positions that dovetail closely with force-planning desiderata and prudent national military strategy. The Joint Chiefs of Staff plays a critical role in contributing to U.S. arms control policy and a literally decisive role in legitimizing the outcome of the policy process. But with only rare exceptions, U.S. defense professionals, let alone uniformed defense professionals, have not exercised much control over the design and negotiation of arms control proposals for close fit with a careful determination of U.S. strategic needs. The lack of autonomy in the arms control process and its significance mean that just as the benefits that might be secured from well-crafted treaties are modest,[14] so necessarily should the damage that could accrue from ill-advised regimes be modest also. That judgment is true at least at the level of useful generalization. There is, however, no law of statecraft or strategy ensuring that the potential damage of arms control must be small. The 1930 London naval arms limitation treaty might have had war-losing consequences, as might the INF treaty, the CFE treaty, and a START follow-on treaty.

The London naval treaty of 1930 left the great maritime powers of Britain and the United States with far too few cruisers and destroyers for convoy duties in a future war. Britain's Royal Navy paid the bill for interwar naval arms control in the first half (which could have been the only half) of World War II.[15] The INF treaty of 1987, discussed below, was strategically unsound for NATO, given both the thoroughgoing incompatibility of the control regime with the Alliance's central strategic concept of flexible response and its comprehensive undermining of the integrity of the then-West German official view of how, and with what, nuclear deterrence should function.[16] The political melt-down of the Warsaw Pact in 1989–1990 and the demise of the Soviet Union in 1991 have perhaps rendered the strategic folly of the INF treaty inconsequential. But one should not conduct arms control policy in the confident expectation that completely unrelated empire-ending political events will "save the patient" from postoperative trauma and infection.

Much of the popularity of the CFE process stemmed from the belief that peace and war are reducible to a military science. The people who find solid ground for peace in proposed force postures that supposedly guarantee a "structural inability to attack" and a nonprovocative and defensive defense saw great merit in the 1990 CFE treaty, which should require, for example, a 47 percent cut in Soviet tanks in Europe compared with 13 percent for NATO.[17] In short, there is no way that a military-technical peace can be mandated and enforced through arms control.

Although it is true that arms control is twice removed from great significance for peace or war, poorly designed control regimes can impact dangerously should hostilities commence. This double removal of arms control points first to the fact that decisions to fight are overwhelmingly driven by political and not military motives, meaning that the absence or the control of weapons is of little importance.[18] Second, even to the degree to which military motives are important, there is nothing about arms control processes likely to prove uniquely friendly to peaceful outcomes. The leading historical, as well as contemporary and future, case where arms control can make and has made a major mark on the course of hostilities is that of naval matters. The maritime dimension to conflict is unusually susceptible to influence by arms control because military value is distributed over so few discrete units in that environment. In the realm of "strategic" forces, discrete assets or *targets* at present number well in excess of a thousand (counting the SLBM force as a small number of submarines). Major naval combatants, by way of the sharpest contrast, are numbered only in tens or the very low hundreds. When combat power is concentrated on, say, thirty-five SSBNs, or on fourteen (or twelve, or nine) fleet aircraft carriers, even modest negotiated arms reductions could promote a geometric rate of increase in military-technical, admittedly not political, risk.[19]

## THE DEBATE: FOUR POSITIONS

General attitudes toward arms control have an important influence in shaping opinions about particular proposals and agreements and some individual weapon systems. The arms control debate is conducted sequentially, issue by issue, but the positions favored by individuals are highly predictable. Four broad alternatives cover the spectrum of attitudes toward arms control, though it should be noted that the strongly hostile option tends to be expressed, time after time, with reference to particular agreements rather than against arms control or the arms control process per se.

First, there is a body of opinion that looks to arms control as to a philosopher's stone that will transmute the base metal of competition into the gold of cooperation. The all-but-instinctive reaction to a new weapon system by those who look upon arms control as a savior is to control it. Anything that might cause grievous military harm to an adversary is likely to be judged destabilizing; hence it becomes a leading candidate for arms control "medicine" or "surgery."[20] Second, the most popular attitude is that which finds arms control modestly useful. This is the sophisticated centrist and politically safe position explained, for example, in the Harvard University study by Albert Carnesale and Richard N. Haass, *Superpower Arms Control.* Third, the centrist alternative to position two is the attitude that finds arms control modestly harmful. Under pressure of debate with generically pro–arms control elements, adherents to the "modestly harmful" school have a way of drifting to the Right, just as their opponents in the "modestly useful" school drift to the Left when under pressure from strong skeptics. It is worth noting that both of these centrist categories provide acceptable political cover for people who, respectively, are really more passionately inclined to favor or to condemn arms control than sounds responsible. Fourth, there are people who praise arms control as a noble cause, but who have yet to find an actual Soviet-American agreement that did not warrant description as a snare and a delusion. It is unusual for an adherent to the fourth position to venture beyond condemnation of particular agreements and question the viability of the central idea of arms control in general. It seems to be the "American way" to approach, or at least appear to approach, each agreement pragmatically "on its merits." To date there has been little reasoned critique of this pragmatic reductionism.

Statecraft and strategy are arts, not sciences. This recognition obliges one to draw back from the brink of declaiming some law of social behavior as it should bear upon arms control. In general, it should be true to argue that only the two centrist positions identified above are inherently compatible with the character of arms control processes. If it is the case, as I believe, that politics are superior to their tools (weapons), then neither the formal control of the tools for conflict nor the absence of such control can have history-turning implications for war or peace.

## OBJECTIVES

If one's operational objective is to annihilate the French battle fleet, secure a landing strip for damaged B-29s on Iwo Jima, or recapture Seoul, the means-ends connection lends itself to close calculation and to focused criticism in terms that all can agree are the correct ones. But it is not so easy to specify how the objectives of arms control can be rendered operational. The history of arms control shows considerable indeterminacy both over tactical goals—indeed, these are settled through the more or less protracted arm wrestling of negotiation processes at home and with the foreign adversary—and over the relationships, if any, among tactical goals, operational objectives, and policy aims.[21]

The 1983 *Report* of the President's Commission on Strategic Forces (the "Scowcroft *Report*") itemized seven claims for arms control.[22] These claims pertain to important aspirations and, at the level of desiderata, are beyond sensible criticism. The questions to be asked of them include the following: Does the historical evidence suggest that they are achievable? Are they sufficiently specific in their implications for policy guidance that the United States knows how to go about achieving them? And, if the past record is disappointing, are there good reasons for believing that arms control performance in the future (learning from past policy errors, perhaps) is likely to be significantly better than in the past? The seven Scowcroft claims are itemized and annotated below. This particular set of claims is chosen for consideration both because it was designed to complement an unusually holistic approach to strategic force modernization and because it was crafted to express and advance political consensus. These claims offer a mix of arguments that is richly textured, extensive, popular and noncontroversial, and plainly good enough to stand comparison with any other sets of claimed objectives for arms control. There is no uniquely correct set of arms control objectives.

*One: Reduce the risk of war.* One must first settle upon a theory of why and how wars occur. If thinking on the "whys" and "hows" of great-war causation is lacking in rigor or in major insights, then there can be no way of knowing whether an arms control proposal or agreement is likely to be effective.

*Two: Limit the spread of nuclear weapons.* Specific objectives for realizing this claim are well understood and have been pursued quite effectively for more than three decades. However, it is not true that superpower nuclear arms control necessarily inhibits nuclear proliferation. Since nuclear disarmament by security guaranteeing super and great powers can reduce local feelings of security, such disarmament could encourage the spread of nuclear weapons.

*Three: Remove or reduce the risk of misunderstanding of particular events or accidents.* As an instrument of communication, an institutionalized arms control process certainly might help reduce misunderstanding. However, explanations may not be believed; even if believed they may not render the events in question tolerable; and states already have many communication channels aside from any specific to an arms control process. Inadvertent war (war launched as a result of erroneous political judgment), as contrasted with accidental war (war triggered in error by a military unit), has more conceptual appeal among defense intellectuals than it has traceable historical reality. Similarly, the accidental war, which has troubled technically minded arms controllers in the United States for thirty-five years, is not easy to illustrate with historical examples.[23] Anyone leaning heavily on this third claim for arms control thus has a double-edged problem. First, the feasibility of the claim needs to be established; second, the prospective importance of misunderstanding and accident as fuel for conflict needs to be argued persuasively, not merely asserted.

*Four: Seal off wasteful, dangerous, or unhelpful lines of technical development.* Many people would argue that the Washington treaty of 1922 and the ABM treaty of 1972 did exactly this.[24] Since the overriding goal of arms control for a Western democracy is reducing the risk of war, it is easy to see why agreement on what is "wasteful" and "unhelpful" ("dangerous" is another matter entirely) does not necessarily mark any gain for international peace and security. Arms control (partial) management of competition can become an aid to the more efficient conduct of that competition. States in competition are liable to place local and heavily political interpretation on the meaning of "dangerous" technical development. Since national armaments are *designed to be dangerous* to the presumed or proclaimed military ambitions of the rival, it should be readily understood why arms control as a hunt to slay dangerous developments rapidly descends into a Quixotic enterprise.

*Five: Channel weapon modernization into stabilizing paths.* If the high contracting parties can agree on what is, and what is not, a "stabilizing path," then all may be well. In practice, however, national strategic cultures and the political context of antagonism deny this claim a sufficiently specific and accepted authority.

*Six: Reduce misunderstanding about the purpose of weapon developments.* States in such an adversary relationship that they find (or say that they find) value in an arms control process are not prone to credit words over deeds. Given that two powers, for example, have endorsed the view that "war-fighting" capability is healthy for deterrence, it follows that military capability tends to an inherent ambiguity (recall the discussion in Chapter 2 of the problems in distinguishing between so-called offensive and allegedly defensive armament).[25]

*Seven: Help make arsenals less destructive and costly.* Superficially, these are worthy objectives. But less destructive arsenals, it can be argued, are more usable arsenals (which, admittedly, can have a deterrent effect); less costly arsenals are economically and socially more bearable arsenals.

A central difficulty with discussion of the objectives of arms control is the misunderstanding of the roles of arms that frequently underpins it. The idea that a malign, synergistically functioning trinity of policy, strategy, and weapons can be disrupted via technical arms control assault upon the weapons leg of this particular triad is rather naive and is contrary to historical experience. History has shown that arms control is worth nowhere near the amount of scarce talent expended upon it,[26] and that it must fail to meet its own more elevated goals because the ideas upon which it is based are fundamentally erroneous.[27] Even if the causes of war were to be revealed beyond reasonable argument by inspired scholarship, arms control could not suffice as the leading edge of a grand-strategic assault upon those causes. Not all that is comprehended can be controlled.

## THE INF TREATY OF 1987

My purpose here is neither to praise nor to condemn the INF treaty. Nonetheless, it is instructive to see how the treaty fares when subjected to strategic analysis and when it is assessed with reference to the classic goals of arms control. This brief treatment of the policy, strategy, and weapons associated with the INF treaty of 1987 is not an exercise in current affairs; instead it endeavors to treat the strategic world as it was visible to negotiators at the time. The fact that the course of political events in East-West relations since late 1987 has been remarkably forgiving of faults in arms control behavior is neither to the credit of the American negotiators nor damaging to the enduring value of case studies that attempt to hold their principals to reasonable standards of prudence. One can hardly establish as a principle for arms control policy that the political context for a control regime must be almost infinitely tolerant of negotiating folly. The merit for international security of the INF treaty can no more be assayed with reference to the political climate from 1987 to the present than the merit in the Washington naval arms limitation system can sensibly be measured with regard to conditions in the 1920s as opposed to the 1930s.

The central pillar of the rationale for the treaty was that it effected a healthily asymmetrical trade between Soviet and NATO weapon systems. Subsidiary rationales included the points that in addition to the novelty of a favorable asymmetry, the verification protocol to the treaty was a real breakthrough and set a precedent for distinctly intrusive on-site inspection of preselected sites; it represented a triumph for the patience and rigor of U.S. (and NATO) arms control policy (the "zero-option" was the position of the United States, not the Soviet Union, for six frustrating years); it achieved not only disarmament, but also the innovation of a clean sweep of an entire class of weapons; and it provided momentum for more important agreements in the future.

None of the rationales just cited necessarily bore upon strategy. Strategic argument, properly labeled, was noticeably absent from the public INF treaty debate of 1988.[28] The fact that strategic argument was not deployed in praise of the treaty told its own story. It might be argued that the Soviet Union's SS-20 force was a strategic "decoupler" for NATO, designed to pose so frightful a theater threat that the European members of the Alliance would lose their traditional appetite for the nuclear threat in flexible response.[29] The ready replacement of SS-20s by the nuclear firepower of variable-range ICBMs, dual-capable strike aircraft, and redeployable sea-based nuclear weapon platforms, however, rendered that argument more than a little fragile. The strategy case against the INF treaty was straightforward and really unanswerable, save to say that deterrence in Europe may have been so stable that the strategic sins of the treaty did not matter—an exception amply, if unpredictably, illustrated by subsequent political events. The treaty required the removal of weapons that were strictly redundant to Soviet strategy but had a uniquely important political role for NATO.[30] U.S. missiles based in Europe, and particularly in continental Europe, were capable of striking at targets on Soviet home territory. The GLCMs and the *Pershing* IIs were weapons of maximum coupling effect, a quality the equivalent of gold in the context of NATO's then-strategic concept of flexible response. The 1980s-style Soviet strategy for the subornment or conquest of Western Europe appeared designed to achieve nonnuclear blitzkrieg success. NATO strategy to dissuade such adventure sought to convince Soviet leaders that they could not conquer Western Europe without waging a very large war in the process against a coalition that included the other superpower—a war more likely than not to become heavily nuclear in character.

Could the INF treaty reduce the prospect of war occurring, reduce the likely damage should war occur, and reduce the burden of defense preparation? Rigorous defense analysis, which by no means encompasses all that should be considered for treaty evaluation, suggests strongly that the INF scored negatively on the first criterion, high on the second, and modestly on the third. The removal of NATO's INF could not fail to encourage—though perhaps not by very much—Soviet defense planners (governed by "old thinking") to believe that their chances of executing a thoroughly nonnuclear campaign in Europe would be improved as a consequence of the arms control regime. By holding out some very uncertain promise to reduce damage in war, the INF treaty regime could reduce deterrent effect. The burden of peacetime defense preparation would be reduced because, in a new era of detente and arms control promise, NATO governments would be unable to hold the line on existing defense budgetary plans, let alone move to augment them (as the antinuclear logic of the treaty implied should be done in a cold war environment). The case for the INF treaty succeeded in reversing the applicable logic of cause and effect. The INF treaty did not play a critical role in promoting the demise of the cold war. Rather, the demise of the cold war rendered the strategic implications of the treaty a matter of practical indifference. Arms control is a beneficiary of detente, not vice versa. Even though the influence relationship may not be wholly unidirectional, there is no basis for claiming that arms control ever has had, or could have, major significance for the reshaping of political relations.

The military implications of the INF treaty were that some mix of conventional or central-strategic substitution be provided for INF. Because NATO depended upon nuclear threats for its security in Europe and the Soviet Union did not, the local effects of the treaty worked wholly to NATO's disadvantage.

The negative military implications of the treaty have been overridden by rapidly evolving political circumstances, though not by positive political consequences attributable persuasively to the treaty. It could always be argued that real security rested not so much on armed forces that could give a good account of themselves in combat, but rather on neighbors who were not motivated to attack. There can be little doubt that the INF treaty was a geostrategic policy success for the Soviet Union. For four decades the Soviet Union had struggled to little avail to encourage the West to dismantle the architecture of the U.S. nuclear guarantee to European security. Prior to the INF treaty of 1987, the greatest advance towards the "decoupling" of the U.S. nuclear deterrent from the security of allies in Europe had been the U.S. acceptance of the parity principle in SALT I in 1972. If one believes that the Soviet threat to Western Europe was the reciprocal of the threat it felt itself, then the removal of the sharpest spears of that threat could be expected to reduce the amount of deterring the Soviet Union would require in the future. Cause and effect is difficult to establish clearly in the rich stew of influences that move history. The INF treaty may have been a political marker in the acceleration of East-West detente processes in the late 1980s; nonetheless, not even the more enthusiastic members of the arms control community have asserted that the treaty played a critical role in the demise of the cold war. In the case of this treaty, high policy clearly dictated zero INF with complete indifference to the means-ends question of strategy and in the absence of a residual weapons story to take up the deterrence slack. The subsequent Soviet breakdown was not reasonably predictable during the period of INF treaty negotiation.

## START

It has often been said of hospitals that even if they cannot cure patients, at the very least they should be required not to spread disease. By analogy, the same admonition should apply to the arms control process. If arms control cannot cure what is popularly viewed as the "disorder" of arms race, at least it should not make that condition worse. With its proclivity for the discrete regulation of selected capabilities (such as INF, central-strategic weapons, and some conventional weapons, in virtual isolation), arms control has demonstrated potential for the exacerbation of military security problems.

START, the redirected and U.S.-renamed successor to SALTs I and II, was intended to be the highest of high-concept approaches to improved management of what used to be the superpower military competition. The weapons at issue comprise the last line of deterrence for both countries, help define what is super about superpower, and undergird the military postures of what used to be called East and West. A fundamental question of strategic purpose, however, remains unsettled. What is START about? As its name shows, the treaty was conceived and advertised as an exercise in arms reduction; indeed, Russian and American leaders are formally committed to the goal of a nuclear-free world. Nonetheless, both sides know that a condition of zero nuclear arms is unverifiable, and that zero nuclear weapons could never be acceptable to a Russia worried both about an ever more powerful China on its long inner-Asian eastern flank and by the prospect of a German-dominated European superstate emerging to the west. Strategic arms reduction on a monumental scale, though halting short of zero-level arsenals, would greatly enhance the strategic value for political leverage of the nuclear arsenals of unregulated third parties. The nominal goal of 50 percent reductions for *treaty-accountable* START cuts—translated into a treaty ceiling of 6,000 warheads, though with Russia moving un-ilaterally well below this level—may or may not be sensible, but its merit cannot be weighed with reference to a goal of nuclear disarma-ment. There is widespread agreement that international security will prosper with a relatively high ceiling for residual nuclear armament. At this time of writing there is admittedly a small but growing U.S. constituency for reductions down to the 1,000 warhead level, but there remains—to repeat, thus far—a working consensus that a START fol-low-on (possibly START II) regime should not mandate strategic force level reductions below a *real*, not just treaty-accountable, level in the 3,000–4,000 warhead range. The ongoing political revolution in what used to be the USSR, not to mention the breakup of the former empire, territorial and hegemonic, and the steps being taken toward conven-tional and tactical nuclear disarmament, have had radical implica-tions for U.S. strategic targeting requirements and the details of the war plans. It is no less obvious, however, that neither the START treaty signed on July 31, 1991, nor suggestions for follow-on agreements on further reductions has been shaped perceptibly by defense analytical arguments. The START treaty should not be viewed or advertised as a large step either toward a nuclear-free world or even toward very low levels of nuclear armament. *START I-accountable* forces should drop by approximately 43 percent (the United States) and 42 percent (the So-viet Union), while total strategic inventories will probably descend by 25–30 percent, though unilateral reductions will certainly lower these figures.[31]

Compared with SALTs I and II, the START treaty might appear to be a major achievement. Unfortunately, the large-scale reductions ne-gotiated in the 1991 START treaty were possible only because peace al-ready had broken out between the United States and the Soviet Union. Prominent among the more potent criticisms of the SALT process was the license that process provided for the expansion of strategic arse-nals. It is true that START will effect a large reduction in forces, but the important question remains: "So what?" If 30 percent or 50 percent cuts in treaty-accountable strategic forces are good, must cuts of 75 per-cent or 95 percent be better still? In other words, what policy road is the country traveling—and why? Is it the U.S. objective to achieve the smallest strategic-nuclear arsenal possible (à la President Reagan at Reykjavik in 1986)? If not, presumably the goal is attainment of the same or more security at lower levels of forces. But is that possible be-low some uncertain range? Is it possible when U.S. strategic weapons are subject to high platform and force-loading ratios? (They were not designed to provide maximum prelaunch security in a world wherein strategic nuclear delivery vehicles would be subject to severe control.)

For two decades the United States sought to alleviate the problem of the (nominal) vulnerability of its silo-housed ICBM force through arms control and unilateral effort. Over the years, U.S. policymakers have repeatedly and correctly maintained that the ICBM vulnerability problem was not created by arms control. Furthermore, the points have been made, again correctly, that Russia will not permit arms control agreements to solve military problems that the United States has been unwilling to solve by sensible and timely unilateral measures and that it is the duty of the United States to its own security to design its strategic force posture in a prudent manner. The problem of silo-based ICBM vulnerability easily lends itself to mischaracterization and exaggeration.[32] But no particular military engineering formula enjoys undiminished utility forever. The difficulties still facing the U.S. silo-based force were predicted in studies as early as 1954 and have been the subject of intensive debate and research since the mid-1960s. START I worsened the high-quality warhead to silo ratio, which was already nominally lethal to fixed-site ICBMs. The solution to this problem was either to seek a radical reshaping of the START treaty or for the United States to exercise its ICBM modernization options so as to deny Russia unilateral advantage in hard-target counterforce.

What is the future of ICBMs under START? Of the 6,000 START I-accountable allowed warheads, no more than 4,900 can be carried by ballistic missiles. The *Trident* force (loaded at 24 × 8) certainly would have had a lock on warhead allocation in the 3,072–3,840 (16–20 *Ohio*-class boats) range, leaving the remainder for ICBM use. To date, there is every indication that the United States intends to preserve a triad in its strategic forces. In June 1992, Presidents Bush and Yeltsin signed a follow-on START agreement which more than doubled the real cuts that were mandated. This functional START II was as striking technically as it was rendered irrelevant by the fact of political peace between Russia and the United States. The START follow-on agreement requires weapon reductions down to the 3,000–4,000 range by 2003, bans multiple warheads on ICBMs, and calls for the phasing-out of the Russian SS-18 heavy ICBM.

Prior to the START II package of June 1992, many defense professionals argued that the treaty was unhelpful for strategic stability at the military-technical level (which is not to deny that the elusive subject of strategic stability should be approached more inclusively than defense analysis is wont to do).[33] From the U.S. perspective, the dubious structure of the START I regime spoke for itself: Russian ICBM warhead-to-target ratios would increase (recall that the United States has denied itself mobile ICBMs); SSBNs would suffer a drastic reduction in number because of the exceedingly high launcher-to-boat and warhead-to-launcher ratios, but ASW capability was unconstrained; and the air-breathing leg of the triad was restricted (albeit relatively generously), but air defense was not. (Air defense increasingly benefits from strategic missile defense "trickle down" capabilities.)

Earlier chapters discussed the uncertain linkage between the strategic offensive force posture and strategic defense. In the 1980s there was a formally integrated grand concept known after its enunciator, Paul Nitze, as the "Nitze Doctrine," which in a notional way provided broad guidance for arms control and strategic force planning. Stripped to its essentials, the doctrine favored the achievement of maximum offensive-force reductions as a necessary prelude to, and facilitator of, the emergence of a condition of defense dominance.[34] The START treaty would be more robust in terms of technical notions of stability if its practice were accompanied by deployment of some strategic missile defenses, and if the U.S. ability to fight for access to and exploitation of outer space were more advanced than is the case at present (ASAT and DSAT questions overlap, but are not wholly synonymous with, SDI issues).[35] Beyond the START follow-on agreement, it is desirable that the fundamental offense-defense relationship be revisited. Admittedly, this seems improbable. There is a reasonable prospect of Russian-American agreement in the 1990s on new ballistic missile defense deployments well beyond the 100-launcher level licensed in the 1972 ABM treaty, but all the political signs point to terminal impatience with grand designs, let alone "redesigns," of arms control. If the relationship between strategic offense and defense is radically transformed over the next decade and more, that outcome will be imposed by unilateral effort, not by formal grand design between states.

The strategy question intrudes. Will the START regime have the net effect of imperiling U.S. security? Will the treaty diminish the strategic effectiveness that could be required of U.S. central systems by more than it reduces the demand for that effectiveness? How does START influence U.S. targeting policy, strategy, and capabilities? Issues such as these require answers before the strategic implications of a START treaty can be understood. The 1991 START treaty and the 1992 agreement have no important negative (*or positive*) implications for U.S. national security. The new, unified U.S. Strategic Command must identify and understand its mission in defense of a very uncertain new world order. Strategic Command's leading problem in the 1990s is not to answer the second-order question of how well it will be able to prosecute the SIOP against what remains of yesterday's foe, but rather to address the first order question of what its duties should be. The chief problem for the START regime is that it addresses yesterday's strategic issues, albeit incompletely. Since there is no Soviet-American  or even Russian-American arms competition any more, who cares about its (!) regulation?

The more detailed and constraining a treaty regime the more likely it is that the flexibility to adjust to changing conditions will be impacted negatively. The U.S. nuclear arsenal has been accumulated, rather than designed, over several decades. At any particular time, the sunk costs in hardware, trained personnel, organizations, plans, and procedures are enormous. Bearing in mind the distinctly limited probable value of the START regime, sunk-cost arguments should not be completely discounted. It is not an example of atavistic "old thinking" to note that the United States does not maintain strategic (nuclear) forces simply because Russia does so—any more than Britain maintained a battle fleet in its Royal Navy simply because of an extant battle fleet owned by the Dutch, the French, or the Germans. Britain knew that it required the services of a navy second to none in fighting ability. The adversary (or two) of the day, the technologies in application, and force planning were all passing matters of detail—important detail, but still detail. The capabilities dimension to a Russian threat ebbs, but the United States must assume that it will need to influence a superpower foe some time, or times, in the future relevant for defense planning today.

VERIFICATION AND COMPLIANCE

No aspect of arms control has tested the political mettle of Western democracies like the twin topics of verification and compliance. Notwithstanding historical experience extending over the course of seventy years, the distinction between verification and compliance has achieved widespread public notice only in recent years. Even today it is common to find people talking as if the two were synonymous. In addition to those who have been genuinely confused about the meaning of verification as contrasted with compliance, there have been many who have been convinced that to verify is to ensure compliance. Allegedly, fear of detection would all but guarantee compliance.[36]

Long experience has revealed that even verification, let alone compliance (or a policy actively to encourage compliance) is a political subject. The defense behavior of an arms control adversary-partner is monitored at a technical working level, but verification of compliance or noncompliance with agreements whose terms may be less than crystal clear requires political rather than technical judgment. At least two levels of political decision give policy shape to this subject, and they interact in ways that the early literature of modern arms control theory did not foresee. First, there must be a political finding as to whether or not a treaty violation has, or may have, occurred. Second, if the finding is positive there must be a political decision as to what, if anything, to do about it. Since an arms control malefactor will rarely oblige by providing a smoking gun, it is necessary for the injured party to weigh the strength of the evidence, the public plausibility of that evidence, the sensitivity of the sources and methods that may be revealed by the evidence, the inherent military significance of the activity at issue, the implications of that activity vis à vis adversary policy attitudes and inferable future intentions, the multidimensional costs of serving what would amount to an indictment, and, last but far from least, the availability of suitably punitive, or at least effectively offsetting, responses.[37]

For substantive military as well as symbolic political reasons, all U.S. opinion leaders say that they care about verification and compliance. Nonetheless, the record of every administration since 1963 (with the ratification of the Partial Nuclear Test Ban Treaty) provides grounds for doubt as to whether the United States has really cared about Soviet treaty violations.[38] Strong official words on the subject do not signify—in fact they make matters worse—when a multidecade-long pattern of Soviet noncompliance with some of the terms of arms control was tolerated by the United States. There are always excuses for policy inaction: more evidence is needed; the violations are not sufficiently important (they are only "technical" in character); Russia is complying with *most* of the agreement; overall, the agreement is of such value to the United States that it is better to live with selective noncompliance than to move out into an unregulated world; or the United States is not ready to respond in suitable ways. Pick the favored mix of excuses.

The strategic argument over compliance policy in the 1930s and the 1980s was stacked heavily in favor of what amounted to the condoning of misbehavior. Typically, though not invariably, violations or probable and possible violations appeared to be of only marginal military significance. A serious U.S. compliance policy, then, could easily have appeared grossly disproportionate in scale to the offense. In theory the United States could adopt a policy of proportionate response, but in practice a popular democracy cannot readily function in such a mode.[39] The strategic argument for insisting upon strict compliance is only marginally military in character. Of course one should move to offset advantages gained by another country through cheating, but the central strategic argument holds that deterrence and peace repose not only in the details of competitive armament, but also, indeed primarily, in the respect that foreign leaders learn to accord U.S. policymakers as a result of the steadiness they demonstrate in protecting officially defined U.S. national interests. In short, compliance policy is strategically significant primarily for the training it provides foreign leaders in expecting U.S. deeds to match solemnly issued U.S. words. If a president has no policy or strategy for coping with cheating, he should not claim zero tolerance for verified misbehavior. President George Bush ventured into dangerous terrain when he stated: "I believe that . . . arms control commitments must be scrupulously observed. Nothing less will do."[40] The report that these words introduce showed that the president's words should not be taken at face value.

Soviet/Russian cheating on agreements has been, and is likely to remain, "cultural" in origin as well as expedient in purpose. The Soviet Union of the cold war era could no more comply rigorously with an arms control treaty than the average professional criminal could change his mode of life. Traditionally the Soviet political system respected neither domestic nor international law. Soviet state behavior was governed by expediency and a duty to compete effectively with the West and was not hindered by legal or moral sanctions against lying, or worse. Political culture is not immutable and there is ample evidence of contemporary upheaval in formerly settled modes of Soviet thought and behavior. To date, however, the evidence for new Russian probity as an arms control partner remains distinctly mixed.[41] It is well to remember that the problem has been as much Russian as it has been Soviet and that the future character of Russia is not confidently predictable at present. The Soviet Union abided by most of the provisions of the agreements that it signed because it was in its self-interest to do so, not because it was "right." It should follow that the United States signed arms control treaties with the Soviet Union in the knowledge that Soviet compliance, to be polite, would be selective. It also follows that assessment of any treaty "on its merits," as the responsible-sounding phrase goes, should take account both of the likelihood that compliance would be unequal and that the United States would not design and execute a sanctions or safeguards policy to deter, offset, or punish noncompliance.

## CRITERIA FOR REGULATION—POLITICAL OR TECHNICAL?

The history of strategic arms control negotiations since 1969—as in the protracted naval precedent in the 1920s and 1930s—has shown a thoroughly unremarkable "pull to parity."[42] Visible, and hence more readily verifiable, measures assume a symbolic importance in legislated military relationships that mandate common ceilings or balanced-looking asymmetries. In the rational world of *Homo strategicus*, military forces are designed and procured to support the distinctive burdens placed upon them by their country's foreign policy. Arithmetical or apparent parity with a putative enemy is unlikely to find support from strategic analysis, but the world of arms control is not the world of strategy. Its external and internal political logic requires that the high contracting parties sign on for equal-looking numbers.

In practice, the operative principle governing policy guidance for arms control negotiations is not usually the application of the *right* criteria, whatever they may be, but the application of the parity principle, in the hope that the permitted forces will be good enough to perform their strategic functions. The arms control process is not driven by strategic argument; instead it is driven by the prudent realization that public support for defense preparation rests upon the political confidence that policymakers are attentive to the dangers of war. Evidence of such attentiveness is equated in important part with arms control activity, not arms control outcomes. In a descriptive and not pejorative sense, arms control is about public relations. Security cannot be ensured through arms control, but it can be secured or undermined by variable public support that holds defense modernization programs hostage to visible, if possibly insincere, official commitment to arms control.

There are few genuinely technical problems of great importance in the arms control process. Generally the subject of arms control discussion is either the quantity and quality of the applied technology of weaponry and weapon support systems, or operational modes or styles for the same. However, issues that too often have been debated in the West as technical problems—such as allegedly "destabilizing, first-strike weapons" (preeminently, Soviet "heavy" ICBMs in silos)—really were nothing of the sort. The problem, if that is the correct expression, was not the so-called first-strike character of silo-housed SS-18 ICBMs. Instead, the problem was a Soviet government whose policies might derive deterrent and coercive value from the prospective war-fighting prowess of those missiles. Save with reference to safety in operation, a subject assiduously well-treated on a unilateral basis, new weapon technologies do not invite scrutiny for regulation according to technical criteria (as if countries could agree that certain weapons were, or were not, inherently destabilizing). Writing of the interwar period, Robert Gordon Kaufman has argued that "arms control will fail without corresponding political détente. No formula, no yardstick sufficed in itself to bring about the naval agreements. Politics, not technologies, caused their breakdown. In the 1920s, political détente made naval arms control possible. In the 1930s, Japan's determination to dominate China made failure inevitable."[43]

What needs regulation, by arms control or any other means, are the incentives to use military force—the policy goals that yield motivation to act. Two questions provide criteria for policy guidance. First, does a policy diminish or increase the adversary's political incentive to fight? Second, does a policy diminish or increase the likelihood of that adversary achieving military success or believing he can achieve it? Arms control must be regarded strictly as an instrument of policy. The regulation of competitive armament is of no inherent interest. What matters is the regulation of the incentive to fight and, in a strongly complementary vein, regulation of the likelihood of victory in the would-be enemy's military calculations.

Few fallacies are more damaging to useful policy discussion than is the posing of the false alternatives of arms control or arms race. The idea has gained ground that arms control can, has, and does (as contrasted with theoretically might) restrain arms competition significantly with benign consequences. A supporting argument holds that in the absence of arms control regulation, arms competition can, might, or will spiral out of control, presumably with the consequences of mutual bankruptcy or war. Arms control has been only one of the factors exercising regulatory restraint upon the urge to compete, and not a very important one at that. More significant have been shifting public moods on the subject of foreign peril, economic constraints, and doctrinally shaped notions of military sufficiency.


## IS IMPROVEMENT POSSIBLE?

Policymakers are at least as likely to do (unintended) harm as to secure benefit to the national security through participation in an arms control process. The record is by no means black, but it does show varying shades of gray with very occasional flashes of white. Sensible skepticism about the promise of arms control is not advanced by shrill predictions of "disaster or surrender through arms control." American policymakers have been neither fools nor traitors, and veiled suggestions that one or the other of those descriptions fits the record have the unfortunate effect of discrediting even balanced critiques of arms control experience. However, optimistic prognoses for arms control do not rest securely upon a record laced with positive precedents.

It is probably safe to say that the American electorate does not think about strategic nuclear weapons at all, save very occasionally during crisis periods. Like death and taxes, nuclear weapons are simply facts beyond the purview of the individual. Unfortunately, strategy expertise almost invariably impacts on the public, not as a way of thinking, but rather as prepackaged certainties in policy recommendation. Strategists do not appear on television advising citizens how to be their own strategists, but rather to sell this or that prewrapped policy preference. Whether or not the general public can be educated in strategy, the United States would perform better in arms control policy if its policymakers functioned more reliably in the strategy mode. In much of the public debate over the INF treaty, for example, the experts were certainly, and by definition, far more knowledgeable than was the public. But the quality, and particularly the coherence, of the genuinely strategic analysis they provided was not obviously superior to the thoughtways of laypersons.

The quality of arms control policy—judged for its fit with national interests and not for its negotiability—can be, though often is not, improved if the policy process is provided with firm leadership from the White House. The president is the only feasible leader if policy is to be balanced and coherent, since the coherence of policy can be fatally damaged by astrategic political compromises among contending bureaucratic interests. It should go without saying that coherence and orderliness in the policy process are only necessary prerequisites for high quality policy. There can be no substitute for sound strategic judgment by policy leaders.

Given the enduring presence of nuclear weapons, the infeasibility of thoroughgoing nuclear disarmament, and the checks and balances built into the structure of U.S. policymaking and policy execution, it is very unlikely indeed that any administration could negotiate, sign, and secure Senate ratification of an arms control treaty whose terms would literally place the Republic in mortal peril. "Op. ed. alarmism" and the plots in pulp fiction notwithstanding, even unwise arms control agreements (to which U.S. history is no stranger) are decidedly limited in their potential to damage the national security. However, that comforting generalization must be policed by national security professionals alert for poor policy performance. The paradoxical logic that sharply confines the practicable accomplishments of the arms control process, also sharply confines the potential of the process to wreak damage.

It is doubly ironic that the dynamic relations among policy, strategy, and weapons that comprise the common thread through these chapters can find either an unusual coherence or quite the reverse as a consequence of an arms control process. On the one hand, the actuality or even the prospect of a sharp reduction in force levels tends to encourage defense planners and some of their political masters to revisit matters of strategy. Like the prospect of being hanged in the morning, a radical scale of arms reduction can focus the mind. The Washington treaty system certainly had this effect, as may the START process in the years ahead. On the other hand, any arms control regime that requires deep cuts will, by definition, be a regime designed and implemented (at first) in a political environment at home and abroad that is not likely to have strategic issues high on its list of active concerns. Even if *strategy* becomes the order of the day the arms control process is not likely to deal strategic hands strongly congruent with the prudent implications of foreign policy for force planning. That is not an immutable truth, but it describes the balance of the experience of the Western democracies in this century. Circumstances differ, but there are no persuasive reasons to predict a more impressive performance in arms control policy in the 1990s and beyond than has been achieved in the past.

# CHAPTER SEVEN

# Nuclear-Age History: "Mislessons" and Lessons

Are the analyses of national security developed by scholars and decision makers part of the solution or part of the problem? Have these exercises actually made the world less safe? Have we called into existence problems that, had we defined them differently, would not have been troublesome?

—Robert Jervis
*Meaning of the Nuclear Revolution*

## THE NUCLEAR REVOLUTION

The apocalyptic premise that mankind faces a clear choice between "one world or none" has been advanced with periodically renewed fervor since the early 1940s. The familiar propositions are that human scientific skills have outrun human political wisdom and that man will either destroy himself or radically reform his political organizations. From time to time distinguished scientists, historians, soldiers, and journalists have lent their prestige to this binary view of the human dilemma. The truth of the matter is that political problems are more difficult to solve than scientific problems, and "one world or none" is not the range of choice before humankind—which is fortunate, since in that case the smart money would have to be on "none."

It so happens that the nuclear age has coincided with what once optimistically was called "the American century."[1] This has been unfortunate in that an already unhistorical, even antihistorical, American political culture was encouraged by the novelty of nuclear events to assume a more decisive breakpoint for statecraft in 1945 than the facts warranted. The absence of a U.S. tradition of active participation in peacetime great-power politics rendered American policymakers and strategic thinkers unusually vulnerable to a shallow pragmatism. There has never been any question but that the atomic weapon and then the nuclear weapon merited the ascription "dominant." Whether or not nuclear weapons would be used in future wars, the possibility of their use must shape defense planning and influence policy choice. The quantum leap in (energy) yield to weight (of explosive) ratio achieved by nuclear weapons did not change the offense-defense dialectic discussed at length in chapters 1 and 2, but that leap did change the required exchange ratios of military effectiveness if any facsimile of victory was to be a probable war outcome. The point is not that there is no defense against nuclear armed forces, which is untrue, but that no defense has yet been devised that could assuredly preclude victory from being Pyrrhic.

It is difficult to overemphasize the fact that nuclear strategy and defense planning for armed conflict in a nuclear context are unusually speculative enterprises. It is impossible to know why particular events did not happen. The presence of nuclear weapons certainly discourages policymakers from settling political differences by force of arms, but the awesomeness of both overt and latent nuclear threats can also encourage crisis generation in the hope of gaining concessions through fear (witness the on-off Berlin crises of 1958–1961). Nuclear war itself is terra incognita (1945 does not count), as is a situation wherein a superpower decides not to be deterred.[2] In this century at least (and, one could argue, in the last century also), war has not been regarded lightly as just another instrument of policy. Carl von Clausewitz's penetrating insights on the unity of war and politics should not be read too literally.[3] The difference that nuclear weapons have made to statecraft and strategy may be gauged if one looks backward and, as an exercise for the imagination, hypothesizes great-power *nuclear* armaments for the 1930s. There have long been inhibitions regarding the decision to resort to war as well as conduct in war.[4] Although nuclear weapons have added mightily to those inhibitions, it is not in the nature of humankind or its political organizations passively to accept the functional outlawing of the resort to force—at least that is the conclusion that must be drawn from historical experience to date. The strategic history of the superpower relationship since the late 1940s is in part a history of attempts to evade some of the undesired implications of the nuclear age.

This chapter offers both a brief critical review of the theory and practice of superpower strategic (largely nuclear) relations in the now-departed cold war era and a stocktaking of some major "mislessons" and lessons that can be derived from this history. The discussion here, as in the book as a whole, seeks to identify and understand enduring structural relationships among policy, strategy, and weapons rather than to prescribe favored solutions to the passing problems of the day. Of course the demise of the cold war casts doubt on the future validity of alleged mislessons or lessons derived from study of that period. It is a postulate of this book, however, that "history can be the window that will allow us to 'know the enemy and know ourselves [sic]'."[5] In this case the history is very recent, but it is still history. Details will not be repeated, but situations will.

## NEW TECHNOLOGIES, OLD STRATEGIES?

There is a large and internally diverse school of thought that holds that nuclear war would not be "war" as the term and the phenomenon have been understood and experienced throughout history thus far. Discussion of nuclear strategy, particularly of nuclear "exchanges," attracts the charge that the radically different nature and consequences of nuclear actions are being discounted or simply ignored. In short, for whatever psychological or other reasons, some defense professionals allegedly have conventionalized that which is inherently unconventional.[6]

The means-ends nexus that defines strategy is threatened with fatal tension by the destructiveness of nuclear weapons and the current impracticality of reliable protection against their large-scale retaliatory use. This is not a wholly novel problem. The poison gas that was used extensively by both sides in World War I from 1915 to 1918 was not employed in World War II (at least not between the great-power combatants). The technical and political taming of the nuclear-armed engines of war (by improved accuracy of delivery, by more efficient yield-to-weight weapon design, and by physical, psychological, and administrative safety procedures, and the like) has proceeded apace, but the possibility of escalation cannot be denied and indeed is essential for deterrence.

Vociferous critics of nuclear weapons and of reported trends in offi-

cial preferences for nuclear weapon employment policy have a poor record of facing up to the realities of a nuclear age. So long as nuclear
weapons exist they must be accommodated strategically in the contingency plans of armed forces acting under political direction.[7] It is easier
to criticize targeting philosophies oriented toward threats to military
forces than it is to devise alternatives that make sense for deterrence
(bearing in mind that deterrence requires a combination of capability
and of perceived political will to act).[8]

It is reasonable and prudent to approach questions of nuclear strategy
with a mind acutely attuned to the perils of large-scale nuclear war. However, given that nuclear weapons cannot safely, and certainly will not, be
abolished, there is literally no intelligent alternative to the ongoing endeavors to render them as precisely responsive to policy needs as technology and the grammar of war permit. The fact that familiarity with nuclear issues can desensitize people to nuclear horrors is no basis for
relaxing efforts to see that nuclear-armed forces are as discriminate a military tool as possible. Just because nuclear war could be waged at a level
of insensate violence that would mock the very concept of strategy, it does
not follow that it would be waged in that manner. Indeed, the obvious perils of a general nuclear catastrophe provide the maximum incentive for all
parties to fashion a policy-responsive nuclear military instrument.

The foreign policy of the United States is the most likely roadblock in
the process of precipitate denuclearization (actual physical or functional
strategic). For sound geopolitical reasons, during the era of the cold war
the United States undertook to lead the organization of regional security
in Europe and South and North East Asia against Soviet continental
threats. For the better part of forty years the Western World judged the
tactically and operationally offensive use of nuclear weapons to be the
centerpiece of its politically defensive deterrence strategy. Since the mid-
1960s at the latest, NATOs nuclear strategy represented anything but
the "conventionalization" of nuclear weapons, as any degree of familiarity with the concept of flexible response makes crystal clear.[9] Nuclear
weapons were defined by NATO primarily as tools to inculcate a healthy
fear of possible catastrophe, not as weapons for the conduct of war.

## THE UTILITY OF NUCLEAR FORCE?

The utility of nuclear force as a threat is questionable in degree but not
in principle. Most careful students of post-1945 history argue that nu-

clear threat has exercised an important net positive influence for international order.[10] Rather more subjective—given that there is an unblemished postwar historical record of nuclear nonuse—is the fashionable judgment that nuclear weapons can have positive utility for statecraft *only* in nonuse.[11] The extreme-sounding belief that any and every nuclear use option carries with it an unacceptable risk of triggering an uncontrollable escalation of violence is by no means confined solely to the strategically illiterate.[12] Such a belief seems unreasonable, if prudent, but defies authoritative refutation in the absence of experience with nuclear conflict.

Contrary to expectations in the 1940s and to official U.S. and NATO-European policy assertions in the mid-1950s, it is reasonable to claim that the passage of nearly five decades without the use of nuclear weapons has produced a tradition of nuclear nonuse. The Eisenhower Administration almost certainly was prepared to use nuclear weapons for coercive effect over Korea in 1953 and Quemoy and Matsu in 1958, had it been necessary.[13] So unfashionable have nuclear weapons become that today it is difficult even to design war games wherein resort to nuclear use is convincing, but it was fairly commonplace in the mid-1950s to assert that nuclear weapons would be used henceforth as if they were conventional. By the late 1980s, however, it was not easy to persuade an audience of defense professionals that either side would see benefit in nuclear use even in the event of a large war in Europe. The nuclear use contingencies that look even semiplausible in the 1990s, following the demise of the Warsaw Pact and the USSR and the reunification of Germany, involve the adventures or desperate exploits of Third World states in regional conflicts.

The reasons for satisfaction with the experience and tradition of nuclear nonuse are too obvious to warrant particular exposition. Nonetheless, one should be aware of the negative, as well as the positive, legacy of this "tradition." Specifically, it is not wholly beneficial for the stability of deterrence and for the international order favored by the West, for the ultimate weapon in the arsenal of the principal guardian to be heavily beset with political-moral (as well as prudential self-regarding) inhibitions against its actual use. The price to be paid for the multidecade success in the prevention or avoidance of nuclear war might be either a fatal nuclear incredulity on the part of some state at a moment of crisis, or an inability on the part of Western policymakers to undertake measured nuclear use when they ought to do so.

The declining public acceptability of nuclear options in defense strategy over the past thirty years has been reflected persuasively in poll data. Indeed, recognition of this trend was an important source of encouragement for the policy demarche of the SDI in 1983.[14] Unfortunately, the opinion polls that recorded the sensible distaste for nuclear risks did not record any offsetting willingness to provide alternative means of deterrence. The risks to the integrity of Western strategy posed by popular nuclearphobia tended to be handled by the conveniently accurate assumption that the Soviet Union was not in need of much deterring. It is as certain as anything can be in international politics that nuclear weapons will one day be used in anger. That use will probably not originate in a superpower conflict, but the ramifications of such use would exercise a major influence over the politics of defense strategy in Western polities. A small-scale nuclear war in South Asia, for example, would probably add fuel to popular demands for nuclear disarmament and encourage the demand for missile-defense deployments.

## THE NEW WISDOM

Energized initially by the first public, official articulation of nuclear strategy in 1953–1954, a group of American civilian social scientists (preponderantly associated with the Rand Corporation) constructed a distinctive strategic theory for the nuclear age.[15] The period 1955–1965 was the most productive decade for strategic thought in all of American history. The so-called intellectual Golden Age of 1955–1965 mapped the field of modern strategic studies and established the lingua franca of debate.[16] Three ideas, though hardly original, were developed, indeed overdeveloped, in original ways for nuclear-age application.

First, the new civilian strategists elevated the ancient concept of *deterrence* to master status. Keyed to the critical distinction between first- and second-strike forces—which is to say those forces that enjoyed prelaunch survivability and those that did not—deterrence was the overriding purpose to be served by U.S. strategic forces.[17] Second, recognition that a stable mutual deterrence precluded freedom of action for the use of strategic forces sparked interest in theories of *limited war*.[18] If central strategic forces were paralyzed by the mutuality of nuclear deterrence, then local and even regional conflicts could be waged carefully by nonstrategic systems. A fundamental assumption underpinning limited war theory was the stability of the central strategic balance. If the central balance was unstable (for example, if a marked first-strike bonus should obtain), then the conduct of regional limited war would be dangerously likely to escalate. Third, the civilian strategists discarded what they saw as old-fashioned, politically and strategically irrelevant notions of disarmament, and (re)discovered *arms control*.[19] They believed that although the political interests that divided the superpowers were beyond near-term resolution, much might be accomplished to help stabilize strategic deterrence through limited technical cooperation.

Many of the concepts, assumptions, and arguments of the 1955–1965 period retain their authority over the minds of American policymakers, defense planners, and commentators today. Fine flourishes have been added since that period, but for good and for ill the ideas of those years educated a generation of policymakers. Many weaknesses in the founding ideas of modern American strategic studies have been exposed or suggested. Preeminently, as some of the foreign friends of the United States were to notice at a comparatively early stage, the "new strategy," for all its formal obeisance to the ever more popular Clausewitz, was actually strongly apolitical.[20] Moreover, the systemic idea of stability that inspired arms control theorizing was noticeably divorced from recognition of the distinctive foreign policy duties that the United States laid upon its central strategic systems. The unhealthy tendency to divorce politics from competitive armaments was complemented by a neglect of political and strategic culture.[21] In practice, as revealed in Vietnam and in the conduct of the strategic arms competition, the neglect of culture translated ethnocentrically into the false assumption of distinctly American-style enemies. In addition, the failure of Americans to understand their own society has been as damaging as the failure to study an enemy on his own terms. In Vietnam, for example, there was a massive American strategy failure. U.S. policymakers and defense planners failed to understand that American society would not tolerate a long, indecisive, and morally ambiguous war. The junior and field-grade officers of the Vietnam era learned from that experience that a country, not an army, goes to war. If the latter is committed to battle without the enthusiastic support of the former, defeat is all but invited. Prominent among the lessons, or mislessons, of Vietnam drawn by those then relatively junior—but now very senior—officers has been rejection of gradualism as a military style. It is not so much that the concept of limited war has been rejected as that a distinctly intellectualized and unmilitary variant of it has been discarded in favor of plans that take strategic reasoning more seriously.

Desert Storm of 1991 was a frontal rejection of Vietnam-era military operational malpractice. The U.S.-led coalition forces went directly for the enemy's jugular, his supposed "center of gravity."[22] For political and ethical reasons the United States persuaded itself that the Iraqi center of gravity was its organized military power rather than its over-centralized political leadership. Although a historic military victory was won, subsequent events demonstrated that the true center of gravity in Iraq was not its military power in the field, or even its military reputation, but Saddam Hussein himself. The United States had learned from Vietnam that its armed forces must be assigned an achievable military victory; it had not learned to use military power to resolve the dominant political problem. Desert Storm was a military campaign "for the ages," but as a war it left too much unresolved.[23]

## IDEAS AND DOGMAS

Military instruments tend to rust or become blunt over the course of a long peace. Furthermore, nothing is so likely to promote failure in the future as a glittering record of past success.[24] The absence of great-power war over a period of record duration is not the kind of history that motivates people to challenge the ideas believed to have been instrumental in producing the long peace. Particularly is this true when the long peace that really was war-in-peace, or cold war, concludes with a burgeoning political peace. This is not to imply that old ideas are necessarily bad ideas, but rather that cause and effect may not be straightforward. For example, to what extent did the evolving nuclear facts help keep the peace? Did the details of the strategic balance matter very much?[25] Was "the deterrent" of either superpower ever really tested?

Debates over strategic ideas cannot sustain themselves for long. Great debates are fueled by such real-world events as speeches by politicians, new military technologies, and military action—actual or threatened. Because strategy is not a branch of philosophy or aesthetics but a practical art, it is understandable and desirable that intellectual debate should refer explicitly to the actual defense business of the nation. Unfortunately this can mean that some relatively ill-considered ideas are applied precipitately and prematurely to the problems faced by policymakers and defense planners. Since the engines that drive strategic debate are real-world problems and the behavior of governments, strategic thought can easily degenerate into a policy faddism. The entropy characteristic of all intellectual debates after the early surge of creativity tends to be arrested and reversed by the fueling agent of actual policy proposals.

It is noticeable that deterrence theory, though it is a branch of policy science explaining, or purporting to explain, the structure of a field of inquiry, long ago degenerated into sets of competing credos with attendant recommendations for policy.[26] Notwithstanding the ambiguity of postwar strategic history, theory has become belief, even dogma, concerning "what deters" (deters whom from doing what?). Moreover, dogma begets competing dogma. In public debate, open-minded skepticism has difficulty competing effectively with dogmatic self-assurance. The plainest example of theory becoming dogma lies in the field of arms control. Thirty years ago the idea of arms control was an exciting novelty to strategic theoreticians. Twenty years ago arms control (the SALT exercise) was a bold, experimental field test of the worth of American ideas. It was painfully apparent in the 1970s and 1980s, however, that healthy skepticism, open-minded willingness to reexamine fundamental ideas in the light of recent historical experience, and even the inclination to think strategically about the purpose of the endeavor all fall victim to the political passions energized by the attempt to practice arms control.

In sharp contrast to the Golden Age of American strategic thought thirty years ago, the U.S. defense cognoscenti in the late 1970s and the 1980s were divided, even polarized, into competing schools of thought on the proper design of U.S. defense posture and its directing strategy. The actual practice of U.S. defense behavior to date always has returned to an even keel, but the ebb and flow in the level of defense effort from the early 1970s to the aftermath of the of cold war in the 1990s have mirrored the fissure between alternative schools of thought among the defense illuminati at large. The U.S. defense debate of the early 1990s has been unusually confused because of the retirement of the Soviet Union and the uncertain implications of the extraordinary yet temporary challenge posed by Iraqi aggression in the Persian Gulf.[27] At present neither maximalist nor minimalist schools of U.S. defense thought have succeeded in framing robust advocacy positions for a new era. The demise of traditional Soviet threats does not foreclose American debate over policy, strategy, and weapons, but opens a new and in some ways more difficult chapter.

There was nothing very new about the polarized character of the 1980s-era debates over U.S. foreign and national security policy. The incivility and contrasting premises that characterized public debate over, for example, the INF treaty, ICBM modernization, the proper occasions for the use of American force in regional quarrels, and the like reflected the interaction between recent U.S. history and the several threads that comprise American political culture.

## THEORIES OF DETERRENCE

Because the ability to deter is a function of capabilities and of perceived political will, manipulation of the latter—if feasible—offers an attractive alternative to military effort. When war is nowhere in sight, there is no recent memory of acute crisis, and the notional enemy is talking peace, important segments of opinion in a democracy are inclined to regard their own country's defense preparations as a dangerous provocation rather than a prudent hedge against uncertainty. The fallacious idea that weapons or technologies move history along has an implication frequently missed by its purveyors. If one holds that weapons make war and their absence makes for peace, then one is driven to argue, at least by inference, that all weapons are created equal and have equivalent consequences according to their technical qualities but regardless of their political ownership. Apart from those relatively rare cases of U.S.-hating Americans, it is noticeable that much of the arms control and peace activist literature reduces the politics of international security to arguments about the better administration of machines.

An ever-popular economical approach to deterrence is to signal enhanced political determination in lieu of enhanced military capabilities. This approach is not entirely foolish, but because politicians deal in words there is always the danger they will overvalue the power of that currency. Given the absolute destructiveness of nuclear weapons and the unknowable risks of escalation, there is a great deal to recommend purposive manipulation of adversary perception of political commitment (consider, for example, the history of the several Berlin crises and of the Cuban Missile Crisis). However, there are limits to the plausibility of commitment.[28] Past reputation for firmness will be a factor, calculation of "the correlation of forces" might play a significant role in whether or not an intended deterree elects to be deterred, and the relative intensity of interests at stake for each of the key players constrains the bounds of policy possibility and the terms of strategy.

Two broad theories of deterrence have played simultaneously in a policy dialogue in the United States for four decades: deterrence by punishment and deterrence by denial. These concepts can be presented as sharp alternatives, although in practice they overlap and are complementary. The punitive theory holds that if the pain is believed by the would-be aggressor to exceed the gain, then he should elect to be deterred. Rather than punish an enemy's society, action that virtually licenses retaliation against our society, the quasi-alternative theory of deterrence holds instead that if the foe is denied military victory, he will also be denied his political objectives. This second theory prescribes counterforce targeting (such as active forces of all kinds, command and control assets including political leadership cadres if they can be located, and war-supporting industry) to deny the enemy military advantage. This idea of victory-denial can be presented as a clear alternative to societal punishment, but in practice, the proximity of military to civilian assets and the likelihood that one would be punishing the enemy's state via its instruments of coercion render these alternatives less than rigorously distinctive.[29]

When considering the deterrence burdens that have been placed upon the strategic force posture, it is useful to bear in mind the three-fold categorization specified by Herman Kahn.[30] Kahn argued that the United States required, or would like to achieve, three types of deterrence. Type I is the deterrence of direct attack upon the U.S. homeland; Type II is the deterrence of extremely provocative attacks upon U.S. interests abroad; and Type III is the deterrence of lesser provocations. The core of the problem through the cold war years was the difficulty of ensuring extended Type-II deterrence through the agency of strategic offensive forces. Though capable of punishing an enemy and damaging his most valued assets, strategic offensive forces were prospectively incapable of protecting U.S. society through their war-fighting prowess. The end of the cold war has left basic deterrence questions unresolved or moot, depending upon one's point of view. Supposed strategic truths really point only to specific terms of engagement. For example, the alleged impracticality of homeland defense in the nuclear age applies only to the case of large-scale nuclear attacks by superpowers. As the superpowers cease to define each other as plausible enemies, their dominant theories and practice of deterrence and coercion should change dramatically (albeit with the caveats that enmity could be renewed and that one day there is likely to be another superstate or coalition foe in need of containment).[31] This point should be as obvious as it is underappreciated. The complex relations among policy, strategy, and weapons that unite the chapters of this book must be woven into a new pattern of interdependencies as the superpowers redefine their deterrence missions in the 1990s. That task has begun.[32] Given the state of flux in formerly "Soviet" domestic affairs, however, the case for not rushing to judgment on U.S. defense needs for the late 1990s and beyond all but makes itself. It is unnecessary for the United States to make bold guesses about the Russian future, and such speculation matters not at all for the argument here.

## THE STALEMATE THESIS

It is a truism that Soviet and American societies were hostages to the mutual restraint shown by policymakers. It has been less of a truism, though a long-standing and still current fact of strategic life, that the mutual hostage relationship is an enduring technical condition. However, the implications of robust mutual nuclear deterrence remain unsettled. Also increasingly unsettled is the question of whether mutual deterrence still has policy relevance to superpowers (at least one current and one lapsed) in a condition of political peace. I decline to speculate about the medium- to long-term future of Russian-American relations except to say, for the limited purposes of this analysis, that it would be imprudent for U.S. policymakers and defense planners to assume that henceforth (for ten, twenty, thirty years?) they will be able to function in the military realm without being checked by another superpower.

Even though superpowers must be presumed capable of inflicting unacceptable damage upon each other, does that fact translate into strategic deadlock?[33] In theory it should, but in practice it may not.[34] If the United States lacks a persuasive theory for a satisfactory end-game to a nuclear war, it is a matter of elementary logic to demonstrate the inadvisability of taking even preliminary steps in such a conflict. In principle, the first use of central nuclear systems should not have "worked" as NATO's strategy of flexible response long envisaged, because a measured Soviet response would have offset any Western military gain and left the burden of the decision to escalate on U.S. shoulders.[35] In the real world of fearful and responsible politicians, however, the absence of some approximation of a calculable escalation dominance may matter far less than would the believable prospect of a slide to catastrophe.

The superpowers competed to secure and deny military advantage in the conduct of strategic nuclear operations, even though the likelihood of either side achieving a decisive edge was long recognized as low. That situation encouraged commentators to conclude that whatever marginal gains might be achievable with respect to nuclear force on nuclear force, those ever-arguable prospective gains must be overshadowed, and decisively overshadowed at that, by the menace of an Armageddon they could not neutralize reliably. Recognizing the possibility of catastrophe should indeed help discipline the conduct of counterforce operations, but it would be unwise simply to assume that the prospect of decisive military advantage has been banished by the existence of nuclear weapons. Although a deadlocked strategic outcome can be expected at the highest level of violence, it does not necessarily follow that any conflicts waged with, and decided by, nuclear weapons must be suicidal.

In the absence of a persuasive theory of victory in war as a whole, it would be exceedingly difficult to attempt to achieve intrawar deterrence through the threat or actual measured use of nuclear weapons. However, this was the story (and dilemma) of NATO strategy. The central strategic systems of the United States and its allies were unable to win a great East-West war at prospectively tolerable cost, but for several reasons intrawar nuclear deterrence was probably not quite the forlorn hope the argument for strategic stalemate asserted. Those reasons included a political determination not to accept defeat and a healthy Soviet fear of the negative consequences of nuclear actions for the political solidarity of their imperium. The events of 1989–1991 were to show just how fragile was that imperium.

Pending the physical realization of almost unimaginably reliable strategic defensive systems to complement a first-class offense,[36] a nuclear war of unbounded scale certainly could not be won. To make that easy admission, however, is to say neither that wars waged in the shadow of nuclear threat cannot be won, nor even that wars wherein nuclear weapons are used cannot be won. In Robert Jervis's words: "The influence of nuclear weapons on world politics is far-reaching. Although *military* victory is impossible, victory is not: nuclear weapons can help reach many important political goals."[37] It is beneficial for international peace and security for statesmen to be horrified at the prospect of the canonical nuclear "war" of the kind envisaged by the deceptively anodyne phrase, a "SIOP-RISOP *exchange*" (as if the subject were an exercise in violent diplomacy). But there is no inherent reason—no law of physics, let alone of history or of the strategic art—why the controlled use and counteruse of nuclear weapons for political or limited military purposes must lead inexorably to a mindless process of runaway escalation.

## TOWARD A "POST-NUCLEAR ERA?"

In the late 1980s some thoughtful defense theorists speculated as to whether or not the superpowers and their security dependents were heading—drifting or moving purposefully—into a "post-nuclear era."[38] Their thesis was that states and coalitions responded to nuclear challenges by grand-strategic evasion. Those challenges included the perils of unbalanced nuclear power on the part of an adversary and, more recently, the challenge of policy paralysis induced by the mutual nature of nuclear deterrence. The argument was that competent statesmen and defense planners have learned to cope with the problems posed by nuclear foes by sidestepping the kind of confrontations in which nuclear weapons might exert effective leverage. In this reading of strategic history, massive cross-border attacks in Europe, or threats to reduce the United States to the condition of Carthage after the Third Punic War, simply were not interesting, because they were not viable (or profitable) strategic options. In the 1990s, as the one-time foe resigns that status for an indefinite period, the problems for strategy posed by nuclear weapons (means disproportionate to ends, as well as means fatally flawed in their ability to deliver success) can be evaded by political cancellation of erstwhile difficulties.

Far from welcoming an apparent paralysis of nuclear action, the principal response of the United States to mutual nuclear deterrence was to seek relief from the threatened deadlock through technological finesse and flexibility in war planning.[39] From the so-called Schlesinger Doctrine of 1974 to *Discriminate Deterrence* in 1988,[40] official or all-but-official American thinking endeavored to combat the perception that U.S. central strategic systems had become irrelevant to the challenges posed by regional security problems. By the mid to late 1980s a critical unresolved question for the United States and its allies was whether a trend toward a functionally, if not literally, "postnuclear era" should be welcomed or resisted. Schizophrenically, the INF treaty of 1987 was praised for its modest accomplishment of nuclear disarmament, but also defended on the grounds that its bite out of the West's nuclear assets would be only marginal. In 1987–1988 the Western Alliance favored partial dismantlement of the nuclear engines of deterrence (or war), but only in such a balanced, or favorably unbalanced, way and to such a modest degree that the existing architecture of nuclear-dependent international security could remain intact. The unexpected collapse of the Soviet imperium in 1989–1990 and of the Soviet Union itself in 1991 effectively sidelined most of the practical significance of arguments within NATO about military strategy.

Prior to the dramatic events of 1989–1990, enhanced conventional stopping power for regional security certainly was favored by NATO, but not to the extent that any European member of the Alliance was willing to engage in a large-scale conventional military buildup. As a matter of basic policy choice, there was never a conventional answer to nuclear dangers. Nuclear weapons can be deterred only by nuclear weapons. However, NATO could have decided to construct a conventional defense posture upon the premise of nuclear no-first-use. The European allies naturally lacked enthusiasm for the status as an expendable campaigning ground in what could become a protracted and global conventional war.[41] Those allies discerned superior merit for deterrence in a relatively early wartime nuclear dependency, particularly since there was no evidence to persuade them that flexible response could not handle the modest threat traffic of the 1970s and 1980s. In the aftermath of the abortive Soviet coup in August 1991, President Bush announced unilateral withdrawal and eventual destruction of all U.S. short-range ground-based nuclear systems (i.e., artillery and short-range missiles).[42] The U.S. plans to retain air-delivered nuclear weapons in Europe. Post–cold war Europe cannot be a postnuclear Europe, given that residual U.S. nuclear weapons, as well as British, French, and Russian nuclear arsenals, will all be retained as national hedges against an unprecedented level of political uncertainty.

The limits to denuclearization are set narrowly but immovably by the permanent need for the United States to retain at least a residual basic Type I deterrent. Zero nuclear armament is not and cannot be a policy objective for the United States, if only because a nuclear-disarmed America would be at the mercy of any state or group that retained or acquired such weapons. Since zero nuclear armament is not a sensible policy, small-scale nuclear armament would not be wise either. Defense analysis demonstrates that cuts in strategic weapon arsenals very much below the levels of the 1992 START follow-on agreement (3,000–6,000 weapons) could entail substantial risks of technical instability. That same analysis flags the potential for awesome dangers were the U.S. arsenal to be reduced to the level of hundreds, let alone tens, of weapons. In practical terms, the limits of denuclearization for the West are set by the unwillingness of U.S. allies in Eurasia to change course from the residual transatlantic and transpacific nuclear guarantees with which all have become familiar, if not comfortable; the possibility, even probability, of nuclear proliferation by polities radically more difficult to deter than was the USSR of the cold-war era; and, finally, by the danger of political reversion within what remains an exceedingly well-armed Russia. Complete nuclear disarmament is not practicable and therefore is not interesting as a policy option. The reasons advanced in support of this position thirty years ago have stood the test of time extremely well. In 1961, Hedley Bull argued:

It is the logic of "the more disarmament the better" that if nuclear weapons cannot be abolished they should be reduced, limited or restricted as far as possible. Various measures of this kind are briefly discussed below [reductions in nuclear arsenals, ceasing nuclear weapons production, ending nuclear testing]. The idea that all of them should be pressed as far as possible stems from a Luddite approach to the problem of security.[43]

### "MISLESSONS"

The judgments provided here are precisely that—judgments. The postulated "mislessons" and "lessons" of nuclear-age history to date could be invalidated tomorrow.

Mutual deterrence often is discussed as though it were an existential fact guaranteed forever by the technology behind nuclear-age international politics.[44] The popular confusion of subject and object encourages people to believe that that which we call the "deterrent" must deter. Deterrence, greatly fortified by historically novel nuclear peril, certainly seems to have existed in the relations among great nuclear-armed states, but it is easy for a military posture to deter if adversaries are only minimally motivated to pose vigorous challenges. (An important reason why the Royal Navy served the Pax Britannica so well through most of the nineteenth century, for example, was that no state or coalition had an overwhelming political interest in challenging British command at sea).[45] This is not to argue that U.S. strategic forces have had an easy passage to policy success since the late 1940s, but that there is no evidence they have been rigorously field-tested for adequacy.

As Clausewitz argued, there can be an enormous difference between "war on paper" and "real war."[46] We do not genuinely know more about nuclear war today than we did thirty or forty years ago. Attitudes toward nuclear weapons have changed radically as doctrinal fashion has altered. However, a repeated opinion, even if it is only a political commitment, can seem to have authority that truly it lacks. The United States and the Soviet Union did not learn from the cold-war years either that a nuclear war could not be won, or that nuclear use must prove futile. Those are prudent beliefs, and they are politically expedient beliefs to expose to domestic and allied view, though not to the putative enemy, but they do not rest upon, or comprise, genuine knowledge. Indeed, the very structure of NATO's now-lapsed strategic concept of flexible response denied their validity. If nuclear use *must* prove futile, why would the Alliance ever have first resort to it?

Nuclear-age history suggests that participation in a so-called arms control process is politically essential if a government is to remain popular. However, there is nothing in recent or more distant history to prove that arms control is essential or even important for peace. As I argued in Chapter 3, the purported connections between arms competition and war are strictly of the "it-stands-to-reason" kind. To date, arms control has inhibited neither the motives for war nor the capability to wage war.

Soviet and American policymakers agreed for decades that nuclear war *could* be a limitless catastrophe. Nonetheless, the United States and its allies did not seriously try to diminish their nuclear dependency, nor did they implement anything remotely resembling a nuclear war survival program. By way of contrast, in the 1970s and 1980s the Soviet Union both acquired a conventional regional striking power that sought to evade the necessity for making nuclear choices and continued its long-standing programs for the physical protection of key political cadres and industrial assets against nuclear attack.[47] The Soviet

Union did not intend to tolerate passively the possibility of an open-ended nuclear disaster. The military effectiveness that Moscow sought through its very expensive strategic programs, both offensive and defensive (active and passive), did not attest to an intention to wage nuclear war, nor to any confidence that nuclear war would be survivable for the Soviet state and society. However, those programs spoke volumes about long-standing Soviet rejection of the mutual hostage thesis that many Americans believe to be a permanent, perhaps desirable, condition of the nuclear age.[48]

Dubious historical extrapolation and ethnocentric and ideological bias encouraged the drawing of the following "mislesson" from nuclear-age history: that as a general rule Moscow backed down in the eyeball-to-eyeball circumstances of acute international crisis. What is the evidence for this conclusion? The Soviet Union allowed itself to lose the Berlin crises of 1948–1949, 1958–1961, the Cuban Missile Crisis of 1962, and the Middle East Crisis of 1973 without pressing its case by force of arms. In the last case, a U.S. strategic-forces alert helped dissuade Leonid Brezhnev from intervening on Egypt's behalf at the turning point of the October War.[49] As remote as the possibility may seem from current Russian-American amity, acute superpower crises can happen. The tolerable outcomes for the West of the now distant crises cited above can be attributed, first, to the relative intensity of interests of the parties in those instances (immediate deterrence), and second, to the favorable "correlation of forces" (general deterrence).[50]

To recap and rephrase the "mislessons" introduced in this section: it has been argued that mutual deterrence may not be eternal; nuclear threat and use need not prove self-defeating; arms control is not essential or even important for peace; the logic of nuclear strategy is subject to cultural variation; and that it would be perilous to assume that Russia, or indeed any other polity, will always back down in an acute crisis.

This final "mislesson" found support in the apparently aberrant misbehavior of Iraq in 1990–1991. Iraq broke many of the rules of conduct deemed prudent and rational in the West. To be specific, Iraq resorted to force to grab what she wanted, declined to blink in an eyeball-to-eyeball confrontation with *the* superpower over the course of six months, purposefully lobbed missiles at a nuclear-armed Israel (what is more, those missiles might have carried chemical agents—a possibility guaranteed to touch the rawest nerve in Jewish sensitivity to threat and damage), and, it later transpired, had a huge nuclear-weapon development program well under way in flagrant violation of her status as a signatory to the Nuclear Non-Proliferation Treaty of 1968. American defense analysts and media commentators are prone to project their own values and their own concept of, and content to, rational behavior on alien political cultures.

## LESSONS

Eras of good feeling ebb and flow with events in domestic and international politics, but policy is driven most consistently by determination to protect or advance national interests. As a great, if currently domestically disturbed, continental state, Russia poses an enduring latent threat to the Eurasian balance of power. Tactics and even grand strategies can alter in short order, particularly if they are heavily dependent on the political preferences of none-too-secure individuals in a polity that continues to move only from the top down. At this time, nothing sensible can be said about the future course of political leadership in Russia. However, threats to an international security order flow most predictably from a maldistribution of power, not from this or that kind of polity or identity of statesman. With rare exceptions it is a mistake to personalize either inter-state conflict or the conditions believed necessary for a tolerable order. This is not to say that individuals do not matter, but to say that circumstances make people rather more than vice versa.

Discussion of U.S. military policy is impoverished by the tunnel vision that afflicts scenario-dependent minds. The rich variety of circumstances, expected and otherwise, to which armed forces may need to be relevant must be expressed in a military posture that is primarily flexible, though disciplined by principles for the guidance of force planning.[51] Contrary to an easy but fallacious assumption, flexibility is not a strategy but a highly variable quality in tactical performance that enables alternative operational and strategic ideas to be implemented (or not) on minimum notice. Nikita Khrushchev was justly criticized for his economical fixation upon "single-variant" war. Public discussion of the U.S. strategic force posture (which capabilities might be needed and in what quantities) and of the U.S. Navy has been particularly hampered by narrowly canonical views of the shape and scale of future conflict. The notion of a dominant scenario is as convenient for orderly defense planning and provision of plausible budgetary rationales as it is irrelevant to historical experience. Such a scenario is unavailable for the post-cold-war world.

A short-term view of the strategic world neglects, or simply discounts, the fact that decisions that are expedient today are a legacy for tomorrow. Confident assertion in the late 1970s that the MX ICBM would be based survivably served to deflect much potential criticism, but in the 1980s it proved difficult to persuade the public that silo-basing for the MX was good enough and did not detract significantly from mission survivability. In 1979 it was expedient for NATO to agree to the twin-track approach to INF of deployment *and* negotiations. To compound the problem, it was expedient in the fall of 1981 for the U.S. government to proclaim the zero option as its negotiating position for INF. The short-term expedient of a radical arms control position on INF could have had the long-term effect of denying NATO the services of an important, indeed unique, link in the great chain of deterrence that was flexible response. NATO's strategy concepts, along with the Alliance itself, are changing in the 1990s, but this is one of those rare cases wherein states have been saved from the consequences of poor policy *and no strategy* by what amounts to historical good fortune.

Technological change and its impact on policy preferences are not reliably predictable. In the same way that tactical offense and tactical defense complement each other in land warfare, so strategic offense and defense synergistically should produce a more formidable deterrent. The SALT I package of 1972 was politically convenient, while its BMD component in particular was perceived, perhaps correctly, as a vital bargaining chip providing U.S. leverage against the visible momentum in the Soviet buildup of strategic offensive forces. Unfortunately, the BMD chip was played to little effect, given the porous character of the Interim Agreement on Offensive Forces (and of the later SALT II design), but its legal surrender remained to inhibit U.S. (and, to a lesser extent, Soviet) freedom of action in the arms competition. Arms control negotiators have a history of prohibiting or confining weapon technologies if they do not, or perhaps cannot, understand the strategic implications of those technologies at the time.

"Apocalypse Soon" has been a recurrent cry in the nuclear age. Nuclear pessimism has been an irregular growth industry whenever superpower relations took a sharp downturn. The history of the nuclear age to date, and particularly the history of the cold war, should encourage respect for the fact that great-power nuclear war is not inevitable, while common sense aided by prudent defense planning suggests that even if nuclear war should occur, it need not resemble Armageddon. Nuclear pessimism tends to be a self-negating prophecy. The reason, one could argue, is that the American and Soviet guardians of the nuclear peace were so aware of the scale of the danger that the danger remained strictly hypothetical. One could also argue that many of the more narrowly military-technical hypothetical dangers have been far more hypothetical than dangerous. There may be nuclear wars in the next few decades, but those are unlikely to be great struggles between superpowers.

The handful of nuclear-age lessons I have singled out for discussion reinforce the general argument of this book. To summarize, I have suggested that the protection of interests in the face of an actual or potential maldistribution of power drives policy most reliably; flexibility, though not a substantive policy, is a cardinal military virtue in an era of great uncertainty; yesterday's solution can be today's problem; technological prediction is an inexact science; and nuclear pessimism is strictly speculative theory. These lessons are completely independent of any particular phase in postwar history. They are as salient for the 1990s as for any of the previous decades. The complex structural relationships among policy, strategy, and weapons are entirely indifferent to the ebb and flow of eras of goodwill and ill will in international politics.

# CHAPTER EIGHT

# Instruments of Policy

No one starts a war—or rather, no one in his senses ought to do so—without first being clear in his mind what he intends to achieve by that war and how he intends to conduct it. The former is its political purpose; the latter its operational objective.

—Carl von Clausewitz
*On War*

But planning for certitude is the greatest of all military mistakes, as military history demonstrates all too vividly.

—J. C. Wylie
*Military Strategy*

## PREPARE PURPOSEFULLY FOR THE UNKNOWN

The tension between the arguments in the quotations above point to a concern central to this text. Policy must be the master, providing guidance and meaning to all other functions, but policy is not always able to deliver orders or even advice of the kind or specificity that will reduce the supportive development of military power or the actual employment of that power to mere administration. The trinity in the title of this book—policy, strategy, and military technology (or weapons)—assuredly should move according to the grand design of a single choreographer. However, the practice of policy-weaponry relations, or of the policy-force planning nexus, often bears little resemblance to design, grand or otherwise.

Today it is far from self-evident what policy guidance ought to be for U.S. strategic forces, to cite the most difficult of cases. Indeed, new and fashionable "certitudes" have a way of disappearing as rapidly as they appeared. For example, the demise of the Soviet "threat" removed much of the necessity for the United States to project the capability for the conduct of heavy ground combat. But huge potholes loomed in the path of Soviet internal reform prior to the abortive August 1991 coup and when a regional bully with a large army required prompt discipline.[1] Carl von Clausewitz's concept of friction has an applicability much wider than a narrow wartime focus.[2] To return to the two quotations that head this final chapter, although Clausewitz's argument for clarity in policy purpose and broad strategic method is unexceptionable, Wylie reminds us, by inference, that military power must be developed and even exercised with a material flexibility and an agility of mind that reflect prudence in the face of uncertainty. The United States can plan to maximize its prospects of succeeding in the future, but it cannot plan the future. The difference is important and fundamental, yet it is frequently disregarded and misunderstood.

## THE ARGUMENT

Any book that comprises a series of complementary yet overlapping explorations of the complex relations among three broad and multifaceted activities of state—the provision of policy, the determination of strategy, and the development of weapons—risks a lack, or periodic loss, of sharp focus. The declamatory title, *Weapons Don't Make War*, illustrates my intention to combat the reductive fallacy that lays upon weapons, or more basically upon military technology, the charge of driving the course of international security affairs. In his magisterial study, *Historians' Fallacies*, David Hackett Fischer advised that

> The *reductive fallacy* reduces complexity to simplicity, or diversity to uniformity, in causal explanations. It exists in several common forms, none of which can be entirely avoided in any historical interpretation. As long as historians tell selected truths, their causal models must be reductive in some degree. But some causal models are more reductive than others. When a causal model is reductive in such a degree, or in such a way, that the resultant dis-

tortion is dysfunctional to the resolution of the causal problem at hand, then the reductive fallacy is committed.[3]

The particular reductive fallacy that this book has assaulted or probed from several different directions is the claim for an autonomous, or all but autonomous, role for weapons or military technology vis à vis policy and strategy. Nonetheless, as was indicated in the Introduction, following Clausewitz again, there is a "grammar" to war (and defense preparation) distinctive from, though subordinate to, the "logic" of policy.[4] I have criticized erroneous beliefs about "the meaning of military technology": for the character of strategy (Chapter 1); for the alleged nature of weapons (Chapter 2); for the claimed dynamics and consequences of arms races (Chapter 3); for the determination of arms acquisition (Chapter 4); for defense planning (Chapter 5); for what arms control needs to, yet cannot, achieve (Chapter 6); and for the course of nuclear-age strategic history to date (Chapter 7). I do not suggest that technology is unimportant. As the Fischer quotation made abundantly clear, "some causal models are more reductive than others." Economy in explanation and simplification to a degree are desirable and unavoidable. The purpose here is to demote technology, or weapons, from candidacy for recognition as prime mover, not to eliminate them from the explanation of how and why security events proceed as they do. In the words of a perceptive study of the 1991 Gulf War:

An effective armed force is not made up of its weapons alone. It is the people that operate those weapons, the supporting technologies that control them, the logistics that sustain them, and a dozen other elements that make the difference between victory and defeat in wartime. Each of those elements requires significant resources. A balanced investment strategy would recognize this and put as much emphasis on people, concepts, battle management, and intelligence as on high-profile weapons. Because, like the Gulf War, the next war will be won by men and women— integrated, cohesive human organizations—not machines.[5]

Accepting some risk of undue simplification, this final chapter presents seven complementary points which, considered in unison, comprise the main body of argument of the book.

1. It is policy that shapes strategy and gives meaning to weapons,

not vice versa. As the title of this book affirms, weapons do not make war. There cannot be such phenomena as offensive or defensive weapons. Weapons and the military technologies that they render operational are the servants, not the masters, of policy and strategy. The tactical defensive may serve an operationally offensive purpose in pursuit of a generally defensive strategy mandated by policy. Questions of offense and defense must always be examined in a context that includes considerations of policy.

Distinctions between offense and defense would warrant prompt dismissal, by and large, as either scholastic irrelevancies or just plain confusions, were it not for the fact that offense and defense have become value-charged concepts, alleged attributes with major implications for policy debate and choice. "Offensive" has long been equated with aggression,[6] while "defensive" has typically been associated with the slippery notion of stability. An important recent exception is in the realm of "strategic" offensive and defensive forces. The dominant school of thought on stability in the West has come to attribute net merit for peace and security to effectively unchallenged strategic offensive forces and to discern the peril of a net instability in moves toward a strategic posture much better endowed with so-called defensive assets.

The popular term "strategic offensive forces" betrays a double confusion that has potentially nontrivial consequences for the quality of policy and strategy. To be specific, no forces of any technical kind are inherently strategic, and whether or not particular forces are offensive is a matter of policy and strategy determination. It is unsound to judge "strategic" quality according to geography (range) or quantity or quality of lethal effect (nuclear/non-nuclear) yet that is what the idea of a strategic offensive weapon purports to accomplish. The reasons for dissatisfaction with these crimes against the English language and common sense have nothing to do with linguistic puritanism. Rather, to think of a weapon as inherently "strategic" is to confuse instrument with effect. Similarly, habitually to call weapons offensive or defensive invites a blurring of critical tactical, operational, strategic, and policy distinctions.

Overall, the attribution to weaponry of strategic or nonstrategic and of offensive or defensive qualities misdirects attention to the tools of security rather than to the brain that acquires and then commands them. This first point highlights the error in the view that problems of regional security can be addressed via the cutting edge of a regional arms control policy.[7] The basis of this view lies in the false assumption that weaponry of allegedly undesirable kinds is a quasi-independent cause of insecurity and even war.

2. The arms race concept is a metaphor,[8] and an unhelpful metaphor at that. Twenty years ago, when Johan J. Holst wrote that "we just do not have an adequate explanatory model for the Soviet-American arms race,"[9] it was plausible to believe that the reason for the deficiency was nothing more fundamental than a lack of scholarly effort. Repetition and sheer familiarity yield an authority all their own. Indeed, in the early and mid 1970s I failed to challenge the existential postulate of "the arms race phenomenon."[10] Understanding dawned late, but dawn it did.

The reason arms race theory has failed to yield anything more valuable than the occasional interesting insight is that it is an impossible mission. As with expeditions mounted greedily in quest of El Dorado, scholarly forays in search of a robust general theory of arms races are condemned to fail, no matter how sophisticated their methodology. El Dorado does not exist, nor do arms races, at least not in forms distinctive enough to lend themselves to discrete theoretical assault. Of course states compete in armaments. One can even refer, if carefully, to arms competitions. However, historical evidence does not support the proposition that at some particularly acute phase an arms competition becomes an arms race, nor does it support the view that an arms race is a distinctive phenomenon in security affairs.

Whereas the first point above challenged the claim that particular weapons have inherent meaning for policy and strategy, this second one counters the argument that states and coalitions somehow become policy and strategy captives to the dynamics or grammar of arms race.

3. Without clear policy guidance, the euphemistically labeled "weapons acquisition process" is reduced to an often protracted, political arm-wrestling contest. There are good and bad reasons why policy guidance tends to be less than fully satisfactory, or even practicable, to those in need of direction. The principal good reason is that when policymakers confront a necessarily unknowable future, they tend to be inclusive rather than exclusive regarding the military capabilities for which they foresee possible need. The principal bad reason is that policymakers are by no means uniformly inclined, or even competent, to reason strategically about matters that require strategic treatment. Consequently strategic logic may not even be seriously attempted.

Policy guidance can be clear without being impracticably specific. Policymakers should identify goals and provide guidance as to tolerable means and methods, but they should not seek to arrogate the role of military strategist, let alone that of military tactician. The grammar of war lies within the expertise of the military professional, but he cannot be entirely confident that his strategy, plans, and forces will be able to perform as policy prefers. War is a realm of chance, though not dominated by it. In Clausewitz's words: "It is now quite clear how greatly the objective nature of war makes it a matter of assessing probabilities. Only one more element is needed to make war a gamble—chance: the very last thing that war lacks. No other human activity is so continuously or universally bound up with chance. And through the element of chance, guesswork and luck come to play a great part in war."[11]

Even when policy guidance is clear and does not intrude beyond its proper sphere into the prospective military conduct of war, a quest for an objectively correct military posture is the pursuit of a chimera. To cite the importance of chance in war, however, and hence to point to some fundamental indeterminacy concerning "correct" force levels and strategy, is not to excuse policy from providing appropriate meaning to the enterprise. One should never forget the importance of the deceptively simple truth noted by Andrew D. Lambert in his outstanding analysis of the Crimean War: "Without agreed war aims, strategy could not be formed."[12] There are no guarantees of success in armed conflict *with worthy enemies*, but peacetime defense preparation as well as strategy for war (or for deterrence and coercion) are literally out of control if policy guidance is lacking.

4. Uncertainty is a condition of, not a problem for, defense planning. Policymakers and defense planners cannot know exactly which demands will be placed upon the U.S. armed forces over the next several months, let alone the next several decades. Thus, strategy-making and force planning are more akin to theoretical physics than to engineering; at best decision-makers can assume that their candidate answers are approximately right. The deeper questions in both physics and strategy do not lend themselves to analysis that will yield answers correct to four or five decimal places. Correct military programs cannot be discretely and objectively identified by careful analysis, but sufficiently correct or "right enough" answers to the question of how much is enough can be provided. One can seek profitably after broad principles for the guidance of force planning and, hence, of weapons acquisition.

Since the future is not predictable in detail, it is important not to waste scarce time and effort on the impossible. The U.S. role in the world is broadly knowable, as are the geostrategic parameters for American military action (such as transoceanic power projection and the need for nuclear "cover") and the capabilities that must be sustained or acquired in order for the country to be effective in its identified policy roles. One cannot plan not to be surprised, but one can plan intelligently to minimize the influence of the undesirable surprise effects of events that can be *broadly* anticipated. In other words, it is entirely possible to plan a defense posture—in the context of a flexible grand strategy—that is not vulnerable to catastrophic defeat or evasion leading to policy failure catalyzed by very unwelcome events. It is an illusion to believe that a truly fireproof national security policy, strategy, or military posture can be identified and implemented. Occasionally "super threats" do appear. Nonetheless, explicit attempts to pursue fault-tolerant planning will pay worthwhile dividends. The necessity of "Red Team" devil's advocacy has long been appreciated. The problem is persuading senior officials of the practical value of expert criticism.

5. The practice of arms control among states is unimportant, and the theory upon which that practice is based is wrong. It would be difficult to improve upon the judgment offered by Louis J. Halle, a wise scholar of international relations:

> In no other organized endeavor of the nations of mankind has so much work been expended to so little effect as in the efforts to achieve arms control. We must suppose that there has been something fundamentally wrong at the conceptual level to account for so consistent a failure on so large a scale over so long a period.[13]

Halle proceeded to the rare, but acute, appreciation that

> When such vast and sustained efforts as went into the pursuit of disarmament between the wars come to nothing [with particular reference to the World Disarmament Conference of 1932], we may properly suspect that the conceptual foundation on which the efforts were based was wrong.[14]

At several junctures in this discussion I have advanced the argument that arms control is an attempted perversion of the true relationship between policy and weapons. Arms control has been analyzed here not for its importance, of which it has little, but rather for its value as negative instruction on broader matters. Arms control provides a classic, persisting example of the fallacy that policy problems can be side-stepped by technical expertise. The hope endures that somehow arms control processes will reduce the difficulties created by politics and opposed national policies to problems of administration, management, and engineering. The national trait of machine-mindedness that can reduce the American practice of war to movement (U.S. forces have tended to be very mobile) and firepower,[15] gives rise to an American version of peace that is inclined to ask of technical fixes much more than they can deliver.

The theory of arms control is fundamentally unsound. The political antagonism that generates the objective need for alleviation via arms control—always assuming, again fallaciously, that arms control could yield such alleviation—is the very reason why arms control must fail to accomplish its most important goal—reducing the risk of war. The theory and practice of arms control is akin to scholarly and practical efforts to map and explore an earth believed falsely to be flat. Scholars, and even many statesmen, mean well, work hard, and exercise great ingenuity, but they cannot succeed.

6. Nuclear-age history does not prove the success, or even the viability, of the dominant ideas of modern Western strategic theory. Strategy is a practical subject wherein truth and beauty are demonstrated through that which works well enough. With the perils of the nuclear age very much in mind, Robert Jervis wrote "In this sort of world, the lack of objective answers to many crucial questions allows unusual scope for the power of the ideas we develop and the concepts we employ."[16]

It is possible that the United States and its security clients endured and eventually triumphed in the cold war of 1947–1989/90 despite rather than because of the dominant strategic ideas of the Western world. Were policy, strategy, and weapons appropriately aligned? Did it matter?

For example, the American war in Vietnam, say from 1964 until 1973, demonstrated a failure of strategy on a heroic scale.[17] America's overconfident military professionals, clever but arrogant civilian defense intellectuals, and overly ambitious politicians all failed to find a mix of policy and force, directed by a purposeful yet agile strategy, that would work. Perhaps such a strategy was not available to be found, let alone consistently and persistently applied, but the U.S. government did not even come close. The current official view of the merit of the limited war theory so fashionable in the 1960s, may be summarized tersely as complete rejection. The U.S. defense establishment entered the 1990s enamored of the attractive concept of Invincible Force (IF, with unintended humor, subsequently changed to Decisive Force). No longer does the United States conduct planning with a view to influencing enemy minds *in war*. In war the United States of the 1990s seeks a clear, favorable outcome. Desert Storm in 1991 was a perfect expression of this U.S. rejection of the old idea of limited war and its replacement with the IF doctrine. As noted already in this text, the political outcome to Desert Storm leaves much to be desired, but the military campaign was a healthy return to the traditional American commitment to achieve clear military victory.[18]

Next, the arms control theory that scholars invented and reinvented in the late 1950s and early 1960s[19] has been applied with great persistence over the better part of the succeeding three decades. Virtually everyone agrees that the results can only be described, even optimistically, as very modestly useful.[20] As Louis J. Halle suggested, the enduring evidence of nonachievement suggests strongly that the theory has been wrong.

With reference to strategy for nuclear weapons and ideas on the policy utility of those weapons as deterrents or compellents, the evidence is thoroughly ambivalent. There is food for thought in the familiar aphorism reportedly uttered in the following form by Lt. General James F. Hollingworth: "Any damned fool can write a plan. It's the execution that gets you all screwed up."[21]

Strategic thinkers sometimes need reminding that the ideas that they manipulate pertain, or might pertain, to the actual plans and operations of governments. I am frequently willing to concede notional political, ethical, military, and intellectual merit to ideas that I nonetheless judge impracticable. For just one example of cold war vintage, the authoritative, if underacknowledged (even among the few who understand it), U.S. theory of damage limitation in central nuclear war was reduced to hopes for reciprocation in targeting restraint. The idea was unexceptionable, though the probable reality would have been failure on a truly grand scale. The theory asked too much of people, organizations, procedures, cultures, weapons, and luck. To say that, however, is not necessarily to condemn the U.S. nuclear planning ideas, procedures, and posture of the 1970s and 1980s. It is always easier to find flaws in official assumptions and practice than it is to advance an unmistakably superior alternative.

Overall, it is more than a little uncertain that the details of official ideas—which might or might not warrant elevation to the status of policy—or of plans or military forces really mattered for the preservation of superpower peace. U.S. nuclear weapons helped create and sustain a general deterrence for forty-plus years, which must have helped discourage local crises. One can speculate that U.S. high policy in the cold war was broadly appropriate, if indeterminately fallible in detail, particularly with reference to the insistence upon massive nuclear armament. Whether or not the ebb and flow of fashion in American strategic ideas for nuclear deterrence and compellence was of any real-world significance, one can but speculate.

7.  Military technology is only one among the many servants of policy, and by no means the most important. Bernard Brodie was surely right to argue that "when war comes, differences in weaponry between the contestants may appear of modest importance compared with other differences."[22] When writing about the relatively unexplored region of "technological surprise in war," Michael I. Handel observed that

> All scientific/technological experts talk more or less in the same language, work with similar concepts, and share a common body of knowledge. The political-strategic analyst, though, must grapple with concepts, perceptions, languages and cultures that differ radically from his own. He does not have as much in common with his adversary as the technological-scientific expert has with his counterpart. The logic or art of analysis must be tailored to each adversary and is not universal, nor can it be studied in relatively objective terms.[23]

Individual weapons, weapon systems, classes of weapons, or combined-arms teams do not direct the traffic of history. The feasible scope of policy ambition admittedly can be driven by the tactical practicality that is the basis of operational art and strategy. But strategic, even military, effectiveness is rarely dominated by weapons to the practical exclusion of other factors. The key to temporary success in war tends to lie in the novel use of new, or newly combined, weapons rather than in those weapons themselves. No major war between industrial powers has been won because one side was technologically superior. The case of Japan in 1945 is not really an exception, given the many areas in which Japanese deficiencies were literally critical.

Weapons do not win or lose wars, either for states that enjoy a comparable level of technological achievement, or even for states with different levels of technological achievement, when the parameters of the conflict (such as triple-cover jungle) place brute force at a large discount. Weapons have a meaning imposed only by the policy that directs them. Save in the mindlessly mechanical sense, weapons do not make war, and their control or elimination does not make peace. War and peace are a political subject.

NOTES

INTRODUCTION

1. See Carl G. Jacobsen, ed., *Strategic Power: USA/USSR* (New York: St. Martin's Press, 1990), pt. 1, "Strategic Culture in Theory and Practice."

2. John Ellis, *Brute Force: Allied Strategy and Tactics in the Second World War* (New York: Viking, 1990), p. 526.

3. Carl von Clausewitz, *On War*, trans. Michael Howard and Peter Paret (Princeton: Princeton University Press, 1976; first pub. 1832), p. 605.

4. Alfred Thayer Mahan, *The Influence of Sea Power upon the French Revolution and Empire, 1793–1812*, vol. 2 (Boston: Little, Brown, 1898; first pub. 1892), p. 391.

5. Clausewitz, *On War*, p. 88 (also see p. 607).

6. Ibid., p. 8; emphasis in original.

7. Ibid., p. 605.

8. Walter Emil Kaegi, Jr., *Some Thoughts on Byzantine Military Strategy* (Brookline, Mass.: Hellenic College Press, 1983), p. 14.

9. Ibid., p. 10.

10. See the comparative judgments offered in Lt. General John H. Cushman, "Challenge and Response at the Operational and Tactical Levels, 1914–45," in Allan R. Millett and Williamson Murray, eds., *Military Effectiveness*, vol. 3, *The Second World War* (Boston: Allen and Unwin, 1988), pp. 320–40.

11. Writing about U.S. problems in the early 1950s, Russell F. Weigley has said that "to seek refuge in technology from hard problems of strategy and policy was already another dangerous American tendency, fostered by the pragmatic qualities of the American character and by the complexity of nuclear-age technology," (*The American Way of War: A History of United States Military Strategy and Policy* [New York: Macmillan, 1973], p. 416).

12. For example, see Herman Hattaway and Archer Jones, *How the North Won: A Military History of the Civil War* (Urbana: University of Illinois Press, 1983). The authors conclude that "all three branches of the art of war—logis-

tics, strategy, and tactics—played crucial and interrelated roles in the Civil War, but more or less their relative importance was in that order," (p. 720).

13. Dick Cheney, *Conduct of the Persian Gulf Conflict: An Interim Report to Congress* (Washington, D.C.: Department of Defense, July 1991), is valuable.

14. See Colin S. Gray, *War, Peace, and Victory: Strategy and Statecraft for the Next Century* (New York: Simon and Schuster, 1990), passim.

15. Edward N. Luttwak, "From Geopolitics to Geoeconomics: Logic of Conflict, Grammar of Commerce," *National Interest*, no. 20 (Summer 1990): 17–23.

16. Clausewitz, *On War*, p. 119.

17. Francis Fukuyama, "The End of History?" *National Interest*, no. 16 (Summer 1989): 3–18. Fukuyama's argument is somewhat muted in his book, *The End of History and the Last Man* (New York: Free Press, 1992).

19. In his remarks to a joint session of Congress on September 11, 1990, President George Bush endorsed the Wilsonian idealist notion that "out of these troubled times . . . a new world order can emerge."

20. Robert Jervis, *The Meaning of the Nuclear Revolution: Statecraft and the Prospect of Armageddon* (Ithaca: Cornell University Press, 1989), p. 22.

21. Edward Rhodes, *Power and MADness: The Logic of Nuclear Coercion* (New York: Columbia University Press, 1989).

22. John Mueller, "The Essential Irrelevance of Nuclear Weapons: Stability in the Postwar World," *International Security* 13 (Fall 1988): 55–79.

23. Daniel A. Baugh, *British Naval Administration in the Age of Walpole* (Princeton: Princeton University Press, 1965), p. 2.

## CHAPTER ONE. OFFENSIVE AND DEFENSE STRATEGIES

1. Strictly speaking, there is a third alternative: isolationist. Until 1917, U.S. foreign policy toward Europe-centered international security politics generally was one of isolation, but isolation is not the same as indifference. The United States could not be indifferent to the balance of power in Europe, since hegemonic success on the part of some state or coalition in that region would free that party to pursue ambitions for influence in North America if it so desired (see Kenneth Bourne, *Britain and the Balance of Power in North America, 1815–1908* [Berkeley: University of California Press, 1967]).

2. Edward Gibbon, *The History of the Decline and Fall of the Roman Empire*, ed. J. B. Bury (London: Methuen, 1909; first pub. 1776–1788), 4:173.

3. Very much to the point is Samuel P. Huntington, "Playing to Win," *National Interest*, no. 3 (Spring 1986): 8–16.

4. See the discussion in Colin S. Gray, *War, Peace, and Victory: Strategy and Statecraft for the Next Century* (New York: Simon and Schuster, 1990), chap. 1.

5. Martin van Creveld, *Fighting Power: German and U.S. Army Performance, 1939–1945* (Westport, Conn.: Greenwood Press, 1982).

6. Aggressive patrolling/raiding and prompt counterattack was standard practice in the German and British armies engaged in trench warfare during World War I even while they were operationally on the defensive (see John Ellis, *Eye-Deep in Hell: Trench Warfare in World War I* [New York: Pantheon Books, 1976], particularly chap. 5). On offense/defense relationships in that war, see William Balck, *Development of Tactics—World War*, trans. Harry Bell (Ft. Leavenworth, Kans.: General Service Schools Press, 1922), and Pascal

M. H. Lucas, *The Evolution of Tactical Ideas in France and Germany during the War of 1914–1918* (Paris: Berger-Levrault, 1923; trans. P. V. Kieffer, 1925). On the British experience, see Tim Travers, *The Killing Ground: The British Army, the Western Front, and the Emergence of Modern Warfare, 1900–1918* (London: Allen and Unwin, 1987).

7. For example, see General D. T. Yazov, "On Soviet Military Doctrine," *RUSI Journal* 134 (Winter 1989): 1–4. Soviet military writing in the 1987–1989 period is analyzed in John G. Hines and Donald Mahoney, *Defense and Counteroffensive under the New Soviet Doctrine*, R-3982-USDP (Santa Monica, Calif.: Rand Corporation, 1991).

8. For a useful discussion, see Samuel P. Huntington, "U.S. Defense Strategy: The Strategic Innovations of the Reagan Years," in Joseph Kruzel, ed., *American Defense Annual, 1987–1988* (Lexington, Mass.: Lexington Books, 1987), particularly pp. 35–42. Also valuable is Marion William Boggs, *Attempts to Define and Limit "Aggressive" Armament in Diplomacy and Strategy*, University of Missouri Studies no. 16 (Columbia: University of Missouri, 1941). Also relevant, but less usefully executed, are Jack S. Levy, "The Offensive/Defensive Balance of Military Technology: Theoretical and Historical Analysis," *International Studies Quarterly* 28 (1984): 219–38, and Lawrence Freedman, *Strategic Defence in the Nuclear Age*, Adelphi Papers no. 224 (London: IISS, Autumn 1987).

9. See Alfred T. Mahan, *Naval Strategy Compared and Contrasted with the Principles and Practice of Military Operations on Land* (Boston: Little, Brown, 1919; first pub. 1911), pp. 141–62, and Wayne P. Hughes, Jr., *Fleet Tactics: Theory and Practice* (Annapolis, Md.: Naval Institute Press, 1986), pp. 34–39.

10. Every space vehicle must pass over the antipodal location of its launch point on its first orbit. See Aadu Karema, "What Would Mahan Say About Space Power," U.S. Naval Institute *Proceedings* 114 (April 1988): 48–49. A useful brief discussion of orbital mechanics is Lynn Dutton et al., *Military Space* (London: Brassey's, 1990), pp. 9–29.

11. When reference is made to a particular general typically waging "defensive" battles, what is meant is that the general in question—the Duke of Wellington is a good example—wins his battles on the counteroffensive, after the enemy has wrought his own destruction in futile assaults. From a vast literature, see particularly Michael Glover, *Wellington as Military Commander* (London: Sphere Books, 1973; first pub. 1968); David Chandler, *Waterloo: The Hundred Days* (New York: Macmillan, 1981; first pub. 1980); and Paddy Griffith, ed., *Wellington, Commander: The Iron Duke's Generalship* (Chichester, Eng.: Antony Bird Publications, n. d. [but 1983 or 1984]).

12. With benefit of hindsight, it is plausible to argue that Germany could have won the First World War in 1917 with a better, certainly a much larger, U-boat force; the same judgment applies to Germany in the Second World War with reference to 1940–1941 (but probably not 1942–1943). The outstanding study is John Terraine, *Business in Great Waters: The U-Boat Wars, 1916–1945* (London: Leo Cooper, 1989). Also see Arthur J. Marder, *From the Dreadnought to Scapa Flow, The Royal Navy in the Fisher Era, 1904–1919*, Vol. 4, *1917: Year of Crisis* (London: Oxford University Press, 1969), and Marc Milner, "The Battle of the Atlantic," *Journal of Strategic Studies* 13 (March 1990): 45–66.

13. An unremarkable fact of which too much is made in Jack Snyder, *The Ideology of the Offensive: Military Decision Making and the Disasters of 1914*

(Ithaca: Cornell University Press, 1984), and "Perceptions of the Security Dilemma in 1914," in Robert Jervis, Richard Ned Lebow, and Janice Gross Stein, *Psychology and Deterrence* (Baltimore: Johns Hopkins University Press, 1985), pp. 153–79. For valuable correctives, see Jonathan Shimshoni, "Technology, Military Advantage, and World War I: A Case for Military Entrepreneurship," *International Security* 15 (Winter 1990/91): 187–215, and Marc Trachtenberg, *History and Strategy* (Princeton: Princeton University Press, 1991), chap. 2.

14. This reasoning was central to the U.S. Navy's maritime strategy as enunciated in the 1980s. See James D. Watkins et al., *The Maritime Strategy*, Supplement to U.S. Naval Institute *Proceedings* (January 1986). Also see Norman Friedman, *The U.S. Maritime Strategy* (London: Jane's, 1988), and Michael A. Palmer, *Origins of the Maritime Strategy: American Naval Strategy in the First Postwar Decade* (Washington, D.C.: U.S. Government Printing Office [for the Naval Historical Center, Department of the Navy], 1988).

15. This argument is challenged in Edward Rhodes, *Power and MADness: The Logic of Nuclear Coercion* (New York: Columbia University Press, 1989). Rhodes struggles to change the focus of the debate from how to design policy-rational nuclear use options to how to enhance the credibility of the commission of irrational acts. He deems any and all nuclear use to be irrational, because of the perils of unintended escalation.

16. Eric Grove, *The Future of Sea Power* (Annapolis, Md.: Naval Institute Press, 1990), pp. 200, 263 (fn. 1). Also see Lawrence Freedman, "British Nuclear Targeting," in Desmond Ball and Jeffrey Richelson, eds., *Strategic Nuclear Targeting* (Ithaca: Cornell University Press, 1986), pp. 109–26.

17. Carl von Clausewitz, *On War*, trans. Michael Howard and Peter Paret (Princeton: Princeton University Press, 1976; first pub. 1832), pp. 119–21 (on "friction"), and 566–73 ("the culminating point of victory").

18. On the paradoxical logic of conflict, see Edward N. Luttwak, *Strategy: The Logic of War and Peace* (Cambridge: Harvard University Press, 1987), passim.

19. Francis Bacon, quoted in Michael Howard, *The Causes of Wars and Other Essays* (London: Unwin Paperbacks, 1983), p. 180.

20. But see the caveats on this subject noted briefly in Robert Jervis, *The Meaning of the Nuclear Revolution: Statecraft and the Prospect of Armageddon* (Ithaca: Cornell University Press, 1989), pp. 33–34.

21. A point well argued in Richard Brody, "Warning and Response," in Andrew W. Marshall, J. J. Martin, and Henry S. Rowen, eds., *On Not Confusing Ourselves: Essays on National Security Strategy in Honor of Albert and Roberta Wohlstetter* (Boulder, Colo.: Westview Press, 1991), pp. 94–113.

22. On inadvertent, as contrasted with accidental, war, see Rhodes, *Power and MADness*, pp. 78–81. George H. Quester, "Crises and the Unexpected," in Robert I. Rotberg and Theodore K. Rabb, eds., *The Origin and Prevention of Major Wars* (Cambridge: Cambridge University Press, 1989), pp. 127–45, is also relevant.

23. See George L. Butler, Anatoli V. Bolyatko, and Scott D. Sagan, *Reducing the Risk of Dangerous Military Activities* (Stanford, Calif.: Center for International Security and Arms Control, July 1991).

24. The best studies are two recent books by Robert Allan Doughty: *The Seeds of Disaster: The Development of French Army Doctrine, 1919–1939* (Hamden, Conn.: Archon Books, 1985), and *The Breaking Point: Sedan and the Fall*

*of France, 1940* (Hamden, Conn.: Archon Books, 1990). Also useful are Barry R. Posen, *The Sources of Military Doctrine: France, Britain, and Germany between the World Wars* (Ithaca: Cornell University Press, 1984), and Mark Jacobsen, Robert Levine, and William Schwabe, *Contingency Plans for War in Western Europe, 1920–1940*, R-3281-NA (Santa Monica, Calif.: Rand Corporation, June 1985).

25. In the early 1980s a proposal for NATO contingency plans for an eastward conventional offensive in the event of war in Europe attracted a lot of attention. It was Samuel P. Huntington's "Conventional Deterrence and Conventional Retaliation in Europe," in Steven E. Miller and Sean M. Lynn-Jones, eds., *Conventional Forces and American Defense Policy: An International Security Reader*, rev. ed. (Cambridge: M.I.T. Press, 1989), pp. 247–71.

26. For example: Baron Antoine Henri de Jomini, *The Art of War* (Westport, Conn.: Greenwood Press, 1971; reprint of 1862 ed.), p. 70, and Clausewitz, *On War*, p. 204.

27. John Keegan is wrong when he claims that "on the day [June 4, 1942], 272 Japanese bombers and fighters would confront 180 Americans. These were extreme odds" (*The Second World War* [London: Hutchinson, 1989], p. 272). In the apposite words of H. P. Willmott, "where it mattered—off Midway on the morning of 4 June—the balance was in favor of the Americans. They had 3 carriers and 22 escorts at sea. With the carriers were 234 aircraft, with another 110 on Midway. For all their massive superiority of numbers spread across thousands of miles of ocean, the Japanese had an unsupported vanguard of 4 carriers, 17 escorts, 229 aircraft and 17 seaplanes" (*The Barrier and the Javelin: Japanese and Allied Pacific Strategies, February to June 1942* [Annapolis, Md.: Naval Institute Press, 1983], p. 343).

28. On the introduction of gunpowder artillery, see T. N. Dupuy, *The Evolution of Weapons and Warfare* (Indianapolis: Bobbs-Merrill, 1980), chaps. 12–13; William H. McNeill, *The Pursuit of Power: Technology, Armed Force, and Society* (Chicago: University of Chicago Press, 1982), pp. 79–102; and Philippe Contamine, *War in the Middle Ages* (Oxford: Basil Blackwell, 1984), chap. 6.

29. See the two books by G. V. Scammell: *The World Encompassed: The First European Maritime Empires, c. 800–1650* (London: Methuen, 1981), and *The First Imperial Age: European Overseas Expansion, c. 1400–1715* (London: Unwin Hyman, 1989). Also useful is the minor classic, Carlo M. Cipolla, *Guns, Sails and Empires: Technological Innovation and the Early Phases of European Expansion, 1400–1700* (New York: Minerva Press, 1965).

30. In "The Geographical Pivot of History" (1904), Halford J. Mackinder predicted that the coming of the railroad would yield to landpower, and particularly to great continental states, a new structural advantage over seapower. See *Democratic Ideals and Reality* (New York: W. W. Norton, 1962) for Mackinder's major geopolitical writings; see also Colin S. Gray, *The Geopolitics of Super Power* (Lexington: University Press of Kentucky, 1988), chap. 2.

31. On the alleged significance of "dominant" weapons, see J. F. C. Fuller, *Armament and History: A Study of the Influence of Armament on History from the Dawn of Classical Warfare to the Second World War* (London: Eyre and Spottiswoode, 1946).

32. For one such noteworthy endeavor, see George H. Quester, *Offense and Defense in the International System* (New York: John Wiley and Sons, 1977).

33. A sound point that undergirds the argument in Jervis, *Meaning of the Nuclear Revolution.*

34. See John Terraine, *The Road to Passchendaele: The Flanders Offensive of 1917, A Study in Inevitability* (London: Leo Cooper, 1984; first pub. 1977), pp. 37–38.

35. See Scott D. Sagan, "1914 Revisited: Allies, Offense, and Instability," *International Security* 11 (Fall 1986): 151–75. Sagan's *Moving Targets: Nuclear Strategy and National Security* (Princeton: Princeton University Press, 1989) is also useful.

36. The Commission on Integrated Long-Term Strategy, *Discriminate Deterrence* (Washington, D.C.: U.S. Government Printing Office, January 11, 1988).

37. A principle recognized in George Bush, *National Security Strategy of the United States* (Washington, D.C.: White House, March 1990), p. 1, but not repeated in George Bush, *National Security Strategy of the United States* (Washington, D.C.: White House, August 1991).

38. Ronald Reagan, "Launching the SDI," in Zbigniew Brzezinski, ed., *Promise or Peril: The Strategic Defense Initiative* (Washington, D.C.: Ethics and Public Policy Center, 1986), pp. 48–50.

39. "New thinking" is well presented in Keith B. Payne, *Missile Defense in the 21st Century: Protection against Limited Threats, Including Lessons from the Gulf War* (Boulder, Colo.: Westview Press, 1991). "Old thinking" pervades Charles L. Glaser, *Analyzing Strategic Nuclear Policy* (Princeton: Princeton University Press, 1990), chap. 9.

40. See Kurt Gottfried and Bruce G. Blair, eds., *Crisis Stability and Nuclear War* (New York: Oxford University Press, 1988).

41. For an outstanding work that was ahead of its time, see Yehezkel Dror, *Crazy States: A Counterconventional Strategic Problem* (Lexington, Mass.: Heath Lexington Books, 1971).

42. Dick Cheney, *Annual Report of the Secretary of Defense to the President and the Congress* (Washington, D.C.: U.S. Government Printing Office, January 1991), pp. 59–60.

43. Clausewitz, *On War*, p. 359; emphasis in original.

CHAPTER TWO. OFFENSIVE AND DEFENSIVE WEAPONS?

1. See "Introduction," fn. 3.

2. "The *material* school rests upon the assumption that the dominant military hardware or weapon—the material strength—at a given time creates such an overwhelming superiority that it alone generally satisfies the nation's defense needs." Clark G. Reynolds, *History and the Sea: Essays on Maritime Strategies* (Columbia: University of South Carolina Press, 1989), pp. 12–13. Emphasis in original.

3. Nonetheless, by the middle of the summer of 1939 even Neville Chamberlain had come to realize both that Hitler would have to be stopped and that he could only be stopped by countervailing force. See Donald Cameron Watt, *How War Came: The Immediate Origins of the Second World War, 1938–1939* (New York: Pantheon Books, 1989), p. 616. Also see Watt, "British Intelligence and the Coming of the Second World War," in Ernest R. May, ed., *Knowing One's*

*Enemies: Intelligence Assessment before the Two World Wars* (Princeton: Princeton University Press, 1984), pp. 237–70, and Wesley Wark, *The Ultimate Enemy: British Intelligence and Nazi Germany, 1933–1939* (Ithaca: Cornell University Press, 1985). Hitler wanted the fruits of victory from war rather than war itself; the course of subsequent history would show just how unready Nazi Germany was for the kind of war she had unleashed.

4. This became the standard verbal formula of the Reagan years after 1981–1982, when a few high officials risked some light speculation about nuclear strategy from a war-fighting perspective. For a typical example of the anodyne verbal formula in context, see Ronald Reagan, *National Security Strategy of the United States* (Washington, D.C.: White House, January 1987), p. 22.

5. See Holger H. Herwig, *"Luxury Fleet": The Imperial German Navy, 1888–1918* (London: George Allen and Unwin, 1980), and Paul Kennedy, *Strategy and Diplomacy, 1870–1945: Eight Studies* (London: George Allen and Unwin, 1983), part 2.

6. See Stephen Roskill, *Naval Policy Between the Wars, I: The Period of Anglo-American Antagonism, 1919–1929* (London: Collins, 1968), and Christopher Hall, *Britain, America and Arms Control, 1921–37* (New York: St. Martin's Press, 1987). Hall's book exaggerates the degree of Anglo-American hostility and thereby inflates the claimed positive effect of the Washington treaty system of naval arms limitation.

7. See Williamson Murray, *The Change in the European Balance of Power, 1938–1939: The Path to Ruin* (Princeton: Princeton University Press, 1984), pp. 239–43, 348–50.

8. See Marion William Boggs, *Attempts to Define and Limit "Aggressive" Armament in Diplomacy and Strategy*, University of Missouri Studies, 16 (Columbia: University of Missouri, 1941).

9. See Christopher Donnelly, *Red Banner: The Soviet Military System in Peace and War* (Coulsdon, Eng.: Jane's Information Group, 1988), pp. 139–45. For a valuable illustration of the quality of strategic education provided for would-be Soviet general staff officers, see Graham Hall Turbiville, ed., *The Voroshilov Lectures, Materials from the Soviet General Staff Academy: Issues of Soviet Military Strategy*, comp. Ghulam D. Wardak, 2 vols. (to date) (Washington, D.C.: National Defense University Press, 1989–1990). For Soviet, now Russian, military developments in the realms of doctrine, strategy, operational art, tactics and organization, see the serial publication *Journal of Soviet Military Studies* (1988–present).

10. In the memorable words of Eliot Cohen, "In no war has an alliance of *independent* states gone to war in lockstep" ("Toward Better Net Assessment: Rethinking the European Conventional Balance," *International Security* 13 [Summer 1988]: 56; emphasis in original).

11. For example, Nazi Germany inadvertently found itself committed to waging war in 1940–1941 against an insular country which could not be damaged fatally by the short-range military instruments that had brought down a succession of continental foes. In 1940–1941, a major capability to execute a strategic bombing campaign, including some long-legged fighter protection; a surface navy of modest proportions with some amphibious skills; or the ability to wage war against Britain's maritime life lines with 200–300 U-boats at sea, instead of 11 (average for October 1940–March 1941) to 33 (average for July–December 1941), most likely would have been critically instrumental in deliv-

ering the victory in the West which would have enabled the USSR to be conquered in 1941–1942. Since Hitler's Germany lacked the aircraft and the ships to defeat Britain, Germany decided to seek a continental solution to its problems. That decision ensured that Germany would never acquire the material means to bring Britain down.

12. See the chapters on the nineteenth century in Kenneth J. Hagan, ed., *In Peace and War: Interpretations of American Naval History, 1775–1984* (Westport, Conn.: Greenwood Press, 1984). On the German menace, real and imagined, see Holger H. Herwig, *Politics of Frustration: The United States in German Naval Planning, 1889–1941* (Boston: Little, Brown, 1976).

13. For an outstanding discussion, see John Shy, "The American Military Experience: History and Learning," in Shy, *A People Numerous and Armed: Reflections on the Military Struggle for American Independence* (London: Oxford University Press, 1976), pp. 225–58. Also useful is Allan R. Millett and Peter Maslowski, *For the Common Defense: A Military History of the United States of America* (New York: Free Press, 1984), chaps. 4–5.

14. Sidney D. Drell has observed that "effective defenses must meet a very much higher standard of performance than at any previous time in the history of warfare. A 10% defense such as won the Battle of Britain—or even a 90% defense—against today's threat of almost 10,000 strategic nuclear warheads, cannot protect a nation from nuclear annihilation" ("What Has Happened to Arms Control," in Catherine McArdle Kelleher, Frank J. Kerr, and George H. Quester, eds., *Nuclear Deterrence: New Risks, New Opportunities* [Washington, D.C.: Pergamon-Brassey's, 1986], pp. 19–20). The absolute ability of missile defenses to protect American society against threats on all scales is not, however, the correct measure of the merit in new missile-defense deployments. For a reasonable, terse presentation of many pro-SDI arguments, see George C. Marshall Institute, *The Concept of Defensive Deterrence: Strategic and Technical Dimensions of Missile Defense* (Washington, D.C.: George C. Marshall Institute, 1988). That publication was, understandably, heavily Soviet oriented. Keith B. Payne makes a strong case for ballistic missile defenses to support a new world order in the 1990s and beyond in *Missile Defense in the 21st Century: Protection against Limited Threats, Including Lessons from the Gulf War* (Boulder, Colo.: Westview Press, 1991).

15. For example, see John Newhouse, *Cold Dawn: The Story of SALT* (New York: Holt, Rinehart and Winston, 1973), pp. 27–28, and Jerome H. Kahan, *Security in the Nuclear Age: Developing U.S. Strategic Arms Policy* (Washington, D.C.: Brookings Institution, 1975), pp. 272–73.

16. I am convinced that a so-called defensive transition, once effected, would be found to have carried the seeds of a succeeding offensive transition. Colin S. Gray, "The Transition from Offense to Defense," *Washington Quarterly* 9 (Summer 1986): 59–72.

17. See Theodore Ropp, *The Development of a Modern Navy: French Naval Policy, 1871–1904* (Annapolis, Md.: Naval Institute Press, 1987), pp. 347–52. Georges Leygues, France's Minister of Marine, argued at the 1930 London Naval Conference that "in particular, she [France] looks on the submarine, as all the lesser naval powers do, as her only protection against a long blockade by surface fleets" (quoted in Hall, *Britain, America and Arms Control, 1921–37*, pp. 102–3). Also see Etienne Taillemite, *L'Histoire ignoré de la marine française* (Paris: Librairie Academique Perrin, 1988), pp. 417–20.

18. The word "strategic" is used variably with "weapons" or "forces" to mean independently decisive, long-range, long-range and nuclear armed, off-battlefield (traditional), or simply very important. For a useful brief note on this subject, see Edward N. Luttwak, *Strategy: The Logic of War and Peace* (Cambridge, Mass.: Harvard University Press, 1987), p. 90.

19. On allegedly offensive and defensive weapon qualities, see George H. Quester, *Offense and Defense in the International System* (New York: John Wiley and Sons, 1977), chap. 1, and the discussion in Jack S. Levy, "The Offensive/Defensive Balance of Military Technology: A Theoretical and Historical Analysis," *International Studies Quarterly* 28 (1984), particularly pp. 225–27.

20. The U.S. defense community has endeavored to study the problems and opportunities of offense-defense integration, but the lack of clear top-down policy and strategy guidance renders the endeavor exceptionally difficult. Other difficulties are explained or suggested in Colin S. Gray, *Policy Implications of Offense/Defense Integration* (Fairfax, Va.: National Security Research, October 1990).

21. An excellent discussion of the critical weakness in the theorizing of the Baron Antoine Henri de Jomini is John Shy, "Jomini," in Peter Paret, ed., *Makers of Modern Strategy: From Machiavelli to the Nuclear Age* (Princeton: Princeton University Press, 1986), pp. 184–85. For complementary points, see Azar Agat, *The Origins of Military Thought from the Enlightenment to Clausewitz* (Oxford: Clarendon Press, 1989), pp. 121–22.

22. "An elementary knowledge of the physical effects of nuclear weapons serves as today's crystal ball" (Joseph S. Nye, Jr., "Old Wars and Future Wars: Causation and Prevention," in Robert I. Rotberg and Theodore K. Rabb, eds., *The Origin and Prevention of Major Wars* [Cambridge: Cambridge University Press, 1989], p. 11).

23. This colorful example is provided in Daniel Deudney, "Unlocking Space," *Foreign Policy* no. 53 (Winter 1983–1984), p. 106.

24. "Technical" arms control is assailed in Robin Ranger, *Arms and Politics, 1958–1978: Arms Control in a Changing Political Context* (Toronto: Macmillan of Canada, 1979), and Colin S. Gray, *House of Cards: Why Arms Control Must Fail* (Ithaca: Cornell University Press, 1992).

25. Scott D. Sagan concludes a generally useful book by endorsing the old adage that "the devil is in the details." Sagan also advises that "not only do U.S. targeting doctrine and war plans determine how the United States is likely to respond to an attack, but they can exert a strong influence themselves on the likelihood of war" (*Moving Targets: Nuclear Strategy and National Security* [Princeton: Princeton University Press, 1989], pp. 182 and 186, respectively). Rather more plausible is Robert Jervis's argument that "mutual vulnerability exists and casts an enormous shadow. This condition is not subtle nor does it depend on the details of the strategic balance or targeting that may loom large to academics or war planners" (*The Meaning of the Nuclear Revolution: Statecraft and the Prospect of Armageddon* [Ithaca: Cornell University Press, 1989], p. 98).

26. For all its scholarly qualifications, Quester, *Offense and Defense in the International System*, encourages the fallacy that there are important distinctions between offensive and defensive armaments and that the latter generally favors peace.

27. For the paradoxical argument that nothing fails like success, see the in-

spired analysis in Luttwak, *Strategy*, chap. 2. Many seemingly successful weapons are successful only until the enemy learns to generate countermeasures of a technical, tactical, or operational kind.

28. For a path-breaking treatment, see Michael I. Handel, "Technological Surprise in War," *Intelligence and National Security* 2 (January 1987): 1–53.

29. This was the lead argument in Walt W. Rostow's very critical review of Paul Kennedy, *The Rise and Fall of the Great Powers: Economic Change and Military Conflict from 1500 to 2000* (New York: Random House, 1987). See Rostow, "Beware of Historians Bearing False Analogies," *Foreign Affairs* 66 (Spring 1988): 863–68; and Kennedy-Rostow, "Comment and Correspondence," *Foreign Affairs* 66 (Summer 1988): 1108–13.

30. The occupation of the Sinai after the Six Day War of 1967 provided a substantial territorial buffer, but at the price of enhancing Israel's susceptibility to surprise attack.

31. "One factor often forgotten when discussing German war aims, or for that matter German military strategy at the outbreak of war, is the factor of geography" (H. W. Koch, "Introduction," in Koch, ed., *The Origins of the First World War: Great Power Rivalry and German War Aims*, 2d ed. (London: Mac-Millan, 1984), p. 10. See Gerhard Ritter, *The Schlieffen Plan: Critique of a Myth* (London: Oswald Wolff, 1958; first pub. 1956), and L. C. F. Turner, "The Significance of the Schlieffen Plan," in Paul M. Kennedy, ed., *The War Plans of the Great Powers, 1880–1914* (London: George Allen and Unwin, 1979), pp. 199–221.

32. There is, however, a great deal to be said in favor of instability when it places military advantage on the side of international order. Writing about the unfavorable impact of the Washington naval arms limitation regime of the interwar years on the ability of the United States to project power across the Pacific, Jervis observed that "extreme stability, then, is an unmitigated blessing only in the rare instances in which the state can always stand on the defensive" (*Meaning of the Nuclear Revolution*, p. 142).

33. See Kahan's presentation on "Stability Principles" in *Security in the Nuclear Age*, pp. 272–76. Kahan is nothing if not direct in his folly. He advises that "in order to establish a mutual stability policy, it is necessary to classify strategic systems as either stabilizing or destabilizing and to avoid the latter" (p. 272).

34. On the new Western policy challenge regarding active missile defense—not that he defines the problem in this manner—see Martin Navias, *Ballistic Missile Proliferation in the Third World*, Adelphi Papers no. 252 (London: IISS, Summer 1990). Very much to the point is Kathleen C. Bailey, "Reversing Missile Proliferation," *Orbis* 35 (Winter 1991): 5–14, and Payne, *Missile Defense in the 21st Century*.

35. For example, Michael I. Handel half-heartedly endorses Clausewitz's view "that tactical mistakes could always be retrieved on the strategic level" ("Clausewitz in the Age of Technology," *Journal of Strategic Studies* 9 [June/September 1986]: 87, fn. 5).

36. The outstanding brief discussion of the assimilation of new weapons is T. N. Dupuy, *The Evolution of Weapons and Warfare* (Indianapolis: Bobbs-Merrill, 1980), pp. 301–7. Also see Martin van Creveld, *Technology and War: From 2000 B.C. to the Present* (New York: Free Press, 1989).

37. The relative importance of man and machine in weapon systems is well treated in historical perspective in Creveld, *Technology and War*.

38. From a large and occasionally bizarre literature, see Nigel Blake and Kay Pole, eds., *Dangers of Deterrence: Philosophers on Nuclear Strategy* (London: Routledge and Kegan Paul, 1983); Joseph S. Nye, Jr., *Nuclear Ethics* (New York: Free Press, 1986); Gregory S. Kavka, *Moral Paradoxes of Nuclear Deterrence* (Cambridge: Cambridge University Press, 1987); and Henry Shue, ed., *Nuclear Deterrence and Moral Restraint: Critical Choices for American Strategy* (Cambridge: Cambridge University Press, 1989). In the same way, and generally for the same reasons, that scientists-as-arms-control theorists tend to be poor strategic thinkers, so moral philosophers-as-policy advisors tend to be less than robust in their grasp of strategic realities. We all have skill biases. The professional philosopher naturally inclines to press his professional concern for the determination of proper conduct (or principles for determination of the same) far beyond the realm of the practicable.

39. See Edward Rhodes, *Power and MADness: The Logic of Nuclear Coercion* (New York: Columbia University Press, 1989), pp. 38, 130–31.

40. The case for deploying MX/MPS was detailed in Colin S. Gray, *The MX ICBM and National Security* (New York: Praeger, 1981).

CHAPTER THREE. THE ARMS RACE METAPHOR

1. This working definition is borrowed from my article, "The Arms Race Phenomenon," *World Politics* 24 (October 1971): 40.

2. A useful analysis of arms races in international relations is Barry Buzan, *An Introduction to Strategic Studies: Military Technology and International Relations* (New York: St. Martin's Press, 1987), part 2. Some readers may find value in Walter Isard, *Arms Races, Arms Control, and Conflict Analysis: Contributions from Peace Science and Peace Economics* (New York: Cambridge University Press, 1988), and Craig Etcheson, *Arms Race Theory: Strategy and Structure of Behavior* (Westport, Conn.: Greenwood Press, 1989).

3. A distinction critical to the argument in Samuel P. Huntington, "Arms Races: Prerequisites and Results," in Carl J. Friedrich and Seymour E. Harris, eds., *Public Policy, 1958* (Cambridge: Graduate School of Public Administration, Harvard University, 1958), pp. 40–86.

4. Notwithstanding the plausible analyses in Patrick Glynn, *Closing Pandora's Box: Arms Races, Arms Control, and the History of the Cold War* (New York: Basic Books, 1992), chap. 1; Samuel R. Williamson, Jr., "The Origins of World War I," and Charles S. Maier, "Wargames: 1914–1919," in Robert I. Rotberg and Theodore K. Rabb, eds., *The Origin and Prevention of Major Wars* (Cambridge: Cambridge University Press, 1989), pp. 225–48, and 249–79, respectively; David Kaiser, *Politics and War: European Conflict from Philip II to Hitler* (Cambridge: Harvard University Press, 1990), pp. 271–325; and Marc Trachtenberg, *History and Strategy* (Princeton: Princeton University Press, 1991), chap. 2. Michael Howard concludes a brilliant essay on "The Edwardian Arms Race" with the following judgment: " 'The arms race' preceded the war and was the result of a rivalry that powerfully contributed to the war. But it did not of itself cause it" (*The Lessons of History* [New Haven: Yale University Press, 1991] p. 96).

5. A proposition advanced and defended robustly in Charles H. Fairbanks, Jr., "Arms Races: The Metaphor and the Facts," *National Interest*, no. 1 (Fall 1985): 75–90. Also useful is Jack S. Levy, "Preferences, Constraints, and Choices in July 1914," *International Security* 15 (Winter 1990/91): 151–86.

6. George W. Downs shows the inconclusiveness of scholarship on the arms race-war connection in "Arms Race and War," in Philip E. Tetlock et al., eds., *Behavior, Society, and Nuclear War*, vol. 2 (New York: Oxford University Press, 1991), pp. 73–109.

7. See the extended discussion in Colin S. Gray, *The Soviet-American Arms Race* (Lexington, Mass.: Lexington Books, 1976).

8. For example, Jonathan Steinberg, *Yesterday's Deterrent: Tirpitz and the Birth of the German Battle Fleet* (London: Macdonald, 1965), p. 28.

9. For a worthy experiment in cross-historical analysis, see Richard Ned Lebow and Barry S. Strauss, eds., *Hegemonic Rivalry: From Thucydides to the Nuclear Age* (Boulder, Colo.: Westview Press, 1991).

10. See David Holloway, *The Soviet Union and the Arms Race* (New Haven: Yale University Press, 1983); Matthew Evangelista, *Innovation and the Arms Race: How the United States and the Soviet Union Develop New Military Technologies* (Ithaca: Cornell University Press, 1988); and Fen Osler Hampson, *Unguided Missiles: How America Buys Its Weapons* (New York: W. W. Norton, 1989). On the problems of industrial conversion from defense to civilian use, see Arthur J. Alexander, *Perestroika and Change in Soviet Weapons Acquisition*, R-3821-USDP (Santa Monica, Calif.: Rand Corporation, June 1990).

11. See Colin S. Gray, "The Urge to Compete: Rationales for Arms Racing," *World Politics* 26 (January 1974): 207–33.

12. There is no substitute for the original. See Herman Kahn, *On Thermonuclear War* (Princeton: Princeton University Press, 1960), and *Thinking About the Unthinkable* (New York: Horizon Press, 1962).

13. Robert Jervis, *The Meaning of the Nuclear Revolution: Statecraft and the Prospect of Armageddon* (Ithaca: Cornell University Press, 1989), p. 22; emphasis in original.

14. Carl von Clausewitz, *On War*, trans. Michael Howard and Peter Paret (Princeton: Princeton University Press, 1976; first pub. 1832), p. 97.

15. See McGeorge Bundy, "Existential Deterrence and Its Consequences," in Douglas MacLean, ed., *The Security Gamble: Deterrence Dilemmas in the Nuclear Age* (Totowa, N.J.: Rowman and Allanheld, 1984), pp. 3–13.

16. Edward Rhodes, *Power and MADness: The Logic of Nuclear Coercion* (New York: Columbia University Press, 1989), p. 229. The concept of the "rationality of irrationality" was first developed in Kahn, *On Thermonuclear War*, pp. 291–95. The central premise in Rhodes's argument is that any use of nuclear weapons must be irrational because the danger that such use would lead to a cataclysm is unacceptably large.

17. For some sophisticated clarification of a conceptual menu designed to obfuscate, see Warner R. Schilling, "U.S. Strategic Nuclear Concepts in the 1970's: The Search for Sufficiently Equivalent Countervailing Parity," *International Security* 6 (Fall 1981): 48–79.

18. In the early 1980s the high end of Western estimates of the percentage of Soviet GNP devoted to imperial security functions lay between twelve and fifteen percent. Today, with the benefit of hindsight, it is not even controversial to estimate that the probable range was 25–30 percent of GNP. Furthermore,

the Soviet economy of the early 1980s was less than one-third the size of the U.S. economy, not approximately one-half as many experts believed at the time.

19. Alfred Thayer Mahan, *The Influence of Sea Power upon History, 1660–1783* (Boston: Little, Brown, 1918; first pub. 1890), p. 29.

20. An excellent interpretative essay is Paul Kennedy, "Strategic Aspects of the Anglo-German Naval Race," in Kennedy, *Strategy and Diplomacy, 1870–1945: Eight Studies* (London: George Allen and Unwin, 1983), pp. 127–60. For the basic history, see E. L. Woodward, *Great Britain and the German Navy* (London: Frank Cass, 1964; first pub. 1935); Arthur J. Marder, *From the Dreadnought to Scapa Flow, The Royal Navy in the Fisher Era, 1904–1919*, Vol. 1, *The Road to War: 1904–1914* (London: Oxford University Press, 1961); and for the political context, Paul Kennedy, *The Rise of the Anglo-German Antagonism, 1860–1914* (London: George Allen and Unwin, 1980).

21. See Arthur J. Marder, *The Anatomy of British Sea Power: A History of British Naval Policy in the Pre-Dreadnought Era, 1880–1905* (Hamden, Conn.: Archon Books, 1964; first pub. 1940), chap. 25; Samuel R. Williamson, Jr., *The Politics of Grand Strategy: Britain and France Prepare for War, 1904–1914* (Cambridge: Harvard University Press, 1969), chap. 1; and J. McDermott, "The Revolution in British Military Thinking from the Boer War to the Moroccan Crisis," in Paul M. Kennedy, ed., *The War Plans of the Great Powers, 1880–1914* (London: George Allen and Unwin, 1979), pp. 107–9.

22. Useful studies include Geoffrey Blainey, *The Causes of War* (London: Macmillan, 1973); the title essay in Michael Howard, *The Causes of Wars and Other Essays* (London: Unwin Paperbacks, 1983), pp. 7–22; Rotberg and Rabb, eds., *The Origin and Prevention of Major Wars*; Kaiser, *Politics and War*; and Jack S. Levy, "The Causes of War: A Review of Theories," in Philip E. Tetlock et al., eds., *Behavior, Society, and Nuclear War*, vol. 1 (New York: Oxford University Press, 1989), pp. 209–33. Kennedy summarized an analysis of "Arms Races and the Causes of War, 1850–1945," as follows: "Arms races and wars are the reflection and the consequence of the fears, suspicions and ambitions within specific societies as they assess their relationship with certain other societies on this planet; [the essay asserts] that they *are* controllable, and can peter out as well as escalate, depending upon the political will existing" (in Kennedy, *Strategy and Diplomacy, 1870–1945*, p. 176; emphasis in original).

23. A sound, recent treatment is Robert Gordon Kaufman, *Arms Control During the Pre-Nuclear Era: The United States and Naval Limitation Between the Two World Wars* (New York: Columbia University Press, 1990). There is also food for thought in Robin Ranger, "Learning from the Naval Arms Control Experience," *Washington Quarterly* 10 (Summer 1987): 47–58.

24. For an excellent, terse critique, see Charles H. Fairbanks, Jr., "The Washington Naval Treaty, 1922–1936," in Robert J. Art and Kenneth Waltz, eds., *The Use of Force: International Politics and Foreign Policy*, 2d ed. (Lanham, Md.: University Press of America, 1983), pp. 473–77. Another unflattering analysis is Colin S. Gray, *House of Cards: Why Arms Control Must Fail* (Ithaca: Cornell University Press, 1992), chap. 4.

25. Bernard Brodie, *Sea Power in the Machine Age* (Princeton: Princeton University Press, 1941), p. 336.

26. "It was the avowed policy of the British Navy during the nineteenth century never to introduce an innovation which would tend to make existing

material obsolete. This principle was later urged against the *Dreadnought* policy. There can be no question that it was often ill-advised. But in respect to underwater attack, where the advantage was clearly on the side of the inferior navy, this theory had real validity" (ibid., p. 443). Brodie proceeds to note the irony in "the frequency with which new devices proved disadvantageous to those very countries which had most energetically furthered their progress" (p. 444).

27. But see Huntington, "Arms Races: Prerequisites and Results," particularly pp. 65–75.

28. "The concept of strategic culture refers to a nation's traditions, values, attitudes, patterns of behavior, habits, symbols, achievements and particular ways of adapting to the environment and solving problems with respect to the threat or use of force" (Ken Booth, "The Concept of Strategic Culture Affirmed," in Carl G. Jacobsen, ed., *Strategic Power: USA/USSR* [New York: St. Martin's Press, 1990], p. 121). Also see Jack L. Snyder, *The Soviet Strategic Culture: Implications for Limited Nuclear Operations*, R-2154-AF (Santa Monica, Calif.: Rand Corporation, September 1977); Ken Booth, *Strategy and Ethnocentrism* (London: Croom, Helm, 1979); Colin S. Gray, *The Geopolitics of Super Power* (Lexington: University Press of Kentucky, 1988), chap. 5; Yitzhak Klein, "The Sources of Soviet Strategic Culture," *Journal of Soviet Military Studies* 2 (December 1989): 453–90; and Klein, "A Theory of Strategic Culture," *Comparative Strategy* 10 (1991): 3–23.

29. On the economic basis for sustained great power status, see Paul Kennedy, *The Rise and Fall of the Great Powers: Economic Change and Military Conflict from 1500 to 2000* (New York: Random House, 1987).

30. Mary Kaldor, *The Baroque Arsenal* (New York: Hill and Wang, 1981).

31. Frank C. Carlucci, *Annual Report to the Congress of the Secretary of Defense, Fiscal Year 1990* (Washington, D.C.: U.S. Government Printing Office, January 17, 1989), pp. 46–48. The idea of "competitive strategies," which was to some extent simply a conceptual elevation of common-sense practice, seemed to die in the course of 1989–1990. In spite of the sincerity of its advocates, it revealed itself to have been a passing fad, as many of us had suspected. Although the political stand-down of the Soviet threat has plainly discouraged, if not thoroughly invalidated, "competitive strategies," it was by no means the leading reason for their demise.

32. In recent years it has come to be fashionable to distinguish between structural arms control—otherwise known as arms limitation—and operational arms control, which focuses on defense behavior instead of force levels or weapon types. See Scott D. Sagan, *Moving Targets: Nuclear Strategy and National Security* (Princeton: Princeton University Press, 1989), p. 181, and Joseph S. Nye, Jr., "Arms Control After the Cold War," *Foreign Affairs* 68 (Winter 1989/90): 45.

33. Thomas C. Schelling and Morton H. Halperin, *Strategy and Arms Control* (New York: Twentieth Century Fund, 1961), p. 1. Also relevant is the argument in Robert Jervis, "Cooperation under the Security Dilemma," *World Politics* 30 (January 1979): 167–214.

34. See John Lewis Gaddis, *Russia, the Soviet Union and the United States: An Interpretive History* (New York: Wiley, 1978).

35. An outstanding recent study is Andrew D. Lambert, *The Crimean War: British Grand Strategy against Russia, 1853–56* (Manchester, Eng.: Manches-

ter University Press, 1990). Also relevant is David Gillard, *The Struggle for Asia, 1828–1914: A Study in British and Russian Imperialism* (London: Methuen, 1977). A sound, brief general diplomatic history, is F. R. Bridge and Roger Bullen, *The Great Powers and the European States System, 1815-1914* (London: Longman, 1980).

36. Howard, *Causes of Wars*, p. 21.

37. Mikhail Gorbachev, *Perestroika: New Thinking for Our Country and the World* (New York: Harper and Row, 1987). A powerful example of Soviet "new thinking" can be found on p. 142. "The new political outlook calls for the recognition of one more simple axiom: security is indivisible. It is either equal security for all or none at all. The only solid foundation for security is the recognition of the interests of all peoples and countries and of their equality in international affairs." Gorbachev attempted to ride the tiger of what became a runaway revolutionary process. When he wrote those words he certainly did not intend that the extended empire in Eastern Europe, and particularly in what then was East Germany, would be subject to genuinely popular local referenda, any more than he welcomed the manifestations of popular sovereignty that brought down the USSR in 1991.

38. James Sherr, *Soviet Power: The Continuing Challenge* (New York: St. Martin's Press, 1987), p. 111.

39. See Colin S. Gray, "The Strategic Forces Triad: End of the Road?" *Foreign Affairs* 56 (July 1978): 771–89; President's Commission on Strategic Forces, *Report* (Washington, D.C.: White House, April 1983); and R. James Woolsey, "The Politics of Vulnerability: 1980–83," *Foreign Affairs* 62 (Spring 1984): 805–19.

40. Brent Scowcroft, John Deutch, and R. James Woolsey, "Come and Get Us," *New Republic*, April 18, 1988, pp. 16, 18.

41. See Chris Bellamy, *Red God of War: Soviet Artillery and Rocket Forces* (London: Brassey's Defence Publishers, 1986). With respect to the United States—in this case with reference to World War II in Europe—Russell F. Weigley has written, "For the sustained combat power that its other components lacked, the American army had to look to its artillery. From the time American divisions first entered the Second World War against Germany in 1942, the same Germans who disparaged American infantry consistently praised American artillery" (*Eisenhower's Lieutenants: The Campaign of France and Germany, 1944–1945* [Bloomington: Indiana University Press, 1981], p. 28). Also see Allan R. Millett, "The United States Armed Forces in the Second World War," in Millett and Williamson Murray, eds., *Military Effectiveness*, vol. 3, *The Second World War* (Boston: Allen and Unwin, 1988), pp. 61, 78.

42. See DeWitt S. Copp, *A Few Great Captains: The Men and Events That Shaped the Development of U.S. Air Power* (Garden City, N.Y.: Doubleday, 1980). W. F. Craven and J. L. Cate, eds., *The Army Air Forces In World War II*, vol. 1, *Plans and Early Operations, January 1939 to August 1942* (Chicago: University of Chicago Press, 1948), chaps. 2 and 16, and Barry D. Watts, *The Foundations of U.S. Air Doctrine: The Problem of Friction in War* (Maxwell AFB, Ala.: Air University Press, December 1984), should also be consulted.

43. Gray, "Arms Race Phenomenon."

44. Over the past twenty years there has been a great deal of social scientific investigation of the arms race phenomenon, but careful historical studies remain short in supply. Much of the social scientific, and particularly "peace

studies," literature on arms races lacks a historical foundation. Writing arms-race theory without a detailed historical base is, in my opinion, making bricks without straw.

45. Winston Churchill in the House of Commons, 13 July 1934 (quoted in Justin Wintle, *The Dictionary of War Quotations* [New York: Free Press, 1989], p. 111).

## CHAPTER FOUR. POLICY GUIDANCE AND WEAPONS ACQUISITION

1. See the comments in Hew Strachan, *European Armies and the Conduct of War* (London: George Allen and Unwin, 1983), p. 174. Also useful are John Keegan, *The Mask of Command* (New York: Viking Press, 1987), pp. 235–310, and, for a focus on the turning point of the war, Geoffrey Jukes, *Hitler's Stalingrad Decisions* (Berkeley: University of California Press, 1985).

2. President Reagan's Director of the Arms Control and Disarmament Agency for five years (1983–1987), Kenneth L. Adelman, has mused ruefully, "My greatest disappointment: We didn't do anything, really, about Soviet cheating. Not from want of answers. We never really found anything much *to do* about Soviet cheating. That's the sad truth" ("Where We Succeeded, Where We Failed," *Policy Review*, no. 43 [Winter 1988]: 45; emphasis in original). For a less than sympathetic analysis of Adelman's professed dilemma, see Colin S. Gray, *House of Cards: Why Arms Control Must Fail* (Ithaca: Cornell University Press, 1992), chap. 6.

3. See Michael I. Handel, "Numbers Do Count: The Question of Quantity Versus Quality," *Journal of Strategic Studies* 4 (September 1981): 225–60.

4. "The two-power standard of naval strength, which was as old as the time of the Earl of Chatham (1770), was rediscovered by Cobden and others after the Crimean War. It was officially accepted by Lord George Hamilton, the First Lord, on 7 March 1889 when he stated that the idea underlying the speeches of all first lords and prime ministers had been 'that our establishment should be on such a scale that it should at least be equal to the naval strength of any two other countries' " (Arthur J. Marder, *From the Dreadnought to Scapa Flow, The Royal Navy in the Fisher Era, 1904–1919*, Vol. 1, *The Road to War, 1904–1914* (London: Oxford University Press, 1961), p. 123. On Britain's formal adoption of the two-power standard in 1889, see Arthur J. Marder, *The Anatomy of British Sea Power: A History of British Naval Policy in the Pre-Dreadnought Era, 1880–1905* (Hamden, Conn.: Archon Books, 1964), chap. 7, "The Two-Power Standard."

5. See G. J. Marcus, *A Naval History of England: I, The Formative Centuries* (Boston: Little, Brown, 1961), chaps. 8–12; J. R. Jones, *Britain and the World, 1649–1815* (London: Fontana Paperbacks, 1980); and Jeremy J. Black and Philip Woodfine, eds., *The British Navy and the Use of Naval Power in the Eighteenth Century* (Leicester, Eng.: Leicester University Press, 1988).

6. See U.S. House of Representatives, Committee on Armed Services, Seapower and Strategic and Critical Materials Subcommittee, *The 600-Ship Navy and the Maritime Strategy, Hearings*, 99th Cong., 1st sess. (Washington, D.C.: U.S. Government Printing Office, 1985). Quasi-"inside" presentations are Norman Friedman, *The U.S. Maritime Strategy* (London: Jane's, 1988), and

Frederick H. Hartmann, *Naval Renaissance: The U.S. Navy in the 1980's* (Annapolis, Md.: Naval Institute Press, 1990). Although these two books lack objectivity, they are authoritative in their knowledge of the U.S. Navy. For a different bias, one could turn to chap. 7, "The Navy and Strategy," in Carl H. Builder's insightful and original work, *The Masks of War: American Military Styles in Strategy and Analysis* (Baltimore: Johns Hopkins University Press, 1989).

7. For a rigorous analysis see Kurt Guthe, *The Military Utility of 100 Peacekeeper ICBM's, and 500 Small ICBM's* (Fairfax, Va.: National Security Research, October 1987).

8. President's Commission on Strategic Forces, *Report* (Washington, D.C.: White House, April 1983).

9. See Edward Beard, *Developing the ICBM: A Study in Bureaucratic Politics* (New York: Columbia University Press, 1976).

10. George Bush, Remarks to the Aspen Institute Symposium, Aspen, Colorado, August 2, 1990.

11. George Bush, *National Security Strategy of the United States* (Washington, D.C.: White House, August 1991), p. 25.

12. George Bush, "The Peace Dividend I Seek Is Not Measured in Dollars," *Washington Post*, September 28, 1991, p. A23.

13. Russell F. Weigley has written, with the early 1950s in mind, that "to seek refuge in technology from hard problems of strategy and policy was already another dangerous American tendency, fostered by the pragmatic qualities of the American character and by the complexity of nuclear-age technology" (*The American Way of War: A History of United States Military Strategy and Policy* [New York: Macmillan, 1973], p. 416). Readers may find some value in Colin S. Gray, "American Strategic Culture: Implications for Defense Technology," in Asa A. Clark IV and John F. Lilley, eds., *Military Technology* (New York: Praeger, 1989), pp. 31–48.

14. Russell F. Weigley notes that Grant "became the most influential figure in the shaping of American strategic thought for the next hundred years, not always with fortunate results" ("American Strategy from Its Beginnings through the First World War," in Peter Paret, ed., *Makers of Modern Strategy: From Machiavelli to the Nuclear Age* [Princeton: Princeton University Press, 1986], pp. 430 ff).

15. Janne E. Nolan, *Guardians of the Arsenal: The Politics of Nuclear Strategy* (New York: Basic Books, 1989); Scott D. Sagan, *Moving Targets: Nuclear Strategy and National Security* (Princeton: Princeton University Press, 1989); and Robert Jervis, *The Meaning of the Nuclear Revolution: Statecraft and the Prospect of Armageddon* (Ithaca: Cornell University Press, 1989).

16. Bush, Remarks to the Aspen Institute Symposium.

17. George Bush, *National Security Strategy of the United States* (Washington, D.C.: White House, March 1990), pp. 24–25; emphasis added.

18. For brilliant development of the proposition that narrowly conceived notions of efficiency can be fatal when applied in the military realm, see Edward N. Luttwak, *Strategy: The Logic of War and Peace* (Cambridge: Harvard University Press, 1987), chap. 3.

19. See the chapters by David Alan Rosenberg and Desmond Ball in Ball and Jeffrey Richelson, eds., *Strategic Nuclear Targeting* (Ithaca: Cornell University Press, 1986), pp. 35–56 and 57–83; Sagan, *Moving Targets*, chap. 1; and

Desmond Ball and Robert C. Toth, "Revising the SIOP: Taking War-Fighting to Dangerous Extremes," *International Security* 14 (Spring 1990): 65–92. For a review of the basic issues, see Colin S. Gray, "War Fighting for Deterrence," *Journal of Strategic Studies* 7 (March 1984): 5–28.

20. "Think Smarter, Not Richer" is Senator Sam Nunn's preferred formulation (*Nunn 1990: A New Military Strategy*, Significant Issues Series 12 [Washington, D.C.: Center for Strategic and International Studies, 1990], p. 58).

21. I assault these errors in *War, Peace, and Victory: Strategy and Statecraft for the Next Century* (New York: Simon and Schuster, 1990), chap. 10. My debt to Richard K. Betts ("Conventional Strategy: New Critics, Old Choices," *International Security* 7 [Spring 1983]: particularly pp. 146–55) is obvious.

22. J. C. Wylie, *Military Strategy: A General Theory of Power Control* (Annapolis, Md.: Naval Institute Press, 1989; first pub. 1967), p. 65.

23. Ibid., p. 72.

24. The most penetrating recent analysis of service cultures, with particular reference to strategic preferences and styles in defense analysis, is Builder, *Masks of War*.

25. See the title essay in Edward N. Luttwak, *On the Meaning of Victory: Essays on Strategy* (New York: Simon and Schuster, 1986), chap. 16.

26. The plausible proposition that Moscow would not permit nuclear weapons to be used in war simply for reason of tactical convenience at sea is advanced in Linton F. Brooks, "Naval Power and National Security: The Case for the Maritime Strategy," *International Security* 11 (Fall 1986): particularly p. 79; and Donald C. F. Daniel, "The Soviet Navy and Tactical Nuclear War at Sea," *Survival* 29 (July/August 1987): 318–35. Also relevant is Robert B. Bathurst, "The Soviet Navy through Western Eyes," in Philip S. Gillette and Willard C. Frank, Jr., eds., *The Sources of Soviet Naval Conduct* (Lexington, Mass.: Lexington Books, 1990), pp. 59–79.

27. In their Introduction to *Crisis Stability and Nuclear War* (New York: Oxford University Press, 1988), the editors, Kurt Gottfried and Bruce G. Blair, comment on the Cuban Missile Crisis of 1962: "This fortunate record has led some to the belief there exists a craft called crisis management, and that the superpowers have mastered it. We do not share this view. Indeed we would attach a warning label to our product" (p 7). The same point needs to be made even more strongly about theories of war termination. It is essential to devise practicable theories of victory for particular wars, but it is a major fallacy to believe that some correct *general* master design for war termination can be discovered by social scientists or historians. An outstanding study that long predates the more recent flurry of theorizing is Fred Charles Iklé, *Every War Must End* (New York: Columbia University Press, 1971).

28. Nelson was writing on October 6, 1805—only fifteen days prior to Trafalgar—expressing his anxiety about the prompt arrival of the reinforcements he had been promised by the Admiralty (quoted in G. J. Marcus, *The Age of Nelson: The Royal Navy, 1793–1815* [New York: Viking Press, 1971], p. 272). Also see Julian S. Corbett, *The Campaign of Trafalgar* (London: Longmans, Green, 1910), pp. 327–28.

29. See Correlli Barnett, *The Swordbearers: Studies in Supreme Command in the First World War* (London: Eyre and Spottiswoode, 1963), part 2, "Sailor with a Flawed Cutlass: Admiral Sir John R. Jellicoe, GCB, KCVO"; Arthur J. Marder, *From the Dreadnought to Scapa Flow, The Royal Navy in the Fisher*

*Era, 1904–1919*, vol. 3, *Jutland and After (May 1916–December 1916)* (London: Oxford University Press, 1966); and John Campbell, *Jutland: An Analysis of the Fighting* (London: Conway Maritime Press, 1986).

30. Arthur J. Marder, *From the Dreadnought to Scapa Flow, The Royal Navy in the Fisher Era, 1904–1919*, Vol. 5, *Victory and Aftermath (January 1918–June 1919)* (London: Oxford University Press, 1970), pp. 332–33. Marder's judgment finds impressive support in Holger H. Herwig, *"Luxury" Fleet: The Imperial German Navy* (London: George Allen and Unwin, 1980).

31. See Builder, *Masks of War*.

32. For example, Bruce W. Menning, "The Deep Strike in Russian and Soviet Military History," *Journal of Soviet Military Studies* 1 (April 1988): 9–28, and David Glantz, *Soviet Military Operational Art: In Pursuit of Deep Battle* (London: Frank Cass, 1990).

33. See Marder, *Dreadnought to Scapa Flow*, Vol. 1, p. 369. He writes, "Mines, torpedoes, submarines, and long-range coastal ordnance had by 1912 blown the idea of close blockade to bits."

34. "The retirement of the Grand Fleet to Scapa [where it functioned to effect the distant blockade] meant that Britain no longer controlled the North Sea. Throughout the war it was a disputed zone, where the Germans were always free and able to make dangerous sallies." Barnett, *Swordbearers*, p. 117.

35. U.S. Department of Defense, *Conduct of the Persian Gulf Conflict: An Interim Report to Congress* (Washington, D.C.: U.S. Department of Defense, July 1991), p. I-4. Two works stand out amidst the torrent of analyses of the Gulf War: James Blackwell, *Thunder in the Desert: The Strategy and Tactics of the Persian Gulf War* (New York: Bantam Books, 1991), and Norman Friedman, *Desert Victory: The War for Kuwait* (Annapolis, Md.: Naval Institute Press, 1991). Since Blackwell understands land warfare, while Friedman is very good on sea and air combat, it is a shame that these authors did not collaborate to produce a single work.

36. The unfortunate Vice Admiral Count Anne Hilarion de Tourville "went to sea [on May 28, 1692] with only forty-four ships [to the Anglo-Dutch eighty-eight], but with a peremptory order from the king to fight when he fell in with the enemy, were they few or many, and come what might." Thus did Alfred Thayer Mahan (*The Influence of Sea Power upon History, 1660–1783* [Boston: Little, Brown, 1918; first pub. 1890], p. 189) explain why the French fleet was committed to hopeless battle (The Battle of La Hogue or Barfleur). See also Etienne Taillemite, *Histoire ignorée de la marine française* (Paris: Librairie Académique Perrin, 1988), p. 122. In the case of the Battle of Trafalgar on October 21, 1805, spurred to action by fear of Napoleon's wrath, Vice Admiral Pierre Charles de Villeneuve broke out of Cadiz with the combined fleet of Spain and France, even though he knew that his prospects for evading Vice Admiral Horatio Nelson were slim and his chances for victory in battle were close to nonexistent. Villeneuve subsequently observed: "Seeing that I had no confidence in the condition of my ships, in their sailing, and in their power of maneuvering together, the concentration of the enemy and the knowledge they possess of all my movements since I reached the coast of Spain leave me no hope of being able to fulfill the grand object for which the fleet was destined [to provide protective cover for the invasion of Britain]" (quoted in John Terraine, *Trafalgar* [New York: Mason/Charter, 1976; first pub. 1975], p. 118). Nelson's tactical plan for Trafalgar—to break the combined fleet's line in two places—showed a well-

founded contempt for the combat effectiveness of the enemy. In 1692 and again in 1805, the fleet movements that concluded with battle were driven by a French commitment to invade Britain; in both cases the French fleet commander was the victim of a policymaker deeply ignorant of sea warfare.

37. Admiral James D. Watkins, then the Chief of Naval Operations, explained in 1986 that "as the battle groups move forward, we will wage an aggressive campaign against all Soviet submarines, including ballistic missile submarines" (Watkins et al., *The Maritime Strategy*, Supplement to U.S. Naval Institute *Proceedings* [Annapolis, Md.: U.S. Naval Institute, January 1986]: 11). On the subject of current strategy Wayne P. Hughes wrote, "Strategy must rest on the rock of combat capability. One builds decisions from the bottom up: tactics affect the efficacy of forces; the correlation of forces reveals what strategy or forces can support" ("Naval Tactics and Their Influence on Strategy," *Naval War College Review* 39 [January–February 1986]: 3).

38. See Michael Brower, "Targeting Soviet Mobile Missiles," *Survival* 31 (September/October 1989): 433–45; and Ball and Toth, "Revising the SIOP."

39. There is much of value in Robert P. Haffa, Jr., *Rational Methods, Prudent Choices: Planning U.S. Forces* (Washington, D.C.: National Defense University Press, 1988). Also see Force Planning Faculty, Naval War College, ed., *Fundamentals of Force Planning*, Vol. 1, *Concepts* (Newport, R.I.: Naval War College Press, 1990), and Colin S. Gray, "From Defense Philosophy to Force Planning: The Strategic Forces," *Defense Analysis* 7 (1991): 363–72.

40. Time as a factor in war is greatly understudied and underappreciated, particularly with reference to the impact of the duration of hostilities.

41. See Fritz Ermarth, "Contrasts in American and Soviet Strategic Thought," *International Security* 3 (Fall 1978): 138–55, and Carl G. Jacobson, ed., *Strategic Power: USA/USSR* (New York: St. Martin's Press, 1990).

42. See Theodore A. Postol, "Targeting," in Ashton B. Carter, John D. Steinbruner, and Charles A. Zraket, eds., *Managing Nuclear Operations* (Washington, D.C.: Brookings Institution, 1987), pp. 373–406, and Haffa, *Rational Methods, Prudent Choices*, chap. 2.

43. The difference between compellence and deterrence was well illustrated by the U.S. policy commitment to expel Iraqi forces from Kuwait in 1990–91—as it had been in 1982 by the British purpose to expel Argentine forces from the Falklands. Much of the "defender's advantage" accrues to an aggressor once he is in possession of his illicit gains.

44. This is another seldom frequented region in need of scholarly attention. Russell E. Dougherty, "The Psychological Climate of Nuclear Command," in Carter, Steinbruner, and Zraket, eds., *Managing Nuclear Operations*, pp. 407–25, is an excellent contribution to this subject.

45. By far the best statement of this thesis is Edward N. Luttwak, *The Pentagon and the Art of War: The Question of Military Reform* (New York: Simon and Schuster 1984), chap. 5, to which I am indebted.

46. See Lawrence H. Holland and Robert A. Hoover, *The MX Decision: A New Direction in U.S. Weapons Procurement Policy?* (Boulder, Colo.: Westview Press, 1985); *International Security* 12 (Fall 1987); and John R. Harvey and Barry E. Fridling, "On the Wrong Track? An Assessment of MX Rail Garrison Basing," *International Security* 13 (Winter 1988/89): 113–41.

47. For an operational view of survivability, see Colin S. Gray, "ICBMs and

Deterrence: The Controversy Over Prompt Launch," *Journal of Strategic Studies* 10 (September 1987): 285–309.

48. See Deputy Undersecretary of Defense for Research and Engineering, *ICBM Basing Options: A Summary of Major Studies to Define a Survivable Basing Concept for ICBM's* (Washington, D.C.: U.S. Department of Defense, December 1980), and Office of Technology Assessment, *MX Missile Basing*, OTA-ISC-140 (Washington, D.C.: Office of Technology Assessment, U.S. Congress, September 1981).

49. In 202 B.C. Carthage was denied the right to own war elephants by the terms of the peace treaty Rome imposed to conclude the Second Punic War. In 1139 the Lateran Council prohibited Christians from using the crossbow against fellow Christians.

50. See chap. 6.

51. See John Robert Ferris, *Men, Money, and Diplomacy: The Evolution of British Strategic Policy, 1919–26* (Ithaca: Cornell University Press, 1989).

52. Richard K. Betts, "The Concept of Deterrence in the Postwar Era," *Security Studies* 1 (Autumn 1991): 35.

53. Allan R. Millett and Williamson Murray, "Lessons of War," *National Interest*, no. 14 (Winter 1988/89): 83–95.

54. See Keith Payne and Jill Coleman, "Nuclear Age Miseducation," *Policy Review*, no. 42 (Fall 1987): 59–64.


CHAPTER FIVE.  DEFENSE PLANNING FOR UNCERTAINTY

1. Notwithstanding contrasting aspirations, as in the following: "The civilized world is now in the process of fashioning the rules that will govern the new world order beginning to emerge in the aftermath of the Cold War" (George Bush, "Why We Are in the Gulf," *Newsweek*, November 26, 1990, p. 28).

2. See Carl H. Builder, *The Masks of War: American Military Styles in Strategy and Analysis* (Baltimore: Johns Hopkins University Press, 1989).

3. Ronald Lewin, *Hitler's Mistakes* (London: Leo Cooper, 1984), p. 32.

4. To sample a rich literature, see Norman F. Dixon, *On the Psychology of Military Incompetence* (London: Futura, 1979; first pub. 1976); Barbara W. Tuchman, *The March of Folly: From Troy to Vietnam* (New York: Ballantine Books, 1984); Eliot A. Cohen and John Gooch, *Military Misfortunes: The Anatomy of Failure in War* (New York: Free Press, 1990); and Barry S. Strauss and Josiah Ober, *The Anatomy of Error: Ancient Military Disasters and Their Lessons for Modern Strategists* (New York: St. Martin's Press, 1990).

5. See Samuel F. Wells, Jr., and Robert S. Litwak, eds., *Strategic Defenses and Soviet-American Relations* (Cambridge, Mass.: Ballinger, 1987), chaps. 6–7, and A. Fenner Milton, M. Scott Davis, and John A. Parmentola, *Making Space Defense Work: Must the Superpowers Cooperate?* (Washington, D.C.: Pergamon-Brassey's, 1989).

6. A similar idea appears in Patrick Glynn, "The Dangers Beyond Containment," *Commentary* 88:2 (August 1989): 15.

7. In characteristically robust language, Carl von Clausewitz judged that "great things alone can make a great mind, and petty things will make a petty mind unless a man rejects them as completely alien" (*On War*, trans. Michael

Howard and Peter Paret [Princeton: Princeton University Press, 1976; first pub. 1832], p. 145).

8. Convoy was standard British wartime practice in the wars with France from the 1680s to the 1810s; usually it was the law for all save heavily armed Indiamen; see Patrick Crowhurst, *The Defence of British Trade, 1689–1815* (Folkestone, Eng.: William Dawson and Sons, 1977), and Alan Pearsall, "The Royal Navy and the Protection of Trade in the Eighteenth Century," in *Guerres et Paix (1660–1815): Journées franco-anglaises d'histoire de la marine* (Vincennes: Service historique de la marine, 1987), pp. 149–62. The long Victorian peace, however, with its absence of substantial strategic challenge to the Royal Navy (Franco-Russian alarms notwithstanding), caused the senior service to forget that it was an instrument of war—as well as of battle—and that the *guerre de course* would be very serious business for trade-dependent Britain. The Royal Navy despised convoy duty as defensive (unglamorous and tedious) and had persuaded itself long before 1914 that the volume and technical character of Britain's seaborne trade had rendered convoy useless. On the clash between dominant service preference and practical necessity (and solid service tradition), see Arthur J. Marder, *From the Dreadnought to Scapa Flow, The Royal Navy in the Fisher Era, 1904–1919*, Vol. 4, *1917: Year of Crisis* (London: Oxford University Press, 1969). It is not true that the Admiralty was obliged by civilians to adopt convoying against its will in 1917. For a vigorous defense of the Royal Navy, see John Terraine, *Business in Great Waters: The U-Boat Wars, 1916–1945* (London: Leo Cooper, 1989), chaps. 4–6.

9. Builder, *Masks of War*, p. 132-33.

10. See J. R. Jones, "The Dutch Navy and National Survival in the Seventeenth Century," *International History Review* 10 (February 1988): 18–32, and Bernard Capp, *Cromwell's Navy: The Fleet and the English Revolution, 1648–1660* (Oxford: Clarendon Press, 1989), pp. 73–86.

11. An excellent treatment is J. R. Jones, "Limitations of British Sea Power in the French Wars, 1689–1815," in Jeremy Black and Philip Woodfine, eds., *The British Navy and the Use of Naval Power in the Eighteenth Century* (Leicester, Eng.: Leicester University Press, 1988), pp. 33–49. Jones writes of English expectations in 1689 that "they started by assuming, on the questionable evidence of the Navy's performance in the three Dutch Wars, that they would easily achieve naval supremacy and that this would have decisive effects on the war as a whole" (p. 35).

12. Among the many reasons for France's defensive military doctrine and posture in the 1930s was the determination not to offend British sensibilities. In the view of Paris, Britain would come to the continental aid only of an unmistakably inoffensive France. See Barry R. Posen, *The Sources of Military Doctrine: France, Britain, and Germany between the World Wars* (Ithaca: Cornell University Press, 1984), pp. 110–11. Also, it is important to recall that Soviet forward defense arrangements were much curtailed in the spring and early summer of 1941 lest they give offense to Adolf Hitler. This sorry story is well told in John Erickson, *Stalin's War with Germany*, Vol. 1, *The Road to Stalingrad* (London: Weidenfeld and Nicolson, 1975), chap. 2.

13. See the essays in Black and Woodfine, eds., *The British Navy and the Use of Naval Power in the Eighteenth Century*, and John Brewer, *The Sinews of Power: War, Money and the English State, 1688–1783* (New York: Alfred A. Knopf, 1989).

14. J. B. Bury, *The Invasion of Europe by the Barbarians* (New York: W. W. Norton, 1967; first pub. 1927), p. 51. Also see Lucien Musset, *The Germanic Invasions: The Making of Europe, AD 400–600* (University Park: Pennsylvania State University Press, 1975; first pub. 1965), pp. 30–33.

15. Otto J. Maenchen-Helfen notes that "as in the eighth and ninth centuries no one thought for a moment that the Magyars could make themselves masters of Europe, so the idea would have been absurd to the Romans that Attila could take Constantinople and hold it" (*The World of the Huns: Studies in Their History and Culture* [Berkeley: University of California Press, 1973], p. 126). Also see C. D. Gordon, *The Age of Attila: Fifth-Century Byzantium and the Barbarians* (Ann Arbor: University of Michigan Press, 1966, first pub. 1960).

16. Maenchen-Helfen, *World of the Huns*, p. 126.

17. See A. H. M. Jones, *The Later Roman Empire, 284–602: A Social Economic, and Administrative Survey*, vol. 1 (Baltimore: Johns Hopkins University Press, 1986; first pub. 1964), pp. 193–94; and J. B. Bury, *History of the Later Roman Empire: From the Death of Theodosius I to the Death of Justinian*, vol. 1 (New York: Dover Publications, 1958; first pub. 1923), p. 275.

18. Romilly Jenkins, *Byzantium: The Imperial Centuries, AD 610–1071* (Toronto: University of Toronto Press, 1987; first pub. 1966), p. 28.

19. Benjamin Isaac, *The Limits of Empire: The Roman Army in the East* (Oxford: Clarendon Press, 1990), p. 268.

20. See Charles J. Halperin, *Russia and the Golden Horde: The Mongol Impact on Medieval Russian History* (Bloomington: Indiana University Press, 1987; first pub. 1985).

21. As well as by a declining Austria-Hungary and by the (Ottoman) succession problems in the Balkans. Marc Trachtenberg offers a perceptive analysis in "The Coming of the First World War: A Reassessment," in Trachtenberg, *History and Strategy* (Princeton: Princeton University Press, 1991), pp. 47–99.

22. Stresemann was Reich chancellor in 1923 and foreign minister from 1924 to 1929; see Hans W. Gatzke, *Stresemann and the Rearmament of Germany* (Baltimore: Johns Hopkins University Press, 1954), and Gordon A. Craig, *Germany, 1866–1945* (New York: Oxford University Press, 1978), chap. 14.

23. Hitler was an outstandingly successful peacetime statesman. Hardly appearing to be a reckless gambler, he had judged his foes perfectly until the fall of 1939. Was it luck or judgment?

24. In addition to the problem of recognizing the character and scale of Hitler's ambitions, foreign statesmen were hindered by cultural barriers from making accurate judgments about distinctly alien "thoughtways." The lack of cultural empathy among the principal statesmen in the late 1930s is identified as an important contributory factor in the slide toward war in 1938–1939 in Richard Overy and Andrew Wheatcroft, *The Road to War: The Origins of World War II* (London: Macmillan, 1989), pp. 297–300.

25. Part of the U.S. problem in Vietnam was cultural. Too many American military professionals and senior civilian officials declined to recognize that they could learn from the painful experience of others and failed to appreciate the expertise of the enemy in waging a thoroughly political unconventional war. The joint chiefs of staff in the mid-1960s told President Johnson how the war should be waged, but they could not accept the serious possibility of national military failure, no matter what political bounds the president imposed

on the war (see Bruce Palmer, Jr., *The 25-Year War: America's Military Role in Vietnam* [Lexington: University Press of Kentucky, 1984], p. 176). Looking back even further, we see that it took a while (to Saratoga in September 1777) for the British (and the French) to take the American colonists seriously in military terms. Had there been an International Institute for Strategic Studies in 1775–1776, publishing an annual *Military Balance*, the military assets of the American colonies would not have compared favorably with those of the crown. However, strategic judgment entails the examination of military power with reference to policy goals in specific geographical and balance-of-power terms. American military power in the Revolutionary War was not at all impressive by "objective" international standards. But, with French (and later Spanish and Dutch) diversion of British strategic focus and energy, that American military power was better able to do what it had to do *in America* (which was to hang on) than were the forces of the mother country. The strategic effectiveness of military capability is not context-free (see John Ferling, ed., *The World Turned Upside Down: The American Victory in the War of Independence* [Westport, Conn.: Greenwood Press, 1988]).

26. See Arthur Ferrill, *The Fall of the Roman Empire: The Military Explanation* (London: Thames and Hudson, 1986), in the light of Ramsay MacMullen, *Corruption and the Decline of Rome* (New Haven: Yale University Press, 1988), p. xi. Ferrill argues that the barbarization of the western army caused it to lose a decisive tactical edge. In short, the Roman army ceased to be good enough to do its job. On why that army was not numerous enough to do its job, see the complexity specified in M. I. Finley, "Manpower and the Fall of Rome," in Finley, *Aspects of Antiquity: Discoveries and Controversies* (New York: Viking Press, 1974; first pub. 1969), pp. 160–61. Finley advises that "the army could not be enlarged because the land could not stand further depletion of manpower; the situation on the land had deteriorated because taxes were too high; taxes were too high because the military demands were increasing; and for that the German pressures were mainly responsible. A vicious circle of evils was in full swing." One could draft an analysis of the internal structure of the Soviet Union's difficulties in the 1980s that would reveal many similarities to the Roman dilemmas described by Finley.

27. See Harold Sprout and Margaret Sprout, *The Ecological Perspective on Human Affairs, With Special Reference to International Politics* (Princeton: Princeton University Press, 1965), chap. 7.

28. See Hedley Bull, *The Anarchical Society: A Study of Order in World Politics* (New York: Columbia University Press, 1977), and Ian Clark, *The Hierarchy of States: Reform and Resistance in the International Order* (Cambridge: Cambridge University Press, 1989; first pub. 1980).

29. Useful studies strongly illustrative of this argument are Michael Mandelbaum, *The Fate of Nations: The Search for National Security in the Nineteenth and Twentieth Centuries* (Cambridge: Cambridge University Press, 1988), and Joseph Lepgold, *The Declining Hegemon: The United States and European Defense, 1960–1990* (New York: Praeger Publishers, 1990).

30. See Felix Gilbert, *To the Farewell Address: Ideas of Early American Foreign Policy* (Princeton: Princeton University Press, 1970; first pub. 1961).

31. On the geostrategic principles behind naval deployment, see "Considerations Governing the Disposition of Navies," in Alfred Thayer Mahan, *Retrospect and Prospect: Studies in International Relations, Naval and Political* (Lon-

don: Sampson Low, Marston, 1902), pp. 139–205. An appreciation of the strategic geography that helped shape Anglo-American relations in the nineteenth century can be gained from the arguments in Kenneth Bourne, *Britain and the Balance of Power in North America, 1815–1908* (Berkeley: University of California Press, 1967).

32. Very much to the point is the article by David French, "The Meaning of Attrition, 1914–1916," *English Historical Review* 102 (April 1988): 358–405.

33. Correlli Barnett has argued that "the strategic mistake which really lost Germany the Great War was not so much the military decision to declare unrestricted submarine warfare or to launch the March 1918 offensive as the industrial decision taken in 1916 to embark on the so-called 'Hindenburg programme.' This entailed converting almost the whole of the German industrial system to munitions production. The result was an immense short-term increase in such production, at the price of making certain that the German economy would later collapse, leading in turn to the country's social and political collapse" (*Strategy and Society*, 1974 Spenser Wilkinson Memorial Lecture [Manchester, Eng.: Manchester University Press, 1975], p. 5).

34. But, see Williamson Murray, *The Change in the European Balance of Power, 1938–1939: The Path to Ruin* (Princeton: Princeton University Press, 1984).

35. Britain's twentieth century problem of imperial defense with too few means may be considered via Michael Howard, *The Continental Commitment: The Dilemma of British Defence Policy in the Era of the Two World Wars* (London: Temple Smith, 1972); James Neidpath, *The Singapore Naval Base and the Defence of Britain's Eastern Empire, 1919–1941* (Oxford: Clarendon Press, 1981); Correlli Barnett, *The Collapse of British Power* (Gloucester, Eng.: Alan Sutton, 1984; first pub. 1972); and Anthony Clayton, *The British Empire as a Superpower, 1919–39* (Athens: University of Georgia Press, 1986).

36. See Paul W. Schroeder, "Alliances, 1815–1945: Weapons of Power and Tools of Management," in Klaus Knorr, ed., *Historical Dimensions of National Security Problems* (Lawrence: University Press of Kansas, 1976), pp. 227–62. The idea that in some important senses countries wage war "against" their allies as well their enemies is developed instructively in David French, *British Strategy and War Aims, 1914–1916* (London: Allen and Unwin, 1986).

37. Although there is some truth to the claim that a country appreciates geographically distant, powerful allies because they are distant, it is not true that they are valued only because they are distant. The first-order attraction of the United States as an ally has been its relative strength. Its distance from Europe and Asia is strictly a second-order advantage but also a logistical inconvenience. States do not select allies on the basis of their distance from the geopolitical temptation to become overbearing. Stephen M. Walt, "Alliance Formation and the Balance of World Power," *International Security* 9 (Spring 1985): 3–43, is not as clear on the distinction between distance and strength as he should be.

38. Francis Fukuyama, "The End of History?" *National Interest*, no. 16 (Summer 1989): 3–18, and *The End of History and the Last Man* (New York: Free Press, 1992).

39. Tibor Szamuely, *The Russian Tradition* (New York: McGraw-Hill, 1974); Richard Pipes, *Russia under the Old Regime* (New York: Charles Scribner's Sons, 1974); Marc Raeff, *Understanding Imperial Russia: State and Society in*

*the Old Regime* (New York: Columbia University Press, 1984); and Marquis de Custine, *Empire of the Czar: A Journey through Eternal Russia* (New York: Doubleday, 1989; first pub. 1839), can be supplemented by the short interpretative essay, George F. Kennan, "Communism in Russian History," *Foreign Affairs* 69 (Winter 1990/91): 168–86.

40. The judgment in the text is close to the opinion of Edward Gibbon. "If a man were called to fix the period in the history of the world during which the condition of the human race was most happy and prosperous, he would, without hesitation, name that which elapsed from the death of Domitian [September 18, 96 A.D.] to the accession of Commodus [co-emperor with his father, Marcus Aurelius, from 177 A.D.]"; see *The History of the Decline and Fall of the Roman Empire*, ed. J. B. Bury (London: Methuen, 1909; first pub. 1776), 1:85–86.

41. One of the best treatments of the force of circumstance (brute empiricism perhaps) over policy and strategy is D. M. Schurman, "Historians and Britain's Imperial Strategic Stance in 1914," in John E. Flint and Glyndur Williams, eds., *Perspectives of Empire: Essays Presented to Gerald S. Graham* (New York: Barnes and Noble, 1973), pp. 172–88.

42. Secretary of Defense Dick Cheney, Prepared statement before the U.S. Congress, House of Representatives, Committee on Armed Services, *Authorization and Oversight, National Defense Authorization Act for Fiscal Year 1991— H.R. 4739, Hearings*, 101st Cong., 2nd sess. (Washington, D.C.: U.S. Government Printing Office, 1990), p. 11.

43. Steven Runciman, *A History of the Crusades*, Vol. 1, *The First Crusade and the Foundation of the Kingdom of Jerusalem* (Cambridge: Cambridge University Press, 1951), p. 51.

44. Samuel P. Huntington, "No Exit—The Errors of Endism," *National Interest*, no. 17 (Fall 1989): 5. Notwithstanding the dramatic changes registered since this article was written, Huntington's judgment is likely to stand the test of time.

45. The menace to American society from this cosmological quarter is statistically nontrivial. A catastrophic asteroid strike is more likely than is achievement of a peaceable new world order.

46. See the path-breaking three-volume study in military history by Allan R. Millett and Williamson Murray, eds., *Military Effectiveness* (Boston: Allen and Unwin, 1988). The volumes address World War I, the interwar years, and World War II, generally via the method of the country case study.

47. See John F. V. Keiger, *France and the Origins of the First World War* (London: Macmillan, 1983).

48. For the best brief explanation available of how the pursuit of national security for one nation can promote the national insecurity of others and incline them to respond with threats to the first country's security—possibly leaving it less secure than it was at the outset—see Robert Jervis, *The Meaning of the Nuclear Revolution: Statecraft and the Prospect of Armageddon* (Ithaca: Cornell University Press, 1989), pp. 53–57.

49. It is widely believed that in arms control agreements, the "devil is in the details." This popular view is not without merit, but it pales in significance compared to the belief that the "terror is in the trends." The details of a prospective treaty do not much matter if the treaty does the wrong things for U.S. security.

50. George Bush, *National Security Strategy of the United States* (Washing-

ton, D.C.: White House, August 1991), p. 31. Dick Cheney, *Annual Report to the President and the Congress* (Washington, D.C.: U.S. Government Printing Office, February 1992), pp. 1–10, and Colin L. Powell (Chairman, Joint Chiefs of Staff), *The National Military Strategy, 1992* (Washington, D.C.: Department of Defense, 1992), also are important.

51. Clausewitz, *On War*, pp. 119–21.

52. James Kurth, "The Shape of the New World Order," *National Interest*, no. 24 (Summer 1991), pp. 3–12, is relevant.

53. A superb case study in the ability and willingness to learn from experience is Williamson Murray, "The German Response to Victory in Poland: A Case Study in Professionalism," *Armed Forces and Society* 7 (Winter 1981): 285–98.

54. SIOP: Single Integrated Operational Plan—the U.S. nuclear war plan.

55. Dick Cheney, *Annual Report of the Secretary of Defense to the President and the Congress* (Washington, D.C.: U.S. Government Printing Office, January 1991), pp. v, 5, 133.

56. See Colin S. Gray, *House of Cards: Why Arms Control Must Fail* (Ithaca: Cornell University Press, 1992), chap. 4.

57. *The War Speeches of William Pitt the Younger* (Oxford: Clarendon Press, 1914), p. 16.

58. Sun Tzu, *The Art of War*, trans. Samuel B. Griffith (Oxford: Clarendon Press, 1963), p. 84.

59. Quoted in Charles Whiting, *The Poor Bloody Infantry, 1939–1945* (London: Arrow Books, 1989; first pub. 1987), pp. 176–77.

60. Ibid., pp. 251–54.

61. In the words of retired U.S. Army Chief of Staff General Fred C. Weyand: "The American way of war is particularly violent, deadly and dreadful. We believe in using 'things'—artillery, bombs, massive firepower—in order to conserve our soldiers' lives" (quoted in Harry G. Summers, *On Strategy: A Critical Analysis of the Vietnam War* [Novato, Calif.: Presidio Press, 1982], p. 40).

62. Clausewitz, *On War*, pp. 566–73.

63. Robert P. Haffa, Jr., *Rational Methods, Prudent Choices: Planning U.S. Forces* (Washington, D.C.: National Defense University Press, 1988), p. 3.

64. Rational behavior need not be sensible behavior. Rationality is a value-neutral concept. See the extensive discussion in Edward Rhodes, *Power and MADness: The Logic of Nuclear Coercion* (New York: Columbia University Press, 1989), pp. 50–52.

65. "The best strategy is always *to be very strong*; first in general, and then at the decisive point" (Clausewitz, *On War*, p. 204; emphasis in original).

66. For example, there is little empirical historical basis for the 3:1 rule: the claim that the offensive in land warfare requires a favorable 3:1 ratio. The alleged 3:1 rule has no meaning whatsoever for unconventional, sea, air, strategic-missile, and space warfare.

67. Fred Charles Iklé, "The Ghost in the Pentagon: Rethinking America's Defense," *National Interest*, no. 19 (Spring 1990): 20.

68. Albert Wohlstetter et al., *Selection and Use of Strategic Air Bases*, R-266 (Santa Monica, Calif.: Rand Corporation, April 1954).

69. Fred Kaplan, *The Wizards of Armageddon* (New York: Simon and Schuster, 1983), pp. 109–10.

70. Dean Wilkening et al., *Strategic Defenses and Crisis Stability*, N-2511-AF (Santa Monica, Calif.: Rand Corporation, April 1989), p. 3.

71. Russell E. Dougherty, "The Psychological Climate of Nuclear Command," in Ashton B. Carter, John D. Steinbruner, and Charles A. Zraket, eds., *Managing Nuclear Operations* (Washington, D.C.: Brookings Institution, 1987), p. 416.

72. Haffa, *Rational Methods, Prudent Choices*, p. 35.

73. See Robert I. Rotberg and Theodore K. Rabb, eds., *The Origin and Prevention of Major Wars* (Cambridge: Cambridge University Press, 1989), and Jack S. Levy, "The Causes of War: A Review of Theories and Evidence," in Philip E. Tetlock et al., eds., *Behavior, Society, and Nuclear War*, vol. 1 (New York: Oxford University Press, 1989), pp. 209–333. Even the arms-control minded contributors to Kurt Gottfried and Bruce G. Blair, eds., *Crisis Stability and Nuclear War* (New York: Oxford University Press, 1988), advise that "the risk that ongoing competition between the superpowers could lead to crisis and then to war is ultimately governed by politics, not technology" (p. 160). They do proceed with the qualification that, "nevertheless, technology can create new military capabilities that could exacerbate a crisis," though convincing evidence in support of this familiar proposition is not forthcoming. Robert Jervis, "Arms Control, Stability, and Causes of War," *Daedalus* 120 (Winter 1991): 167–81, provides a superior treatment.

## CHAPTER SIX. TECHNOLOGICAL PEACE AND POLITICAL PEACE

1. See Donald G. Brennan, "Setting and Goals of Arms Control," in Brennan, ed., *Arms Control, Disarmament, and National Security* (New York: George Braziller, 1961), pp. 19–42; Thomas C. Schelling and Morton H. Halperin, *Strategy and Arms Control* (New York: Twentieth Century Fund, 1961), pp. 1–5; Hedley Bull, *The Control of the Arms Race: Disarmament and Arms Control in the Missile Age* (London: Weidenfeld and Nicolson, 1961), pp. 3–29; Bernard Brodie, "On the Objectives of Arms Control," *International Security* 1 (Summer 1976): 17–36; and of particular note, Thomas C. Schelling, "From an Airport Bench," *Bulletin of the Atomic Scientists* 45 (May 1989): 29–31.

2. This argument is developed in detail in Patrick Glynn, *Closing Pandora's Box: Arms Races, Arms Control, and the History of the Cold War* (New York: Basic Books, 1992), chap. 1, and Colin S. Gray, *House of Cards: Why Arms Control Must Fail*, (Ithaca: Cornell University Press, 1992).

3. In *Icarus Restrained: An Intellectual History of Nuclear Arms Control, 1945–1960* (Boulder, Colo.: Westview Press, 1990), Jennifer E. Sims shows that less was invented in the late 1950s than is typically asserted. The fact remains that the principal thrust behind modern arms control theory and practice was provided by the Rand Corporation's "vulnerability" studies on U.S. bomber and ICBM survivability and the alleged implications of vulnerability for the perils of preemptive attack. Modern arms control theory has had as its centerpiece the determination to alleviate the theoretical perils of "the reciprocal fear of surprise attack." The modern theory of crisis stability is the immediate offspring of the Rand studies, which saw the danger of war in the military postures themselves. In the chapter entitled "Strategic Thought in America,

1952–1966," in Marc Trachtenberg, *History and Strategy* (Princeton: Princeton University Press, 1991), pp. 3–46, Trachtenburg argues that there is a direct link between the Rand studies and modern arms control theory.

4. Benjamin Isaac, *The Limits of Empire: The Roman Army in the East* (Oxford: Clarendon Press, 1990), pp. 261, 263–64.

5. See Philippe Contamine, *War in the Middle Ages* (Oxford: Basil Blackwell, 1984; first pub. 1980), chap. 10.

6. An outstanding treatment is Geoffrey Best, *Humanity in Warfare* (New York: Columbia University Press, 1980). Michael Howard, ed., *Restraints on War: Studies in the Limitation of Armed Conflict* (Oxford: Oxford University Press, 1979), is also useful.

7. This concern pervades Schelling and Halperin, *Strategy and Arms Control*; Scott D. Sagan, "Nuclear Alerts and Crisis Management," *International Security* 9 (Spring 1985): 99–139; and Kurt Gottfried and Bruce G. Blair, eds., *Crisis Stability and Nuclear War* (New York: Oxford University Press, 1988).

8. See Colin S. Gray, *The Geopolitics of Super Power* (Lexington: University Press of Kentucky, 1988).

9. A superior example of analysis in this genre is Mary LeCron Foster and Robert A. Rubinstein, *Peace and War: Cross-Cultural Perspectives* (New Brunswick, N.J.: Transaction Books, 1986). On the relevance, or alleged relevance, of psychology to security problems, see Robert Jervis, Richard Ned Lebow, and Janice Gross Stein, *Psychology and Deterrence* (Baltimore: Johns Hopkins University Press, 1985), and Robert Jervis, *The Meaning of the Nuclear Revolution: Statecraft and the Prospect of Armageddon* (Ithaca: Cornell University Press, 1989).

10. For a very different view, see Ralph K. White, *Nobody Wanted War: Misperception in Vietnam and Other Wars* (New York: Anchor Books, 1970; first pub. 1968). It is relevant to note than White is a social psychologist. The most powerful and persuasive case for the importance of perception and misperception in security affairs is Robert Jervis, *Perception and Misperception in International Politics* (Princeton: Princeton University Press, 1976).

11. Schelling and Halperin, *Strategy and Arms Control*, p. 1.

12. Ibid., p. 4.

13. Joseph S. Nye, Jr., argues that "arms control is part of a political process. Too often the experts judge arms control proposals on their technical details rather than on their political significance" ("Arms Control After the Cold War," *Foreign Affairs* 68 [Winter 1989/90]: 44). By way of some contrast, Michael Howard has offered the thought that "strategic arms control is driven by a logic of its own that bears little relation to political circumstances. . . . As the political climate changes, the calculations of strategic analysts, however logical, become increasingly remote from real probabilities. Eventually a point is reached when the calculus of military capabilities is overtaken by that of perceived intentions; intentions shaped not only by state interests but by political culture" ("The remaking of Europe," *Survival* 32 [March/April 1990]: 101).

14. The view of Albert Carnesale and Richard N. Haass, eds., *Superpower Arms Control: Setting the Record Straight* (Cambridge, Mass.: Ballinger, 1987). Arms control has been described pejoratively as "this piecemeal approach to peace" in Harry B. Hollins, Averill L. Powers, and Mark Sommer, *The Conquest of War: Alternative Strategies for Global Security* (Boulder, Colo.: Westview Press, 1989), p. 14.

15. An excellent discussion is Paul M. Kennedy, *The Rise and Fall of British Naval Mastery* (New York: Charles Scribner's Sons, 1976), chaps. 10–11. Also persuasive is Correlli Barnett, *The Collapse of British Power* (Gloucester, Eng.: Alan Sutton, 1984; first pub. 1972), chap. 5. For a detailed indictment of naval arms control in terms of its potential war-losing consequences, see Correlli Barnett, *Engage the Enemy More Closely: The Royal Navy in the Second World War* (New York: W. W. Norton, 1991), pp. 15, 22, 24, 36, 37, 43, 64–65, 78.

16. The "double-zero" of the INF treaty—banning ground-launched ballistic and cruise missiles with ranges between 500 and 5,500 kms—was a frontal challenge to Bonn's concepts and material preferences for nuclear deterrence in Europe. In 1987 Germans objected to the "singularization" of their homeland (then homelands) by a treaty regime that implied a putative nuclear battlefield defined geographically by weapons with ranges of less than 500 kms; in other words, a *German* battlefield, given the geopolitics and geostrategy of European security in 1987–1988. Whether or not arguments of this kind were valid, they were widely accepted in West Germany. Incredible though it may seem, the implications for Germany of the INF were not considered carefully by U.S. negotiators.

17. NATO and what used to be the Warsaw Pact may each maintain no more than 20,000 tanks in Europe. NATO's treaty-accountable tank holdings totalled 22,900 at the time of treaty signature, while the composite figure for the Warsaw Pact was *approximately* 36,798 (11,900 non-Soviet and 24,898 Soviet). Subsequent to the CFE treaty signing on November 19, 1990, disturbing evidence surfaced that the Soviet accounting of their treaty-accountable equipment holdings was far too low. The mass movement of equipment, plainly treaty-evasive, from European locations to sites beyond the Urals was impossible to miss or to ignore.

18. As Charles S. Maier has written of German policy and strategic choices in 1914: "Again, we come to the irreducible primacy of political determinants of war: political in the assessment of the respective threats to security (the danger to Austrian statehood or to the two alliance systems) and political in the failure of mediation" ("Wargames: 1914–1919," in Robert I. Rotberg and Theodore K. Rabb, eds., *The Origin and Prevention of Major Wars* [Cambridge: Cambridge University Press, 1989], p. 263).

19. In 1990 the U.S. Navy expected to reduce its total size from about 550 ships to perhaps 450, with the number of deployable carriers descending from 14 to 12 (Department of the Navy, *Meeting the Challenges of a Dynamic World: Naval Policy for the '90s and Beyond* [Washington, D.C.: Department of the Navy, 1990]). These ideas on "naval policy for the '90s" formally replaced the maritime strategy of the 1980s. A year later, in 1991, the carrier force was expected to descend to 9 rather than to 12. By mid-1992, best guess estimates for the future size of the Navy were at levels in the 300–600 range. In the absence of the discipline of a clear and present foreign danger of superpower proportions, U.S. Navy force levels could go into a free-fall mode, driven by politics and economics rather than by strategic thinking and planning. See Sam J. Tangredi, *The Means to Deliver: Implications of the New National Strategy for Maritime Forces*, Working Papers in International Studies 1-91-8 (Stanford, Calif.: Hoover Institution, Stanford University, May 1991); Harlan K. Ullman, *In Harm's Way: American Seapower and the 21st Century* (Silver Spring, Md.:

Bartleby Press, 1991); and particularly Donald C. F. Daniel, *Beyond the 600-Ship Navy*, Adelphi Papers no. 261 (London: IISS, Autumn 1991).

20. This sentence may read like a parody, but it is not. Skeptics are invited to peruse these house journals of the arms control advocacy community, *Arms Control Today* and *Bulletin of the Atomic Scientists*. Of course the polar opposite of this view also exists. Specifically, there are people who will advocate any and every weapon idea that promises to be, from a military-technical viewpoint, highly lethal, whether or not there is plausible strategic need for it.

21. This problem for arms control parallels the force-planning and weapons acquisition dilemmas that, as noted in chapter 5 above, are sidestepped in Robert P. Haffa, Jr., *Rational Methods, Prudent Choices: Planning U.S. Forces* (Washington, D.C.: National Defense University Press, 1988). A useful annotated bibliography is Gregory Rattray, "Force Planning," in Schuyler Foerster and Edward N. Wright, eds., *American Defense Policy*, 6th ed. (Baltimore: Johns Hopkins University Press, 1990), pp. 518–24.

22. President's Commission on Strategic Forces, *Report* (Washington, D.C.: White House, April 1983), p. 3.

23. Bernard Brodie once observed, tartly and accurately, that "no such thing as accidental war has happened within the last three hundred years, if ever" ("On the Objectives of Arms Control," p. 26). Also see Paul Bracken, "Accidental Nuclear War," in Graham T. Allison, Albert Carnesale, and Joseph S. Nye, Jr., eds., *Hawks, Doves, and Owls: An Agenda for Avoiding Nuclear War* (New York: W. W. Norton, 1985), pp. 25–53.

24. For generally negative assessments of the Washington treaty system, see Christopher Hall, *Britain, America and Arms Control, 1921–37* (New York: St. Martin's Press, 1987), and Robert Gordon Kaufman, *Arms Control during the Pre-Nuclear Era: The United States and Naval Limitation between the Two World Wars* (New York: Columbia University Press, 1990). Also useful is chapter 2, "Does Arms Control Control Arms?" in Bruce D. Berkowitz, *Calculated Risks: A Century of Arms Control, Why It Has Failed, and How It Can be Made to Work* (New York: Simon and Schuster, 1987). Two arguments, the first generally in praise of the ABM treaty and the second generally critical of it may be found, respectively, in Antonia Handler Chayes and Paul Doty, eds., *Defending Deterrence: Managing the ABM Treaty Regime into the 21st Century* (Washington, D.C.: Pergamon-Brassey's, 1989), and Keith B. Payne, *Strategic Defense: "Star Wars" in Perspective* (Lanham, Md.: Hamilton Press, 1986), particularly chap. 8.

25. See Lothar Rühle, "Offensive Defence in the Warsaw Pact," *Survival* 33 (September/October 1991): 442–500.

26. See the observation to this effect in Kenneth L. Adelman, *The Great Universal Embrace: Arms Summitry—A Skeptic's Account* (New York: Simon and Schuster, 1989), p. 34.

27. My thesis in *House of Cards*.

28. Readers can judge for themselves from U.S. Congress, Senate Committee on Foreign Relations, *The INF Treaty, Hearings*, 100th Cong., 2nd sess. (Washington, D.C.: U.S. Government Printing Office, 1988).

29. Prominent among the better analyses of nuclear weapons in the grand strategic thinking of NATO-Europe, is David N. Schwartz, *NATO's Nuclear Dilemmas* (Washington, D.C.: Brookings Institution, 1983). The policy and strategic meanings of the SS-20 are analysed interestingly and controversially in

Jonathan Haslam, *The Soviet Union and the Politics of Nuclear Weapons in Europe, 1969–87* (Ithaca: Cornell University Press, 1990), particularly chap. 4.

30. "The Soviet Union does not need nuclear weapons to conquer Western Europe; NATO does need them to deter and to defeat a Soviet attack." Samuel P. Huntington, "Coping with the Lippmann Gap," *Foreign Affairs* 66 (Winter 1987/88): 466.

31. U.S. Arms Control and Disarmament Agency, *Fact Sheet, The Strategic Arms Reduction Treaty, START Data Base*, August 1, 1991. An authoritative "package" on START is U.S. Arms Control and Disarmament Agency, *START, The Strategic Arms Reduction Treaty, U.S.-Soviet Summit, Moscow, July 30-31, 1991.* Some of that ACDA material is reproduced in *Survival* 33 (September/October 1991): 466–70.

32. For example, as in Brent Scowcroft, John Deutch, and R. James Woolsey, "Come and Get Us," *New Republic*, April 18, 1988, pp. 16, 18. A different view is taken in Colin S. Gray, "ICBM's and Deterrence: The Controversy Over Prompt Launch," *Journal of Strategic Studies* 10 (September 1987): 285–309.

33. A richly textured discussion that finds more to praise than to criticize about START is Walter B. Slocombe, "Strategic stability in a restructured world," *Survival* 32 (July/August 1990): 299–312. Kenneth L. Adelman, "Just a Sideshow," *Bulletin of the Atomic Scientists* 47 (November 1991): 19–21, and Alexei G. A. Arbatov, "We Could Have Done Better," *Bulletin of the Atomic Scientists* 47 (November 1991): 36–40, 47, also are useful. Arbatov, a member of the Soviet START delegation, writes: "While negotiating START in 1987–91, the parties were not operating on any mutual understanding of the meaning of 'stability'." He notes that "only at the final stage of talks did the Americans and Soviets arrive at a common definition of strategic stability, *albeit a general and vague one. We can infer* that at the Washington summit in June 1990, U.S.-Soviet strategic stability was defined as a state in which the incentives for a first strike have been removed" (p. 37); emphasis added.

34. We must remember that in addition to being a principal author of the ABM treaty of 1972, Paul Nitze also tackled the heroic ground-breaking task, in the mid-1980s, of specifying three exacting and controversial criteria a strategic defensive system (SDS) would have to meet if it were to be approved. Nitze stipulated that an SDS must be technologically effective against the offense, survivable, and cost effective at the margin. See Paul H. Nitze, "On the Road to a More Stable Peace" [address to the Philadelphia World Affairs Council, February 20, 1985], reprinted in Samuel F. Wells, Jr., and Robert S. Litwak, eds., *Strategic Defenses and Soviet-American Relations* (Cambridge, Mass.: Ballinger, 1987), pp. 193–99.

35. DSAT: defense of satellite (systems). This is a compound acronym embracing all measures, active and passive, designed to protect all three segments of satellite systems (that is, platforms on-orbit, up and down links, and ground facilities).

36. Fred Charles Iklé, "After Detection—What?" *Foreign Affairs* 39 (January 1961): 208–20, remains an excellent fundamental discussion. The classic texts on modern arms control theory, for all their sophistication and ingenuity, failed to grasp the nature and persistence of the problem of noncompliance. They also failed to appreciate the severity of the difficulty democracies would face in designing and executing a response policy. For example, see Schelling and Halperin, *Strategy and Arms Control*, pp. 100–101. This is not simply a

case of being wise after the event. After all, the United States and Britain had grappled with the problem of policy in response to arms control treaty violations in the 1930s. See Robin Ranger, "Learning from the Naval Arms Control Experience," *Washington Quarterly* 10 (Summer 1987): 47–58, and Kaufman, *Arms Control during the Pre-Nuclear Era*, passim.

37. See Kenneth L. Adelman's lament in "Where We Succeeded, Where We Failed," *Policy Review*, no. 43 (Winter 1988): 44–45.

38. An argument I have advanced in some detail in "Does Verification Really Matter? Facing Political Facts about Arms Control Non-Compliance," *Strategic Review* 17 (Spring 1990): 32–42.

39. The scope of the U.S. problem was graphically outlined in a November 15, 1985, memorandum by Secretary of Defense Caspar Weinberger to President Reagan. This instructive document was published as " 'Dear Mr. President': A Confidential Memorandum in Washington," *Encounter* 66 (May 1986): 71–75. Also relevant is Robin Ranger, *The Naval Arms Control Record, 1919–1939: Axis Violations Versus Democratic Compliance Policy Failures* (Fairfax, Va.: National Security Research, 1987).

40. George Bush, "Report to the Congress on Soviet Noncompliance with Arms Control Agreements" (Washington, D.C.: White House, February 6, 1991), p. 2.

41. See Kerry M. Kartchner, "Soviet Compliance with a START Agreement: Prospects under Gorbachev," *Strategic Review* 17 (Fall 1989): 47–57, and Sven F. Kraemer, "The Krasnoyarsk Saga," *Strategic Review* 18 (Winter 1990): 25–38.

42. Bernard Brodie wrote of Anglo-American naval disarmament in connection with the 1930 London treaty: "Great Britain and the United States, between whom no antagonism worth mentioning existed, proceeded to disarm each other in an unsettled world, relying completely, as Admiral Beamish put it, 'upon faith, hope, and parity, with parity said to be the most important of all' " (*Sea Power in the Machine Age* [Princeton: Princeton University Press, 1941], p. 336). Also see Hedley Bull, "Strategic Arms Limitation: The Precedent of the Washington and London Naval Treaties," in Morton A. Kaplan, ed., *SALT: Problems and Prospects* (Morristown, N.J.: General Learning Press, 1973), pp. 27–28, 42, 50–51; John Newhouse, *Cold Dawn: The Story of SALT* (New York: Holt, Rinehart and Winston, 1973), pp. 4–5; and Kaufman, *Arms Control during the Pre-Nuclear Era*, p. 196.

43. Kaufman, *Arms Control during the Pre-Nuclear Era*, p. 4.

CHAPTER SEVEN. NUCLEAR-AGE HISTORY

1. Henry R. Luce, "The American Century," *Life*, February 17, 1941, pp. 61–65.

2. The distinctly technological peace that many people believe has been imposed by mutual nuclear deterrence—witness the popularity of the concept of *the* nuclear deterrent—is all too easily analyzed with scant reference to the strength of the political motives extant for the promotion of disorder. Discussion of nuclear strategy and of the strategic forces posture typically is abstracted from any pertinent, let alone plausible, political context.

3. Carl von Clausewitz, *On War*, trans. Michael Howard and Peter Paret

(Princeton: Princeton University Press, 1976; first pub. 1832), particularly pp. 605–10. The uncritical parroting of the translated words—which may or may not represent the thought accurately—of a long dead strategic philosopher is a phenomenon that should not be greeted with enthusiasm. Clausewitz's greatness is not in question, but his theorizing should not be confused with divine inspiration. Michael I. Handel, ed., *Clausewitz and Modern Strategy, Journal of Strategic Studies* 9 (June/September 1986), is useful, as are Raymond Aron, *Penser la guerre, Clausewitz*, 2 vols. (Paris: Éditions Gallimard, 1976); Michael Howard, *Clausewitz* (New York: Oxford University Press, 1983); Peter Paret, "Clausewitz," in Paret, ed., *Makers of Modern Strategy: From Machiavelli to the Nuclear Age* (Princeton: Princeton University Press, 1986), pp. 186–213; Azar Gat, *The Origins of Military Thought: From the Enlightenment to Clausewitz* (Oxford: Clarendon Press, 1989), chaps. 6–7; and Michael I. Handel, *Sun Tzu and Clausewitz:* The Art of War *and* On War *Compared* (Carlisle Barracks, Pa.: Strategic Studies Institute, U.S. Army War College, 1991).

4. See Michael Howard, ed., *Restraints on War: Studies in the Limitation of Armed Conflict* (Oxford: Oxford University Press, 1979), and Geoffrey Best, *Humanity in Warfare* (New York: Columbia University Press, 1980).

5. Barry S. Strauss and Josiah Ober, *The Anatomy of Error: Ancient Military Disasters and Their Lessons for Modern Strategists* (New York: St. Martin's Press, 1990), p. 9. This misquotation (it should be "know the enemy and know yourself") is from Sun Tzu, *The Art of War*, trans. Samuel B. Griffith (Oxford: Clarendon Press, 1963), p. 84.

6. This criticism (of myself, among others) is leveled in Robert Jervis, *The Illogic of American Nuclear Strategy* (Ithaca: Cornell University Press, 1984), pp. 56–63, and Charles Philippe David, *Debating Counterforce: A Conventional Approach in a Nuclear Age* (Boulder, Colo.: Westview Press, 1987), passim. According to Professor David, I am guilty of "conventional nuclear strategic thinking" (see pp. 24–28, in particular). Readers must judge for themselves where the balance of prudence or wisdom lies. They could try Colin S. Gray: "Nuclear Strategy: What Is True, What Is False, What Is Arguable," *Comparative Strategy* 9 (1990): 1–32, and *War, Peace, and Victory: Strategy and Statecraft for the Next Century* (New York: Simon and Schuster, 1990), chap. 9, "Nuclear Weapons and Strategy." Some readers may find utility in Stephen Kull, *Minds at War: Nuclear Reality and the Inner Conflicts of Defense Policymakers* (New York: Basic Books, 1988).

7. "Weapons are impotent without an organization that can decide whether, when, and how they are to be employed. Those decisions can only be a selection from among a set of detailed plans that have already been incorporated into lengthy military training programs" (Kurt Gottfried and Bruce G. Blair, eds., *Crisis Stability and Nuclear War* [New York: Oxford University Press, 1988], p. 20).

8. A brave, though only partially successful, endeavor to square the circle of military effectiveness with orthodox views of crisis stability is Scott D. Sagan, *Moving Targets: Nuclear Strategy and National Security* (Princeton: Princeton University Press, 1989), chap. 2, "Second-Strike Counterforce."

9. See J. Michael Legge, *Theater Nuclear Weapons and the NATO Strategy of Flexible Response*, R-2964-FF (Santa Monica, Calif.: Rand Corporation, April 1983).

10. But see the fascinating debate: John Mueller, "The Essential Irrele-

vance of Nuclear Weapons: Stability in the Postwar World," *International Security* 13 (Fall 1988): 55–79, as contrasted with Robert Jervis, "The Political Effects of Nuclear Weapons: A Comment," *International Security* 13 (Fall 1988): 80–90.

11. Bernard Brodie, *War and Politics* (New York: Macmillan, 1973), chap. 9.

12. On the contrary, it drives the strategically literate, if unpersuasive, argument in Edward Rhodes, *Power and MADness: The Logic of Nuclear Coercion* (New York: Columbia University Press, 1989).

13. See Richard K. Betts, *Nuclear Blackmail and Nuclear Balance* (Washington, D.C.: Brookings Institution, 1987), pp. 54–62, 68–79.

14. See Keith B. Payne, *Strategic Defense: "Star Wars" in Perspective* (Lanham, Md.: Hamilton Press, 1986), pp. 37–38, and Robert C. McFarlane, "Effective Strategic Policy," *Foreign Affairs* 67 (Fall 1988): 41, 47.

15. Bruce Smith, *The Rand Corporation: Case Study of a Nonprofit Advisory Corporation* (Cambridge: Harvard University Press, 1966), is a distinctly friendly history. Less friendly is Fred Kaplan, *The Wizards of Armageddon* (New York: Simon and Schuster, 1983). Marc Trachtenberg, "Strategic Thought in America, 1952–1966," in Trachtenberg, *History and Strategy* (Princeton: Princeton University Press, 1991), pp. 3–46, is generally persuasive.

16. A late-1980s bibliographical essay was comfortable with, and perhaps even complacent about, the judgment that "the early classics of postwar strategic thought, *little improved on since*, have been reproduced in this book" (Philipp Bobbitt, Lawrence Freedman, and Gregory F. Treverton, eds., *U.S. Nuclear Strategy: A Reader* [New York: New York University Press, 1989], p. 520; emphasis added).

17. See Bernard Brodie, "Implications for Military Policy," in Brodie, ed., *The Absolute Weapon: Atomic Power and World Order* (New York: Harcourt Brace, 1946), p. 76. Colin S. Gray, *Strategic Studies and Public Policy: The American Experience* (Lexington: University Press of Kentucky, 1982), is an analytical history of the subject. Somewhat different in focus is Lawrence Freedman, *The Evolution of Nuclear Strategy*, 2d ed. (New York: St. Martin's Press, 1989).

18. See Morton H. Halperin, *Limited War in the Nuclear War* (New York: John Wiley and Sons, 1963), and Robert E. Osgood, *Limited War Revisited* (Boulder, Colo.: Westview Press, 1979).

19. See Hedley Bull, *The Control of the Arms Race: Disarmament and Arms Control in the Missile Age* (London: Weidenfeld and Nicolson, 1961), parts 1–2.

20. See Hedley Bull, "Strategic Studies and Its Critics," *World Politics* 20 (July 1968): 600, and the discussion in Colin S. Gray, *Strategic Studies: A Critical Assessment* (Westport, Conn.: Greenwood Press, 1982), chap. 4. When developed apart from politics, strategy is necessarily reduced to an operational artistry which, bereft of policy guidance, is mere military technique.

21. An outstanding treatment is Ken Booth, "The Concept of Strategic Culture Affirmed," in Carl G. Jacobsen, ed., *Strategic Power: USA/USSR* (New York: St. Martin's Press, 1990), pp. 121–28.

22. See Clausewitz, *On War*, p. 595.

23. These judgments are offered notwithstanding empathetic appreciation of President Bush's dilemma. Two reasons, above all others, drove him to terminate hostilities when he did. First, he did not want the legitimacy of the military victory of Desert Storm sullied by further mass killing of helpless Iraqi

soldiery on the run. Second, he did not want to assume responsibility for the administration and political integrity of a *totally* defeated Iraq. The fact remains that the United States greatly overestimated Saddam Hussein's political vulnerability and failed to secure a satisfactory policy outcome. Lawrence Freedman and Efrain Karsh, "How Kuwait Was Won: Strategy in the Gulf War," *International Security* 16 (Fall 1991): 5–41, is useful but rather weak.

24. See the apposite comments in Edward N. Luttwak, *Strategy: The Logic of War and Peace* (Cambridge: Harvard University Press, 1987), p. 20.

25. The belief that mutual vulnerability to an intolerable level of nuclear damage discounts the significance of military details pervades Robert Jervis, *The Meaning of the Nuclear Revolution: Statecraft and the Prospect of Armageddon* (Ithaca: Cornell University Press, 1989); pp. 9, 22, 43, and 98 are particularly explicit on this point.

26. The superior study is Robert A. Levine, *Still the Arms Debate* (Brookfield, Vt.: Dartmouth Publishing, 1990).

27. William W. Kaufmann and John D. Steinbruner pointedly entitled a subsection in a recent study, "How Many Iraqs?" (*Decisions For Defense: Prospects for a New Order* [Washington, D.C.: Brookings Institution, 1991], pp. 44–45).

28. See Thomas C. Schelling, *Arms and Influence* (New Haven: Yale University Press, 1966), chap. 2.

29. Desmond Ball has argued that "much of the discrimination that has been programmed into U.S. nuclear war plans in recent years is probably significant only to U.S. target planners themselves; it is most unlikely to be unmistakably obvious to the adversary" ("Toward a Critique of Strategic Nuclear Targeting," in Desmond Ball and Jeffrey Richelson, eds., *Strategic Nuclear Targeting* [Ithaca: Cornell University Press, 1986], p. 19).

30. Herman Kahn, *On Thermonuclear War* (New York: Free Press, 1969; first pub. 1960), p. 126.

31. See Eliot Cohen, "The Future of Force," *National Interest*, no. 21 (Fall 1990): particularly p. 15.

32. For two interesting analyses of change on the Soviet side *prior to the August 1990 coup attempt*, see Raymond L. Garthoff, *Deterrence and the Revolution in Soviet Military Doctrine* (Washington, D.C.: Brookings Institution, 1990), and Harry Gelman, *Gorbachev and the Future of the Soviet Military Institution*, Adelphi Papers no. 258 (London: IISS, Spring 1991).

33. Strategic deadlock has been the theme of many studies over the past three decades. For examples many years apart, see Neville Brown, *Nuclear War: The Impending Strategic Deadlock* (London: Pall Mall Press, 1964); Michael Krepon, *Strategic Stalemate: Nuclear Weapons and Arms Control in American Politics* (New York: St. Martin's Press, 1984); and Michael Nacht, *The Age of Vulnerability: Threats to the Nuclear Stalemate* (Washington, D.C.: Brookings Institution, 1985).

34. Writing about U.S. extended nuclear deterrence on behalf of NATO-Europe, Lawrence Freedman advised that "this is one of those areas where a policy has worked far better in practice than an assessment of the theory might lead one to expect" (*The Evolution of Nuclear Strategy* [London: Macmillan, 1981], p. xvi).

35. Lawrence Freedman, "On the Tiger's Back: The Development of the Concept of Escalation," in Roman Kolkowicz, ed., *The Logic of Nuclear Terror*

(Boston: Allen and Unwin, 1987), pp. 109–52, and Colin S. Gray, "Strategic De-Escalation," in Stephen J. Cimbala and Joseph D. Douglass, Jr., eds., *Ending a Nuclear War: Are The Superpowers Prepared?* (Washington, D.C.: Pergamon-Brassey's, 1988), pp. 60–78.

36. It is possible, if far short of probable, that in the 1990s the United States and Russia could elect to celebrate the maturing of political peace between them by negotiating a condition of reciprocal defense dominance in strategic forces. In the context of a burgeoning defensive architecture, were such allowed, the START follow-on regime which permits no more than 3,000–4,000 warheads would begin to usher in this novel condition. If U.S. and Russian policymakers proceed progressively to disarm their countries of most of the long-range nuclear arsenals of today *and* develop and deploy strategic and theater missile defenses to cope with emerging regional threats, defense dominance will slowly emerge.

37. Jervis, *The Meaning of the Nuclear Revolution*, p. 22.

38. Edward N. Luttwak, "An Emerging Postnuclear Era?" *Washington Quarterly* 11 (Winter 1988): 5–15. In his article, "Essential Irrelevance of Nuclear Weapons," Mueller speculates that the character of the so-called nuclear age actually may have been significantly less nuclear as far as international security is concerned than has been popularly assumed.

39. See Henry S. Rowen and Richard Brody, "The Development of U.S. Nuclear Strategy and Employment Policy," in Andrew W. Marshall, J. J. Martin, and Henry S. Rowen, eds., *On Not Confusing Ourselves: Essays on National Security Strategy in Honor of Albert and Roberta Wohlstetter* (Boulder, Colo.: Westview Press, 1991), pp. 29–53; Jervis, *Illogic of American Nuclear Strategy*; Ball and Richelson, eds., *Strategic Nuclear Targeting*; William C. Martel and Paul L. Savage, *Strategic Nuclear War: What the Superpowers Target and Why* (Westport, Conn.: Greenwood Press, 1986); Sagan, *Moving Targets*; and Janne E. Nolan, *Guardians of the Arsenal: The Politics of Nuclear Strategy* (New York: Basic Books, 1989).

40. For the "Schlesinger Doctrine" of limited nuclear options, see Secretary of Defense James R. Schlesinger's testimony in U.S. Congress, Senate Committee on Foreign Relations, Subcommittee on Arms Control, International Law and Organization, *U.S.-U.S.S.R. Strategic Policies, Hearing*, 93rd Cong., 2d sess. (Washington, D.C.: U.S. Government Printing Office, March 1974). See also The Commission on Integrated Long-Term Strategy, *Discriminate Deterrence* (Washington, D.C.: U.S. Government Printing Office, January 1988).

41. On this possibility, even probability—given the geostrategic and geopolitical conditions of the 1980s—see F. J. West, Jr., "The Maritime Strategy: The Next Step," U.S. Naval Institute *Proceedings* 113 (January 1987): 40–49; D. J. Pay, "The U.S. Navy and the Defence of Europe," *Naval Forces* 9 (1988): 28–35; and Colin S. Gray, "The Maritime Strategy in U.S.-Soviet Strategic Relations," *Naval War College Review* 42 (Winter 1989): 7–18.

42. George Bush, "The Peace Dividend I Seek Is Not Measured in Dollars," *Washington Post*, September 28, 1991, p. A23.

43. Bull, *Control of the Arms Race*, p. 102.

44. See Wolfgang K. H. Panofsky, "The Mutual Hostage Relationship between America and Russia," *Foreign Affairs* 52 (October 1973): 109–18. This belief also pervades Jervis's treatment of the *Meaning of the Nuclear Revolution*, particularly chaps. 1–3.

45. See Paul M. Kennedy, *The Rise and Fall of British Naval Mastery* (New York: Charles Scribner's Sons, 1976), pp. 162–63. This thesis is generally true, but it lends itself to overstatement, as does its obverse—exaggerated claims for a substantially fictitious Pax Britannica.

46. Clausewitz, *On War*, p. 119.

47. "The Soviet passive defense program is a major element in an integrated system of strategic defense designed to lessen the effects of a nuclear attack" (U.S. Department of Defense, *Soviet Military Power: Prospects for Change, 1989* [Washington, D.C.: U.S. Department of Defense, September 1989], p. 52). The value of this program is arguable, but the fact of its existence is not.

48. Overall and notwithstanding the phenomenon of "new thinking," one should probably be slow to discard the history- and culture-based view of new Russian strategic attitudes that drives Christopher Donnelly, *Red Banner: The Soviet Military System in Peace and War* (Alexandria, Va.: Jane's, 1988).

49. See Barry M. Blechman and Douglas M. Hart, "The Political Utility of Nuclear Weapons: The 1973 Middle East Crisis," *International Security* 7 (Summer 1982): 132–56.

50. On general as contrasted with immediate deterrence, see Patrick Morgan, *Deterrence: A Conceptual Analysis* (Beverly Hills, Calif.: Sage Publications, 1977), chap. 2.

51. See Henry C. Bartlett, "Approaches to Force Planning," *Naval War College Review* 38 (May/June 1985): 37–48; Henry C. Bartlett and G. Paul Holman, Jr., "Strategy as a Guide to Force Planning," *Naval War College Review* 41 (Autumn 1988): 15–25; and Colin S. Gray, "From Defense Philosophy to Force Planning: The Strategic Forces," *Defense Analysis* 7 (December 1991): 363–72.

## CHAPTER EIGHT.  INSTRUMENTS OF POLICY

1. For the particular purposes of this book, it does not matter how the course of Russian history unfolds. It is clear enough, however, that each polity constructs, or invents, its future with the materials that are the legacy of its past, interacting with the challenges and opportunities of the present. In principle, all kinds of Russias are possible—they are certainly conceivable—but all kinds of Russias are not equally likely to emerge. To predict, for example, that liberal reform will fail on its own terms (or, indeed, on anybody else's terms) would be neither to deny the fact of change nor to assert a return to the political relations of the worst years of the cold war. U.S. foreign and defense policies frequently are praised or blamed, depending on the news of the day, by the small army of instant commentators who write opinion editorials or appear on television talk shows. However, world politics cannot be understood by means of a serial focus on the "play of the day," and neither can trends, or the fuel for trends, be identified that way.

2. Carl von Clausewitz, *On War*, trans. Michael Howard and Peter Paret (Princeton: Princeton University Press, 1976; first pub. 1832), book 1, chap. 7.

3. David Hackett Fischer, *Historians' Fallacies: Toward a Logic of Historical Thought* (New York: Harper and Row, 1970), p. 172; emphasis in original.

4. Clausewitz, *On War*, p. 605.

5. James Blackwell, Michael J. Mazarr, and Don M. Snider, *The Gulf War: Military Lessons Learned*, Interim Report of the CSIS Study Group on Lessons

Learned from the Gulf War (Washington, D.C.: Center for Strategic and International Studies, July 1991), p. 53.

6. See Marion William Boggs, *Attempts to Define and Limit "Aggressive" Armament in Diplomacy and Strategy*, University of Missouri Studies 16 (Columbia: University of Missouri, 1941).

7. Geoffrey Kemp has noticed that "thus, we have a Catch-22 situation. High-level arms-control initiatives on major weapon systems prior to an on-going peace process are unlikely to work unless the countries of the region agree to them." A little earlier Kemp advised, "if there is a lesson to be learned from the European experience on conventional arms-control negotiations, it is that until there is movement toward the resolution of basic political and geographic aspects of the problem, detailed blueprints for arms control will not succeed" ("Regional Security, Arms Control, and the End of the Cold War," *Washington Quarterly* 13 [Autumn 1990]: 47). W. Seth Carus, *Ballistic Missiles in the Third World: Threat and Response* (New York: Praeger Publishers, 1990), is also useful.

8. See Charles H. Fairbanks, Jr., "Arms Races: the Metaphor and the Facts," *National Interest*, no. 1 (Fall 1985): 75–90.

9. Johan J. Holst, "Comparative U.S. and Soviet Deployments, Doctrines, and Arms Limitation," in Morton A. Kaplan, ed., *SALT: Problems and Prospects* (Morristown, N.J.: General Learning Press, 1973), p. 68.

10. As in the following articles by Colin S. Gray: "The Arms Race Phenomenon," *World Politics* 24 (October 1971): 39–79; "Social Science and the Arms Race," *Bulletin of the Atomic Scientists* 39 (June 1973): 23–26; and "The Urge to Compete: Rationales for Arms Racing," *World Politics* 26 (January 1974): 207–33.

11. Clausewitz, *On War*, p. 85. See Katherine L. Herbig, "Chance and Uncertainty in *On War*," *Journal of Strategic Studies* 9 (June/September 1986): 95–116.

12. Andrew D. Lambert, *The Crimean War: British Grand Strategy against Russia, 1853–56* (Manchester, Eng.: Manchester University Press, 1990), p. 97.

13. Louis J. Halle, *The Elements of International Strategy: A Primer for the Nuclear Age* (Lanham, Md.: University Press of America, 1984), p. 73.

14. Ibid., p. 95.

15. For example, Britain's leading expert on counterinsurgency and counterrevolutionary war, Sir Robert Thompson, wrote in his memoirs of General Westmoreland's approach to the war in South Vietnam that, "when asked to give an answer to insurgency in one word it was 'fire-power' " (*Make for the Hills: Memoirs of Far Eastern Wars* [London: Leo Cooper, 1989], p. 151).

16. Robert Jervis, *The Meaning of the Nuclear Revolution: Statecraft and the Prospect of Armageddon* (Ithaca: Cornell University Press, 1989), p. 183.

17. The most useful single study is Bruce Palmer, Jr., *The 25-Year War: America's Military Role in Vietnam* (Lexington: University Press of Kentucky, 1984). Also valuable amidst a large and rapidly growing literature are Harry G. Summers, Jr., *On Strategy: A Critical Analysis of the Vietnam War* (Novato, Calif.: Presidio Press, 1982); Andrew F. Krepinevich, Jr., *The Army and Vietnam* (Baltimore: Johns Hopkins University Press, 1986); and Lawrence E. Grinter and Peter M. Dunn, eds., *The American War in Vietnam: Lessons, Legacies, and Implications for Future Conflicts* (Westport, Conn.: Greenwood Press, 1987).

18. The 1980s and now the 1990s have witnessed a intentional U.S. rejection of its Vietnam experience. Brute force, invincible brute force if possible, has been the traditional American way of war. See Russell F. Weigley, *The American Way of War: A History of United States Military Strategy and Policy* (New York: Macmillan, 1973), and John Ellis, *Brute Force: Allied Strategy and Tactics in the Second World War* (New York: Viking, 1990). The latter book, though generally sound, betrays some lack of empathy for historical figures.

19. See Donald G. Brennan, ed., *Arms Control, Disarmament, and National Security* (New York: George Braziller, 1961); Hedley Bull, *The Control of the Arms Race: Disarmament and Arms Control in the Missile Age* (London: Weidenfeld and Nicolson, 1961); and Thomas C. Schelling and Morton H. Halperin, *Strategy and Arms Control* (New York: Twentieth Century Fund, 1961).

20. For example, see Albert Carnesale and Richard N. Haass, eds., *Superpower Arms Control: Setting the Record Straight* (Cambridge, Mass.: Ballinger, 1987), p. 355. "What emerges above all else is the modesty of what arms control has wrought."

21. Quoted in Summers, *On Strategy*, p. 46.

22. Bernard Brodie," Technological Change, Strategic Doctrine, and Political Outcomes," in Klaus Knorr, ed., *Historical Dimensions of National Security Problems* (Lawrence: University Press of Kansas, 1976), p. 300.

23. Michael I. Handel, "Technological Surprise in War," *Intelligence and National Security* 2 (January 1987): 42–43.

# SELECTED BIBLIOGRAPHY

Allison, Graham T., Albert Carnesale, and Joseph S. Nye, Jr., eds. *Hawks, Doves, and Owls: An Agenda for Avoiding Nuclear War*. New York: W. W. Norton, 1985.

Arbatov, Alexei G. "We Could Have Done Better [in START]." *Bulletin of the Atomic Scientists* 47 (November 1991): 36–41, 47.

Ball, Desmond, and Robert C. Toth. "Revising the SIOP: Taking War-Fighting to Dangerous Extremes." *International Security* 14 (Spring 1990): 65–92.

Ball, Desmond, and Jeffrey Richelson, eds. *Strategic Nuclear Targeting*. Ithaca: Cornell University Press, 1986.

Barnett, Correlli. *Engage the Enemy More Closely: The Royal Navy in the Second World War*, New York: W. W. Norton, 1991.

_____. *The Collapse of British Power*. Gloucester, Eng.: Alan Sutton, 1984; first published 1972.

_____. *The Swordbearers: Studies in Supreme Command in the First World War*. London: Eyre and Spotiswoode, 1963.

Bartlett, Henry C. "Approaches to Force Planning." *Naval War College Review* 38 (May/June 1985): 37–48.

Bartlett, Henry C., and G. Paul Holman, Jr. "Strategy as a Guide to Force Planning." *Naval War College Review* 41 (Autumn 1988): 15–25.

Berkowitz, Bruce D. *Calculated Risks: A Century of Arms Control; Why It Has Failed and How It Can be Made to Work*. New York: Simon and Schuster, 1987.

Best, Geoffrey. *Humanity in Warfare*. New York: Columbia University Press, 1980.

Betts, Richard K. "The Concept of Deterrence in the Postwar Era." *Security Studies* 1 (Autumn 1991): 25–36.

_____. *Nuclear Blackmail and Nuclear Balance*. Washington, D.C.: Brookings Institution, 1987.

_____. "Conventional Strategy: New Critics, Old Choices." *International Security* 7 (Spring 1983): 140–62.

Black, Jeremy, and Philip Woodfine, eds. *The British Navy and the Use of Naval*

*Power in the Eighteenth Century*. Leicester, Eng.: Leicester University Press, 1988.

Blackwell, James, Michael J. Mazarr, and Don M. Snider. *The Gulf War: Military Lessons Learned*. Interim Report of the CSIS Study Group on Lessons Learned from the Gulf War. Washington, D.C.: Center for Strategic and International Studies, July 1991.

Blainey, Geoffrey. *The Causes of War*. London: Macmillan, 1973.

Boggs, Marion William. *Attempts to Define and Limit "Aggressive" Armament in Diplomacy and Strategy*. University of Missouri Studies, no. 16. Columbia: University of Missouri, 1941.

Booth, Ken. *Strategy and Ethnocentrism*. London: Croom, Helm, 1979.

Bourne, Kenneth. *Britain and the Balance of Power in North America, 1815–1908*. Berkeley: University of California Press, 1967.

Brennan, Donald G., ed. *Arms Control, Disarmament, and National Security*. New York: George Braziller, 1961.

Brewer, John. *The Sinews of Power: War, Money, and the English State, 1688–1783*. New York: Alfred A. Knopf, 1989.

Brodie, Bernard. "On the Objectives of Arms Control." *International Security* 1 (Summer 1976): 17–36.

_____. *War and Politics*. New York: Macmillan, 1973.

_____. *Sea Power in the Machine Age*. Princeton: Princeton University Press, 1941.

Brodie, Bernard, ed. *The Absolute Weapon: Atomic Power and World Order*. New York: Harcourt, Brace, 1946.

Brooks, Linton H. "Naval Power and National Security: The Case for the Maritime Strategy." *International Security* 11 (Fall 1986): 58–88.

Brzezinski, Zbigniew, ed. *Promise or Peril: The Strategic Defense Initiative*. Washington, D.C.: Ethics and Public Policy Center, 1986.

Builder, Carl H. *The Masks of War: American Military Styles in Strategy and Analysis*. Baltimore: Johns Hopkins University Press, 1989.

Bull, Hedley. *The Anarchical Society: A Study of Order in World Politics*. New York: Columbia University Press, 1977.

_____. "Strategic Studies and Its Critics." *World Politics* 20 (July 1968): 593–605.

_____. *The Control of the Arms Race: Disarmament and Arms Control in the Missile Age*. London: Weidenfeld and Nicolson, 1961.

Bundy, McGeorge. "Existential Deterrence and Its Consequences." In Douglas MacLean, ed., *The Security Gamble: Deterrence Dilemmas in the Nuclear Age*, pp. 3–13. Totowa, N.J.: Rowman and Allanheld, 1984.

Buzan, Barry. *An Introduction to Strategic Studies: Military Technology and International Relations*. New York: St. Martin's Press, 1987.

Carnesale, Albert, and Richard N. Haass, eds. *Superpower Arms Control: Setting the Record Straight*. Cambridge, Mass.: Ballinger, 1987.

Carter, Ashton B., John D. Steinbruner, and Charles A. Zraket, eds. *Managing Nuclear Operations*. Washington, D.C.: Brookings Institution, 1987.

Chayes, Antonia Handler, and Paul Doty, eds. *Defending Deterrence: Managing the ABM Treaty Regime into the 21st Century*. Washington, D.C.: Pergamon-Brassey's, 1989.

Clark, Ian. *The Hierarchy of States: Reform and Resistance in the International Order*. Cambridge: Cambridge University Press, 1989; first published 1980.

Clausewitz, Carl von. *On War*. Translated by Michael Howard and Peter Paret. Princeton: Princeton University Press, 1976; first published 1832.

Cohen, Eliot A. "The Future of Force and American Strategy." *National Interest*, no. 2 (Fall 1990): 3–15.

Cohen, Eliot A., and John Gooch. *Military Misfortunes: The Anatomy of Failure in War*. New York: Free Press, 1990.

Commission on Integrated Long-Term Strategy. *Discriminate Deterrence*. Washington, D.C.: U.S. Government Printing Office, January 11, 1988.

Contamine, Philippe. *War in the Middle Age*. Oxford: Basil Blackwell, 1984.

Creveld, Martin van. *Technology and War: From 2000 B.C. to the Present*. New York: Free Press, 1989.

_____. *Fighting Power: German and U.S. Army Performance, 1939–1945*. Westport, Conn.: Greenwood Press, 1982.

Daniel, Donald C. F. *Beyond the 600-Ship Navy*. Adelphi Papers no. 261. London: IISS, Autumn 1991.

Donnelly, Christopher. *Red Banner: The Soviet Military System in Peace and War*. Coulsdon, Eng.: Jane's Information Group, 1989.

Doughty, Robert Allan. *The Seeds of Disaster: The Development of French Army Doctrine, 1919–1939*. Hamden, Conn.: Archon Books, 1985.

Downs, George W. "Arms Race and War." In Philip E. Tetlock et al., eds., *Behavior, Society, and Nuclear War*, 2:73–109. New York: Oxford University Press, 1991.

Dror, Yehezkel. *Crazy States: A Counterconventional Strategic Problem*. Lexington, Mass.: Heath Lexington Books, 1971.

Dupuy, T. N. *The Evolution of Weapons and Warfare*. Indianapolis: Bobbs-Merrill, 1980.

Ellis, John. *Brute Force: Allied Strategy and Tactics in the Second World War*. New York: Viking, 1990.

Evangelista, Matthew. *Innovation and the Arms Race: How the United States and the Soviet Union Develop New Military Technologies*. Ithaca: Cornell University Press, 1988.

Fairbanks, Charles H., Jr. "Arms Races: The Metaphor and the Facts." *National Interest*, no. 1 (Fall 1985): 75–90.

_____. "The Washington Naval Treaty, 1922–1936." In Robert J. Art and Kenneth Waltz, eds., *The Use of Force: International Politics and Foreign Policy*, pp. 473–77. 2d ed. Lanham, Md.: University Press of America, 1983.

Falloden, viscount of. *See* Grey.

Fischer, David Hackett. *Historians' Fallacies: Toward a Logic of Historical Thought*. New York: Harper and Row, 1970.

Freedman, Lawrence. *The Evolution of Nuclear Strategy*. 2d ed. New York: St. Martin's Press, 1989.

_____. "On the Tiger's Back: The Concept of Escalation." In Roman Kolkowicz, ed., *The Logic of Nuclear Terror*, pp. 109–52. Boston: Allen and Unwin, 1987.

_____. *Strategic Defence in the Nuclear Age*, Adelphi Papers no. 224. London: IISS, Autumn 1987.

French, David. *British Strategy and War Aims, 1914–1916*. London: Allen and Unwin, 1986.

Fukuyama, Francis. *The End of History and the Last Man*. New York: Free Press, 1992.

————. "The End of History?" *National Interest* (Summer 1989): 3–18.

Fuller, J. F. C. *Armament and History: A Study of the Influence of Armament on History from the Dawn of Classical Warfare to the Second World War*. London: Eyre and Spotiswoode, 1946.

Glynn, Patrick. *Closing Pandora's Box: Arms Races, Arms Control, and the History of the Cold War*. New York: Basic Books, 1992.

Gottfried, Kurt, and Bruce G. Blair, eds. *Crisis Stability and Nuclear War*. New York: Oxford University Press, 1988.

Gray, Colin S. *House of Cards: Why Arms Control Must Fail*. Ithaca: Cornell University Press, 1992.

————. *War, Peace, and Victory: Strategy and Statecraft for the Next Century*. New York: Simon and Schuster, 1990.

————. *The Geopolitics of Super Power*. Lexington: University Press of Kentucky, 1988.

————. "ICBM's and Deterrence: The Controversy over Prompt Launch." *Journal of Strategic Studies* 10 (September 1987): 285–309.

————. "The Transition from Offense to Defense." *Washington Quarterly* 9 (Summer 1986): 59–72.

————. *Strategic Studies and Public Policy: The American Experience*. Lexington: University Press of Kentucky, 1982.

————. *The Soviet-American Arms Race*. Lexington, Mass.: Lexington Books, 1976.

————. "The Urge to Compete: Rationales for Arms Racing." *World Politics* 26 (January 1974): 207–33.

————. "The Arms Race Phenomenon." *World Politics* 24 (October 1971): 39–79.

Grey (Viscount of Falloden). *Twenty-Five Years, 1892–1916*. New York: Frederick A. Stokes, 1925.

Grove, Eric. *The Future of Sea Power*. Annapolis, Md.: Naval Institute Press, 1990.

Haffa, Robert P., Jr. *Rational Methods, Prudent Choices: Planning U.S. Forces*. Washington, D.C.: National Defense University Press, 1988.

Hall, Christopher. *Britain, America and Arms Control, 1921–37*. New York: St. Martin's Press, 1987.

Halle, Louis J. *The Elements of International Strategy: A Primer for the Nuclear Age*. Lanham, Md.: University Press of America, 1984.

Halperin, Morton H. *Limited War in the Nuclear Age*. New York: John Wiley, 1963.

Hampson, Fen Osler. *Unguided Missiles: How America Buys Its Weapons*. New York: W. W. Norton, 1989.

Handel, Michael I. "Technological Surprise in War." *Intelligence and National Security* 2 (January 1987): 1–53.

————. "Numbers Do Count: The Question of Quantity Versus Quality." *Journal of Strategic Studies*, 4 (September 1981): 225–60.

Handel, Michael I., ed. "Clausewitz and Modern Strategy." *Journal of Strategic Studies* 9 (June/September 1986).

Haslam, Jonathan. *The Soviet Union and the Politics of Nuclear Weapons in Europe, 1969–87*. Ithaca: Cornell University Press, 1990.

Herwig, Holger H. *"Luxury Fleet": The Imperial German Navy, 1888–1918*. London: George Allen and Unwin, 1980.

Holland, Lawrence H., and Robert A. Hoover. *The MX Decision: A New Direction in U.S. Weapons Procurement Policy?* Boulder, Colo.: Westview Press, 1985.

Holloway, David. *The Soviet Union and the Arms Race.* New Haven: Yale University Press, 1983.

Howard, Michael. *The Lessons of History.* New Haven: Yale University Press, 1991.

———. "The Remaking of Europe." *Survival* 32 (March/April 1990): 99–106.

———. *The Causes of Wars and Other Essays.* London: Unwin Paperbacks, 1983.

———. *Studies in War and Peace.* London: Temple Smith, 1970.

Howard, Michael, ed. *Restraints on War: Studies in the Limitation of Armed Conflict.* Oxford: Oxford University Press, 1979.

Huntington, Samuel P. "No Exit—The Errors of Endism." *National Interest*, no. 17 (Fall 1989): 3–11.

———. "U.S. Defense Strategy: The Strategic Innovations of the Reagan Years." In Joseph Kruzel, ed., *American Defense Annual, 1987–1988*, pp. 23–43. Lexington, Mass.: Lexington Books, 1987.

———. "Playing to Win." *National Interest*, no. 3 (Spring 1986): 8–16.

———. "Arms Races: Prerequisites and Results." In Carl J. Friedrich and Seymour E. Harris, eds., *Public Policy, 1958*, pp. 40–86. Cambridge: Graduate School of Public Administration, Harvard University, 1958.

Iklé, Fred Charles. "The Ghost in the Pentagon: Rethinking America's Defense." *National Interest*, no. 19 (Spring 1990): 13–20.

———. *Every War Must End.* New York: Columbia University Press, 1971.

———. "After Detection—What?" *Foreign Affairs* 39 (January 1961): 208–20.

Jacobsen, Carl G., ed. *Strategic Power: USA/USSR.* New York: St. Martin's Press, 1990.

Jervis, Robert. "Arms Control, Stability, and Causes of War." *Daedalus* 120 (Winter 1991): 167–81.

———. *The Meaning of the Nuclear Revolution: Statecraft and the Prospect of Armageddon.* Ithaca: Cornell University Press, 1989.

———. "The Political Effects of Nuclear Weapons: A Comment." *International Security* 13 (Fall 1988): 80–90.

———. *The Illogic of American Nuclear Strategy.* Ithaca: Cornell University Press, 1984.

———. "Cooperation under the Security Dilemma." *World Politics* 30 (January 1979): 167–214.

———. *Perception and Misperception in International Politics.* Princeton: Princeton University Press, 1976.

Jervis, Robert, Richard Ned Lebow, and Janice Gross Stein. *Psychology and Deterrence.* Baltimore: Johns Hopkins University Press, 1985.

Jomini, Baron Antoine Henri de. *The Art of War.* Westport, Conn.: Greenwood Press, 1971; reprint of 1862 ed.

Kahan, Jerome H. *Security in the Nuclear Age: Developing U.S. Strategic Arms Policy.* Washington, D.C.: Brookings Institution, 1975.

Kahn, Herman. *On Thermonuclear War.* Princeton: Princeton University Press, 1960.

Kaplan, Fred. *The Wizards of Armageddon.* New York: Simon and Schuster, 1983.

Kaplan, Morton H., ed. *SALT: Problems and Prospects*. Morristown, N.J.: General Learning Press, 1973.

Kartchner, Kerry M. "Soviet Compliance with a START Agreement: Prospects under Gorbachev." *Strategic Review* 17 (Fall 1989): 47–57.

Kaufman, Robert Gordon. *Arms Control during the Pre-Nuclear Era: The United States and Naval Limitation between the Two World Wars*. New York: Columbia University Press, 1990.

Keegan, John. *The Second World War*. London: Hutchinson, 1989.

Kemp, Geoffrey. "Regional Security, Arms Control, and the End of the Cold War." *Washington Quarterly* 13 (Autumn 1990): 33–51.

Kennedy, Paul. *The Rise and Fall of the Great Powers: Economic Change and Military Conflict from 1500 to 2000*. New York: Random House, 1987.

_____. *Strategy and Diplomacy, 1870–1945: Eight Studies*. London: George Allen and Unwin, 1983.

_____. *The Rise and Fall of British Naval Mastery*. New York: Charles Scribner's Sons, 1976.

Kennedy, Paul, ed. *The War Plans of the Great Powers, 1880–1914*. London: George Allen and Unwin, 1979.

Klein, Yitzhak. "A Theory of Strategic Culture." *Comparative Strategy* 10 (1991): 3–23.

_____. "The Sources of Soviet Strategic Culture." *Journal of Soviet Military Studies* 2 (December 1989): 453–90.

Knorr, Klaus, ed. *Historical Dimensions of National Security Problems*. Lawrence: University Press of Kansas, 1976.

Kraemer, Sven. "The Krasnoyarsk Saga." *Strategic Review* 18 (Winter 1990): 25–38.

Kurth, James. "The Shape of the New World Order." *National Interest*, no. 24 (Summer 1991): 3–12.

Lambert, Andrew D. *The Crimean War: British Grand Strategy against Russia, 1853–56*. Manchester, Eng.: Manchester University Press, 1990.

Legge, J. Michael. *Theater Nuclear Weapons and the NATO Strategy of Flexible Response*, R-29-64-FF. Santa Monica, Calif.: Rand Corporation, April 1983.

Levine, Robert A. *Still the Arms Debate*. Brookfield, Vt.: Dartmouth Publishing, 1990.

Levy, Jack S. "Preferences, Constraints, and Choices in July 1914." *International Security* 15 (Winter 1990/91): 151–86.

_____. "The Causes of War: A Review of Theories and Evidence." In Philip E. Tetlock et al., eds., *Behavior, Society, and Nuclear War*, 1:209–333. New York: Oxford University Press, 1989.

_____. "The Offensive/Defensive Balance of Military Technology: Theoretical and Historical Analysis." *International Studies Quarterly* 28 (1984): 219–38.

Luttwak, Edward N. "From Geopolitics to Geoeconomics: Logic of Conflict, Grammar of Commerce." *National Interest*, no. 20 (Summer, 1990): 17–23.

_____. "An Emerging Postnuclear Era?" *Washington Quarterly* 11 (Winter 1988): 5–15.

_____. *Strategy: The Logic of War and Peace*. Cambridge: Harvard University Press, 1987.

_____. *The Pentagon and the Art of War: The Question of Military Reform*. New York: Simon and Schuster, 1984.

Mackinder, Halford J. *Democratic Ideals and Reality*. New York: W. W. Norton, 1962.

McNeill, William H. *The Pursuit of Power: Technology, Armed Force, and Society*. Chicago: University of Chicago Press, 1982.

Mahan, Alfred Thayer. *Retrospect and Prospect: Studies in International Relations, Naval and Political*. London: Sampson Low, Marston, 1902.

_____. *The Influence of Sea Power upon History, 1660–1783*. Boston: Little, Brown, 1918; first published 1890.

Mandelbaum, Michael. *The Fate of Nations: The Search for National Security in the Nineteenth and Twentieth Centuries*. Cambridge: Cambridge University Press, 1988.

Marder, Arthur J. *From the Dreadnought to Scapa Flow, The Royal Navy in the Fisher Era*. 5 vols. London: Oxford University Press, 1961–1970.

_____. *The Anatomy of British Sea Power: A History of British Naval Policy in the Pre-Dreadnought Era, 1880–1905*. Hamden, Conn.: Archon Books, 1964.

Marshall, Andrew W., J. J. Martin, and Henry S. Rowen, eds. *On Not Confusing Ourselves: Essays on National Security Strategy in Honor of Albert and Roberta Wohlstetter*. Boulder, Colo.: Westview Press, 1991.

May, Ernest R., ed. *Knowing One's Enemies: Intelligence Assessment before the Two World Wars*. Princeton: Princeton University Press, 1984.

Mearsheimer, John J. "Back to the Future: Instability in Europe after the Cold War." *International Security* 15 (Summer 1990): 5–56.

Millett, Allan R., and Peter Maslowski. *For the Common Defense: A Military History of the United States of America*. New York: Free Press, 1984.

Millett, Allan R., and Williamson Murray, eds. *Military Effectiveness*. 3 vols. Boston: Allen and Unwin, 1988.

Milner, Marc. "The Battle of the Atlantic." *Journal of Strategic Studies* 13 (March 1990): 45–66.

Morgan, Patrick. *Deterrence: A Conceptual Analysis*. Beverly Hills, Calif.: Sage Publications, 1977.

Mueller, John. "The Essential Irrelevance of Nuclear Weapons: Stability in the Postwar World." *International Security* 13 (Fall 1988): 55–79.

Naval War College, Force Planning Faculty. *Fundamentals of Force Planning*, Vol. 1, *Concepts*. Newport, R.I.: Naval War College Press, 1990.

Newhouse, John. *Cold Dawn: The Story of SALT*. New York: Holt, Rinehart and Winston, 1973.

Nolan, Janne E. *Guardians of the Arsenal: The Politics of Nuclear Strategy*. New York: Basic Books, 1989.

Nye, Joseph S., Jr. *Bound to Lead: The Changing Nature of American Power*. New York: Basic Books, 1990.

_____. "Arms Control after the Cold War." *Foreign Affairs* 6 (Winter 1989/90): 42–64.

_____. *Nuclear Ethics*. New York: Free Press, 1986.

Odom, William E. "The Soviet Military in Transition." *Problems of Communism* 39 (May/June 1990): 51–71.

Palmer, Bruce, Jr. *The 25-Year War: America's Military Role in Vietnam*. Lexington: University Press of Kentucky, 1984.

Payne, Keith B. *Missile Defense in the 21st Century: Protection against Limited Threats, Including Lessons from the Gulf War*. Boulder, Colo.: Westview Press, 1991.

_____. *Strategic Defense: "Star Wars" in Perspective.* Lanham, Md.: Hamilton Press, 1986.

Pipes, Richard. *Russia under the Old Regime.* New York: Charles Scribner's Sons, 1974.

Posen, Barry. *The Sources of Military Doctrine: France, Britain, and Germany between the Wars.* Ithaca: Cornell University Press, 1984.

President's Commission on Strategic Forces. *Report.* Washington, D.C.: White House, April 1983.

Quester, George H. *Offense and Defense in the International System.* New York: John Wiley and Sons, 1977.

Ranger, Robin. "Learning from the Naval Arms Control Experience." *Washington Quarterly* 10 (Summer 1987): 47–58.

_____. *Arms and Politics, 1958–1978: Arms Control in a Changing Political Context.* Toronto: Macmillan of Canada, 1979.

Rattray, Gregory. "Force Planning." In Schuyler Foerster and Edward N. Wright, eds., *American Defense Policy,* pp. 518–24. 6th ed. Baltimore: Johns Hopkins University Press, 1990.

Reynolds, Clark G. *History and the Sea: Essays on Maritime Strategies.* Columbia: University of South Carolina Press, 1989.

Rhodes, Edward. *Power and MADness: The Logic of Nuclear Coercion.* New York: Columbia University Press, 1989.

Roskill, Stephen. *Naval Policy Between the Wars.* 2 vols. London: Collins, 1968–1976.

Rotberg, Robert I., and Theodore K. Rabb, eds. *The Origin and Prevention of Major Wars.* Cambridge: Cambridge University Press, 1989.

Sagan, Scott D. *Moving Targets: Nuclear Strategy and National Security.* Princeton: Princeton University Press, 1989.

_____. "1914 Revisited: Allies, Offense, and Instability." *International Security* 11 (Fall 1986): 151–75.

_____. "Nuclear Alerts and Crisis Management." *International Security* 9 (Spring 1985): 99–139.

Schelling, Thomas C. "From an Airport Bench." *Bulletin of the Atomic Scientists* 45 (May 1989): 29–31.

_____. *Arms and Influence.* New Haven: Yale University Press, 1966.

Schelling, Thomas C., and Morton H. Halperin. *Strategy and Arms Control.* New York: Twentieth Century Fund, 1961.

Schwartz, David N. *NATO's Nuclear Dilemmas.* Washington, D.C.: Brookings Institution, 1983.

Scowcroft, Brent, John Deutch, and R. James Woolsey. "Come and Get Us." *New Republic,* April 18, 1988, pp. 16, 18.

Seiler, George J. *Strategic Nuclear Force Requirements and Issues.* Maxwell AFB, Ala.: Air University Press, February 1983.

Shimshoni, Jonathan. "Technology, Military Advantage, and World War I: A Case for Military Entrepreneurship." *International Security* 15 (Winter 1990/91): 187–215.

Shy, John. "Jomini." In Peter Paret, ed., *Makers of Modern Strategy: From Machiavelli to the Nuclear Age,* pp. 143–85. Princeton: Princeton University Press, 1986.

_____. *A People Numerous and Armed: Reflections on the Military Struggle for American Independence.* London: Oxford University Press, 1976.

Slocombe, Walter B. "Strategic Stability in a Restructured World." *Survival* 32 (July/August 1990): 299–312.

Snyder, Jack. *The Ideology of the Offensive: Military Decision Making and the Disasters of 1914*. Ithaca: Cornell University Press, 1984.

———. *The Soviet Strategic Culture: Implications for Limited Nuclear Operations*, R-2154-FF. Santa Monica, Calif.: Rand Corporation, September 1977.

Stone, Jeremy J. *Strategic Persuasion: Arms Limitations through Dialogue*. New York: Columbia University Press, 1967.

Strachan, Hew. *European Armies and the Conduct of War*. London: George Allen and Unwin, 1983.

Strauss, Barry S., and Josiah Ober. *The Anatomy of Error: Ancient Military Disasters and Their Lessons for Modern Strategists*. New York: St. Martin's Press, 1990.

Summers, Harry G. *On Strategy: A Critical Analysis of the Vietnam War*. Novato, Calif.: Presidio Press, 1982.

Sun Tzu. *The Art of War*. Translated by Samuel B. Griffith. Oxford: Clarendon Press, 1963.

Terraine, John. *Business in Great Waters: The U-Boat Wars, 1916–1945*. London: Leo Cooper, 1989.

Trachtenberg, Marc. *History and Strategy*. Princeton: Princeton University Press, 1991.

Weigley, Russell F. *The American Way of War: A History of United States Military Strategy and Policy*. New York: Macmillan, 1973.

Wells, Samuel F., Jr., and Robert S. Litwak, eds. *Strategic Defenses and Soviet-American Relations*. Cambridge, Mass. Ballinger, 1987.

Williamson, Samuel R., Jr. *The Politics of Grand Strategy: Britain and France Prepare for War, 1904–1914*. Cambridge: Harvard University Press, 1969.

Woolsey, R. James. "The Politics of Vulnerability: 1980–83." *Foreign Affairs* 62 (Spring 1984): 805–19.

Wylie, J. C. *Military Strategy: A General Theory of Power Control*. Annapolis, Md.: Naval Institute Press, 1989; first published 1967.

Yazov, D. T. "On Soviet Military Doctrine." *RUSI Journal* 134 (Winter 1989): 1–4.

INDEX